To

RUDOLF CARNAP

Teacher and Friend

Word and Object

Word and Object

Willard Van Orman Quine

Edgar Pierce Professor of Philosophy

Harvard University

THE M.I.T. PRESS

Massachusetts Institute of Technology

Cambridge, Massachusetts

Wie Schiffer sind wir, die ihr Schiff auf offener See umbauen müssen, ohne es jemals in einem Dock zerlegen und aus besten Bestandteilen neu errichten zu können.

—OTTO NEURATH

Ontology recapitulates philology.

—JAMES GRIER MILLER

Preface

Language is a social art. In acquiring it we have to depend entirely on intersubjectively available cues as to what to say and when. Hence there is no justification for collating linguistic meanings, unless in terms of men's dispositions to respond overtly to socially observable stimulations. An effect of recognizing this limitation is that the enterprise of translation is found to be involved in a certain systematic indeterminacy; and this is the main theme of Chapter II.

The indeterminacy of translation invests even the question what objects to construe a term as true of. Studies of the semantics of reference consequently turn out to make sense only when directed upon substantially our language, from within. But we do remain free to reflect, thus parochially, on the development and structure of our own referential apparatus; and this I do in ensuing chapters. In so doing one encounters various anomalies and conflicts that are implicit in this apparatus (Chapter IV), and is moved to adopt remedies in the spirit of modern logic (Chapters V and VI). Clarity also is perhaps gained on what we do when we impute existence, and what considerations may best guide such decisions; thus Chapter VII.

My six Gavin David Young Lectures in Philosophy at the University of Adelaide, June 1959, will have consisted of portions of this book. Similarly for various of my lectures at the University of Tokyo in July and August. An abridgment of the last chapter figured as the Howison Lecture in Philosophy at the University of California in Berkeley, May 1959, and parts of Chapters II through

VI went to make up five lectures that I gave at Stanford University in April.

A year earlier I drew on the work in progress for my paper at the fourth Colloque Philosophique de Royaumont and for my presidential address to the Eastern Division of the American Philosophical Association. The year before that, 1956–57, I presented portions of interim versions of Chapter II as single lectures at four institutions: Princeton University, the Institute for Advanced Study, Columbia University, and the University of Pennsylvania. My course in the philosophy of language, which I have given ten times at Harvard since VJ-day, has represented ten phases in the development of the book; and a further intervening phase was represented by courses that I gave at Oxford as George Eastman Visiting Professor in 1953–54 and by my A. T. Shearman Lectures at University College, London, in 1954.

Three publications overlap the present text of the book, having stemmed from the work in progress. Two of them are indicated at the beginnings of §§ 7 and 19. The third is "Le mythe de la signification," presumed forthcoming in the acts of the Royaumont colloquium. Three further recent papers bear mention as having conveyed some of the developing notions of the book in other phrasing. One is "The scope and language of science," which formed part of the Columbia Bicentennial program in 1954 and appeared in the *British Journal for the Philosophy of Science* in 1957. The others are "Quantifiers and propositional attitudes," *Journal of Philosophy*, 1956, and "Logical truth," in Hook's *American Philosophers at Work*.

The benefits of a Harvard sabbatical, combined with a generous grant in aid from the Institute for Advanced Study at Princeton, enabled me to devote the year 1956–57 to the book as a member of that Institute. Similar generosity on the part of the Ford Foundation enabled me to devote the year 1958–59 to the same effort, as a Fellow of the Center for Advanced Study in the Behavioral Sciences at Stanford. I gratefully acknowledge all this support. In addition I have the Rockefeller Foundation to thank for a grant which provided secretarial help in keeping up the flow of typescript during years when the secretarial services of the Institute and the Center were not at my disposal.

Last winter I enjoyed the close collaboration of Donald Davidson, who studied drafts of the book and gave me the benefit of his able criticism and his knowledge of the literature. The book has gained much from his help, and much also, in its first half, from the wise scrutiny of my colleague Burton Dreben. At various points in the book I have been helped also by advice and criticism from many other friends, including J. L. Austin, C. A. Baylis, L. J. Binkley, Alonzo Church, J. C. Cooley, Raymond Firth, Nelson Goodman, Joseph Greenberg, H. P. Grice, C. G. Hempel, Roman Jakobson, J. A. Jenkins, Georg Kreisel, T. S. Kuhn, C. E. Osgood, Hilary Putnam, P. F. Strawson, Morton White, Oscar Zariski, and Paul Ziff. I am grateful further to Jakobson for frequent encouragement and varied helpfulness in his capacity of editor of this series.

WILLARD VAN ORMAN QUINE

Stanford, California
June 3, 1959

Contents

Chapter III. The Ontogenesis of Reference

Chapter IV. Vagaries of Reference

Chapter V. Regimentation

Chapter VI. Flight from Intension

Chapter VII. Ontic Decision

Contents

CHAPTER ONE

Language and Truth

§ 1. BEGINNING WITH ORDINARY THINGS

This familiar desk manifests its presence by resisting my pressures and by deflecting light to my eyes. Physical things generally, however remote, become known to us only through the effects which they help to induce at our sensory surfaces. Yet our common-sense talk of physical things goes forward without benefit of explanations in more intimately sensory terms. Entification begins at arm's length; the points of condensation in the primordial conceptual scheme are things glimpsed, not glimpses. In this there is little cause for wonder. Each of us learns his language from other people, through the observable mouthing of words under conspicuously intersubjective circumstances. Linguistically, and hence conceptually, the things in sharpest focus are the things that are public enough to be talked of publicly, common and conspicuous enough to be talked of often, and near enough to sense to be quickly identified and learned by name; it is to these that words apply first and foremost.

Talk of subjective sense qualities comes mainly as a derivative idiom. When one tries to describe a particular sensory quality, he typically resorts to reference to public things—describing a color as orange or heliotrope, a smell as like that of rotten eggs. Just as one sees his nose best in a mirror, removed to half the optimum focal distance, so also he best identifies his sense data by reflecting them in external objects.

Impressed with the fact that we know external things only mediately through our senses, philosophers from Berkeley onward have undertaken to strip away the physicalistic conjectures and bare the sense data. Yet even as we try to recapture the data, in all their innocence of interpretation, we find ourselves depending upon sidelong glances into natural science. We may hold, with Berkeley, that the momentary data of vision consist of colors disposed in a spatial manifold of two dimensions; but we come to this conclusion by reasoning from the bidimensionality of the ocular surface, or by noting the illusions which can be engendered by two-dimensional artifacts such as paintings and mirrors, or, more abstractly, simply by noting that the interception of light in space must necessarily take place along a surface. Again we may hold that the momentary data of audition are clusters of components each of which is a function of just two variables, pitch and loudness; but not without knowledge of the physical variables of frequency and amplitude in the stimulating string.

The motivating insight, viz. that we can know external things only through impacts at our nerve endings, is itself based on our general knowledge of the ways of physical objects—illuminated desks, reflected light, activated retinas. Small wonder that the quest for sense data should be guided by the same sort of knowledge that prompts it.

Aware of the points thus far set forth, our philosopher may still try, in a spirit of rational reconstruction, to abstract out a pure stream of sense experience and then depict physical doctrine as a means of systematizing the regularities discernible in the stream. He may imagine an ideal "protocol language" which, even if in fact learned after common-sense talk of physical things or not at all, is evidentially prior: a fancifully fancyless medium of unvarnished news. Talk of ordinary physical things he would then see as, in principle, a device for simplifying that disorderly account of the passing show.

But this is a misleading way of depicting matters, even when the idea of a sense-datum "language" is counted frankly as metaphor. For the trouble is that immediate experience simply will not, of itself, cohere as an autonomous domain. References to physical things are largely what hold it together. These references are not just inessential vestiges of the initially intersubjective character of language, capable of being weeded out by devising an artificially subjective language for sense data. Rather they give us our main continuing access to past sense data themselves; for past sense data are mostly gone for good except as commemorated in physical posits. All we would have apart from posits and speculation are present sense data and present memories of past ones; and a memory trace of a sense datum is too meager an affair to do much good. Actual memories mostly are traces not of past sensations but of past conceptualization or verbalization.[1]

There is every reason to inquire into the sensory or stimulatory background of ordinary talk of physical things. The mistake comes only in seeking an implicit sub-basement of conceptualization, or of language. Conceptualization on any considerable scale is inseparable from language, and our ordinary language of physical things is about as basic as language gets.

Neurath has likened science to a boat which, if we are to rebuild it, we must rebuild plank by plank while staying afloat in it. The philosopher and the scientist are in the same boat. If we improve our understanding of ordinary talk of physical things, it will not be by reducing that talk to a more familiar idiom; there is none. It will be by clarifying the connections, causal or otherwise, between ordinary talk of physical things and various further matters which in turn we grasp with help of ordinary talk of physical things.

On the face of it there is a certain verbal perversity in the idea that ordinary talk of familiar physical things is not in large part understood as it stands, or that the familiar physical things are not real, or that evidence for their reality needs to be uncovered. For surely the key words 'understood', 'real', and 'evidence' here are too ill-defined to stand up under such punishment. We should only be depriving them of the very denotations to which they mainly owe such sense as they make to us. It was a lexicographer, Dr. Johnson, who demonstrated the reality of a stone by kicking it; and to begin with, at least, we have little better to go on than Johnsonian usage. The familiar material objects may not be all that is real, but they are admirable examples.

There are, however, philosophers who overdo this line of thought, treating ordinary language as sacrosanct. They exalt ordinary language to the exclusion of one of its own traits: its disposition to keep on evolving. Scientific neologism is itself just linguistic evolution gone self-conscious, as science is self-conscious common sense. And philosophy in turn, as an effort to get clearer on things, is not

[1] See Chisholm, *Perceiving*, p. 160.

to be distinguished in essential points of purpose and method from good and bad science.

In particular we shall find, as we get on with organizing and adjusting various of the turns of phrase that participate in what pass for affirmations of existence, that certain of these take on key significance in the increasingly systematic structure; and then, reacting in a manner typical of scientific behavior, we shall come to favor these idioms as the existence affirmations "strictly so-called." One could even end up, though we ourselves shall not, by finding that the smoothest and most adequate overall account of the world does not after all accord existence to ordinary physical things, in that refined sense of existence. *Such* eventual departures from Johnsonian usage could partake of the spirit of science and even of the evolutionary spirit of ordinary language itself.

Our boat stays afloat because at each alteration we keep the bulk of it intact as a going concern. Our words continue to make passable sense because of continuity of change of theory: we warp usage gradually enough to avoid rupture. And such, in the beginning, is the case for Johnsonian usage itself, since our questioning of objects can coherently begin only in relation to a system of theory which is itself predicated on our interim acceptances of objects. We are limited in how we can start even if not in where we may end up. To vary Neurath's figure with Wittgenstein's, we may kick away our ladder only after we have climbed it.

So the proposition that external things are ultimately to be known only through their action on our bodies should be taken as one among various coordinate truths, in physics and elsewhere, about initially unquestioned physical things. It qualifies the empirical meaning of our talk of physical things, while not questioning the reference. There remains abundant reason to inquire more closely into the empirical meaning or stimulatory conditions of our talk of physical things, for we learn in this way about the scope of creative imagination in science; and such inquiry is none the worse for being conducted within the framework of those same physical acceptations. No inquiry being possible without some conceptual scheme, we may as well retain and use the best one we know—right down to the latest detail of quantum mechanics, if we know it and it matters.

Analyze theory-building how we will, we all must start in the middle. Our conceptual firsts are middle-sized, middle-distanced

objects, and our introduction to them and to everything comes midway in the cultural evolution of the race.   In assimilating this cultural fare we are little more aware of a distinction between report
and invention, substance and style, cues and conceptualization, than
we are of a distinction between the proteins and the carbohydrates
of our material intake.   Retrospectively we may distinguish the
components of theory-building, as we distinguish the proteins and
carbohydrates while subsisting on them.   We cannot strip away
the conceptual trappings sentence by sentence and leave a description of the objective world; but we can investigate the world, and
man as a part of it, and thus find out what cues he could have of
what goes on around him.   Subtracting his cues from his world
view, we get man's net contribution as the difference. This difference marks the extent of man's conceptual sovereignty—the domain
within which he can revise theory while saving the data.

In a general way, therefore, I propose in this introductory chapter
to ponder our talk of physical phenomena as a physical phenomenon, and our scientific imaginings as activities within the world
that we imagine.   Later chapters will treat more closely of details.

§ 2.   THE OBJECTIVE PULL; OR,
E PLURIBUS UNUM

'Ouch' is a one-word sentence which a man may volunteer from
time to time by way of laconic comment on the passing show.   The
correct occasions of its use are those attended by painful stimulation.
Such use of the word, like the correct use of language generally,
is inculcated in the individual by training on the part of society;
and society achieves this despite not sharing the individual's pain.
Society's method is in principle that of rewarding the utterance of
'Ouch' when the speaker shows some further evidence of sudden
discomfort, say a wince, or is actually seen to suffer violence, and of
penalizing the utterance of 'Ouch' when the speaker is visibly untouched and his countenance unruffled.

For the man who has learned his language lesson, some of the
stimuli evocative of 'Ouch' may be publicly visible blows and
slashes, while others are hidden from the public eye in the depths
of his bowels.   Society, acting solely on overt manifestations, has
been able to train the individual to say the socially proper thing in
response even to socially undetectable stimulations.   The trick has

depended on prior concomitances between covert stimulation and overt behavior, notably the wincing instinct.

We can imagine a primitive use of 'Red' as a one-word sentence somewhat on a par with 'Ouch'. Just as 'Ouch' is the appropriate remark on the occasion of painful stimulation, so 'Red', under the usage which I am now imagining, is the appropriate remark on the occasion of those distinctive photochemical effects which are wrought in one's retina by the impact of red light. This time society's method of training consists in rewarding the utterance of 'Red' when the individual is seen looking at something red, and penalizing it when he is seen looking at something else.

Actually the uses of 'Red' are less simple. Commonly 'red', unlike 'ouch', turns up as a fragment of longer sentences. Moreover, even when 'Red' is used by itself as a one-word sentence, what evokes it is usually not the mere apprehension of something red; more commonly there has been a verbal stimulus, in the form of a question. But let us keep for a moment to the fictitious usage described in the preceding paragraph; for it, by its similarity to 'Ouch', will help to bring out also a certain contrast.

The critic, society's agent, approves the subject's utterance of 'Red' by observing the subject and his viewed object and finding the latter red. In part, therefore, the critic's cue is red irradiation of his own retina. A partial symmetry obtains between the subject's cue for utterance and the critic's cue for approval in the case of 'Red', which, happily for the critic, was lacking in the case of 'Ouch'. The partial symmetry in the one case, and the lack of it in the other, suggest a certain superficial sense in which 'Ouch' may be spoken of as more subjective in reference than 'Red'; 'Red' more objective than 'Ouch'.

Exceptions are possible on either side. If the critic and the subject are fighting a fire and are scorched by the same sudden gust, then the critic's approval of the subject's 'Ouch' does not differ significantly from the imagined case of 'Red'. Conversely, a critic may approve a subject's 'Red' on indirect evidence, failing to glimpse the object himself. If we call 'Ouch' more subjective than 'Red', we must be taken as alluding thereby only to the most characteristic learning situations. In the case of 'Red', typically one's mentor or critic sees red; in the case of 'Ouch', typically he does not get hurt.

'Ouch' is not independent of social training. One has only to prick a foreigner to appreciate that it is an English word. But in its subjectivity it is a little unusual. Words being social tools, objectivity counts toward their survival. When a word has considerable currency despite the subjective twist, it may be expected, like the pronouns 'I' and 'you', to have a valuable social function of some exceptional sort. The survival value of 'Ouch', from a social point of view, is as a distress signal. And the word is of only marginal linguistic status, after all, being incapable of integration into longer sentences.

The usual premium on objectivity is well illustrated by 'square'. Each of a party of observers glances at a tile from his own vantage point and calls it square; and each of them has, as his retinal projection of the tile, a scalene quadrilateral which is geometrically dissimilar to everyone else's. The learner of 'square' has to take his chances with the rest of society, and he ends up using the word to suit. Association of 'square' with just the situations in which the retinal projection is square would be simpler to learn, but the more objective usage is, by its very intersubjectivity, what we tend to be exposed to and encouraged in.

In general, if a term is to be learned by induction from observed instances where it is applied, the instances have to resemble one another in two ways: they have to be enough alike from the learner's point of view, from occasion to occasion, to afford him a basis of similarity to generalize upon, and they have to be enough alike from simultaneous distinct points of view to enable the teacher and learner to share the appropriate occasions. A term restricted to squares normal to the line of sight would meet the first requirement only; a term applying to physical squares in all their scalene projections meets both. And it meets both in the same way, in that the points of view available to the learner from occasion to occasion are likewise the points of view available to teacher and learner on simultaneous occasions. Such is the way with terms for observable physical objects generally; and thus it is that such objects are focal to reference and thought.

'Red', unlike 'square', is a happy case where a nearly uniform stimulatory condition is shared by simultaneous observers. All the assembled retinas are irradiated by substantially the same red light, whereas no two of them receive geometrically similar projections of the square. The pull toward objectivity is thus a strong pull away from the subjectively simplest rule of association in the case of 'square', and much less so in the case of 'red'. Hence our readiness to think of color as more subjective than physical shape. But some pull of the same kind occurs even in the case of 'red', insofar as reflections from the environment cause the red object to cast somewhat different tints to different points of view. The objective pull will regiment all the responses still as 'red', by activating myriad corrective cues. These corrective cues are used unconsciously, such is the perfection of our socialization; a painter has even to school himself to set them aside when he tries to reproduce his true retinal intake.

The uniformity that unites us in communication and belief is a uniformity of resultant patterns overlying a chaotic subjective diversity of connections between words and experience. Uniformity comes where it matters socially; hence rather in point of intersubjectively conspicuous circumstances of utterance than in point of privately conspicuous ones. For an extreme illustration of the point, consider two men one of whom has normal color vision and the other of whom is color-blind as between red and green. Society has trained both men by the method noted earlier: rewarding the utterance of 'red' when the speaker is seen fixating something red, and penalizing it in the contrary case. Moreover the gross socially observable results are about alike: both men are pretty good about attributing 'red' to just the red things. But the private mechanisms by which the two men achieve these similar results are very different. The one man has learned 'red' in association with the regulation photochemical effect. The other man has painfully learned to be stimulated to 'red' by light in various wavelengths (red and green) in company with elaborate special combinations of supplementary conditions of intensity, saturation, shape, and setting, calculated e.g. to admit fire and sunsets and to exclude grass; to admit blossoms and exclude leaves; and to admit lobsters only after boiling.

Different persons growing up in the same language are like different bushes trimmed and trained to take the shape of identical elephants. The anatomical details of twigs and branches will fulfill the elephantine form differently from bush to bush, but the overall outward results are alike.

§ 3.   THE INTERANIMATION OF SENTENCES[1]

'Ouch' was a one-word sentence. 'Red' and 'Square', when used in isolation in the ways lately imagined, are likewise best looked upon as sentences. Most sentences are longer. But even a longer sentence may still be learned as a single unit, like 'Ouch', 'Red', and 'Square', by a direct conditioning of the whole utterance to some sensory stimulation. Characteristically Humean problems, of how we acquire various ideas, may often be by-passed by representing the words in question simply as fragments of sentences which were learned as wholes.

Not that all or most sentences are learned as wholes. Most sentences are built up rather from learned parts, by analogy with the way in which those parts have previously been seen to occur in other sentences which may or may not have been learned as wholes.[2] What sentences are got by such analogical synthesis, and what ones are got directly, is a question of each individual's own forgotten history.

It is evident how new sentences may be built from old materials and volunteered on appropriate occasions simply by virtue of the analogies. Having been directly conditioned to the appropriate use of 'Foot' (or 'This is my foot') as a sentence, and 'Hand' likewise, and 'My foot hurts' as a whole, the child might conceivably utter 'My hand hurts' on an appropriate occasion, though unaided by previous experience with that actual sentence.

But think how little we would be able to say if our learning of sentences were strictly limited to those two modes: (1) learning sentences as wholes by a direct conditioning of them to appropriate non-verbal stimulations, and (2) producing further sentences from the foregoing ones by analogical substitution as in the preceding paragraph. The sentences afforded by mode (1) are such that each has its particular range of admissible stimulatory occasions, independently of wider context. The sentences added by (2) are more of the same sort—learned faster thanks to (2), but no less capable of being learned in mode (1). Speech thus confined would be strikingly like bare reporting of sense data.

[1] The phrase is adapted from Richards.

[2] This process, and the primacy of the sentence, were already appreciated in ancient India. See Brough, "Some Indian theories of meaning," pp. 164–167.

The objective pull described in § 2 would indeed be there. The stimulations eliciting 'It is square' would indeed take in the odd lot of suitably circumstanced skew projections that social pressure requires. Yet the effect of this objective pull by itself is superficial: a mere warping of the pigeonholes; a gerrymandering, in the public interest, of the range of stimulations which each report embraces. Our idiom would remain very much the inadequate sort of idiom imagined in § 1: the fancifully fancyless medium of unvarnished news. As there remarked, there would be no access to the past, beyond the negligible yield of an occasional memory trace of an unconceptualized stimulation.

What more is needed in order to capitalize the riches of past experience is hinted in the remark (§ 1) that actual memories are mostly traces not of past sensation but of past conceptualization. We cannot rest with a running conceptualization of the unsullied stream of experience; what we need is a sullying of the stream. Association of sentences is wanted not just with non-verbal stimulation, but with other sentences, if we are to exploit finished conceptualizations and not just repeat them.

Mode (2) above is already, in a way, an associating of sentences with sentences; but only in too restrained a way. Further interverbal associations are required which provide for the use of new sentences without tying them, even derivatively, to any fixed ranges of non-verbal stimuli.

The most obvious case of the verbal stimulation of verbal response is interrogation. It was already remarked in § 2 that 'Red' as a one-word sentence usually needs a question for its elicitation. The question may be simply 'What color is this?'. In this case the stimulus eliciting 'Red' is a compound one: the red light assails the eye and the question the ear. Or the question may be 'What color will you have?' or 'What color did it use to be?'. In such a case the stimulus eliciting 'Red' is the verbal one unaccompanied by red light; though its power to elicit 'Red' depends, of course, on an earlier association of 'Red' with red light.

The opposite dependence is also common: the power of a nonverbal stimulus to elicit a given sentence commonly depends on earlier associations of sentences with sentences. And in fact it is cases of this kind that best illustrate how language transcends the confines of essentially phenomenalistic reporting. Thus someone mixes the contents of two test tubes, observes a green tint, and says

germane to all topics and thus provide connections.[5] However, some middle-sized scrap of theory usually will embody all the connections that are likely to affect our adjudication of a given sentence.

The firmness of association to non-verbal stimuli, the power of such association to withstand the contrary pull of a body of theory, grades off from one sentence to another. Roughly imaginable sequences of nerve hits can confirm us in the statement that there is a brick house on Elm Street, beyond the power of secondary associations to add or detract. Even where the conditioning to non-verbal stimulation is so firm, however, there is no telling to what extent it is original and to what extent it results from a shortcutting, by transitivity of conditioning, of old connections of sentences with sentences. Beneath the uniformity that unites us in communication there is a chaotic personal diversity of connections, and, for each of us, the connections continue to evolve. No two of us learn our language alike, nor, in a sense, does any finish learning it while he lives.

§ 4. WAYS OF LEARNING WORDS

At the beginning of § 3 we noted the contrast between learning sentences as wholes and building them of parts. The first ones learned are learned as wholes, we saw, some being indeed one-word sentences. As the child progresses, he tends increasingly to build his new sentences from parts; and thus it is that one usually speaks of learning a new word rather than a new sentence. But even the sophisticated learning of a new word is commonly a matter of learning it in context—hence learning, by example and analogy, the usage of sentences in which the word can occur. It therefore remained appropriate, throughout § 3 and not just at the beginning of it, to treat sentences and not words as the wholes whose use is learned—though never denying that the learning of these wholes proceeds largely by an abstracting and assembling of parts. Now let us think more specifically about the parts.

What counts as a word, as against a string of two or more, is less evident than what counts as a sentence. The principles behind the printer's use of spaces are dim, and the relevance of such principles to any considerations of our own is doubly so. We

[5] This point has been lost sight of, I think, by some who have objected to an excessive holism espoused in occasional brief passages of mine. Even so, I think their objections largely warranted. See e.g. Hofstadter, pp. 408 ff.

might even be tempted to throw printers' precedent to the winds and call any sentence a word, on a par with 'Ouch', if it is learned as a whole rather than by building from parts. But this plan is poor; it would cause wordhood to vary capriciously from person to person and it would make wordhood for each person a function of his own forgotten infantile history. Actually no rationalization of the word will be needed here. Printers' practice, however accidental, gives the word 'word' a denotation good enough for anything that I shall have to say.

The learning of words, in this rough and ready sense of the word, partakes of a contrast correlative to that between learning sentences as wholes and building them of parts. In the case of words it is a contrast between learning a word in isolation—i.e., in effect, as a one-word sentence—and learning it contextually, or by abstraction, as a fragment of sentences learned as wholes. Prepositions, conjunctions, and many other words are bound to have been learned only contextually; we get on to using them by analogy with the ways in which they have been seen to turn up in past sentences. It is mostly just substantives, adjectives, and verbs that will occasionally have been learned in isolation. Which of them are learned thus, and which only contextually, will vary from person to person. Some, certainly, e.g. 'sake', will be learned only contextually.

The same would seem plausible for terms like 'molecule', which, unlike 'red', 'square', and 'tile', do not refer to things that can be distinctively pointed out. Such terms can, however, be inculcated also by yet a third method: description of the intended objects. This method could be grouped under the head of the contextual, but it deserves separate notice.

What makes insensible things intelligibly describable is analogy, notably the special form of analogy known as extrapolation. Thus consider molecules, which are described as smaller than anything seen. This term 'smaller' is initially meaningful to us through some manner of association with such observable contrasts as that of a bee to a bird, a gnat to a bee, or a mote of dust to a gnat. The extrapolation that leads to talk of wholly invisible particles, microbes for example, can be represented as an analogy of relation: microbes are supposed to compare in size to the motes of dust as these do to the bees. If microbes elude scrutiny, no wonder; so does the dust most of the time. Microscopes confirm the doctrine of microbes, but are not at all needed in understanding it; and the descent to yet smaller particles, molecules and others, taxes the imagination equally little.

Once we have imagined molecules with the help thus of size analogies, we bring other analogies to bear. Thus, applying dynamical terms first learned in connection with visible things, we represent molecules as moving, bumping, bouncing. Such is analogy's power to make sense of the insensible.

But analogy in the primary sense, as we might call it, relates things that are already known apart from the analogy. To say that molecules are conceived by analogy to motes or other observed particles is evidently to depart from that sense of analogy. If we locate the analogy rather in the relation of smallerness, as I have done in suggesting that the smallerness relation of molecules or microbes to motes is understood by analogy to the observed smallerness relation of motes to gnats and the like, we still depart from analogy in the primary sense; the analogy is still not one between things (or relations) known apart from the analogy. We can, however, put the matter as an analogy also in the primary sense. What stand in this analogy are the whole observable solids on the one hand and observable swarms ordinarily so-called, e.g. of motes or gnats, on the other.

This analogy is of course very limited. A supplementary aid to appreciating the dynamics of the molecules of a solid is found in the different analogy of a stack of bedsprings. And the fact is that what one learns of molecules by analogy at all is meager. One must see the molecular doctrine at work in physical theory to get a proper notion of molecules, and this is not a matter of analogy, nor of description at all. It is a matter of learning the word contextually as a fragment of sentences which one learns to bring forth as wholes under appropriate circumstances.

In the case of some of the terms that refer or purport to refer to physical objects, the value of analogy is more limited still than in the molecular instance. Thus in the physics of light, with its notoriously mixed metaphor of wave and particle, the physicist's understanding of what he is talking about must depend almost wholly on context: on knowing when to use various sentences which speak jointly of photons and of observed phenomena of light. Such sentences are like cantilever constructions, anchored in what they say of familiar objects at the near end and supporting the recondite objects at the far end. Explanation becomes oddly reciprocal: photons are posited to help explain the phenomena, and it is those phenomena and the theory concerning them that explain what the physicist is driving at in his talk of photons.[1]

One tends to imagine that when someone propounds a theory concerning some sort of objects, our understanding of what he is saying will have two phases: first we must understand what the objects are, and second we must understand what the theory says about them. In the case of molecules two such phases are somewhat separable, thanks to the moderately good analogies which implement the first phase; yet much of our understanding of "what the objects are" awaits the second phase. In the case of the wavicles there is virtually no significant separation; our coming to understand what the objects are *is* for the most part just our mastery of what the theory says about them. We do not learn first what to talk about and then what to say about it.

Picture two physicists discussing whether neutrinos have mass. Are they discussing the same objects? They agree that the physical theory which they initially share, the preneutrino theory, needs emendation in the light of an experimental result now confronting them. The one physicist is urging an emendation which involves positing a new category of particles, without mass. The other is urging an alternative emendation which involves positing a new category of particles with mass. The fact that both physicists use the word 'neutrino' is not significant. To discern two phases here, the first an agreement as to what the objects are (viz. neutrinos) and the second a disagreement as to how they are (massless or massive), is absurd.

The division between the words that are to be viewed as referring to objects of some sort, and the words that are not, is not to be drawn on grammatical lines. 'Sake' provided an extreme illustration of this point. An illustration in another vein is 'centaur'. An illustration in a third vein is 'attribute', there being philosophical disagreement over whether there are attributes. The question what there is will be scrutinized later (Ch. VII). But meanwhile we see that the differences in ways of learning words cut across

[1] On the indirectness of the connection between theoretical terms and terms of observation see Braithwaite, *Scientific Explanation*, Ch. 3; Carnap, "Methodological character of theoretical concepts"; Einstein, p. 289; Frank, Ch. 16; Hempel, both works.

the grammatical differences and also across the referential ones. 'Centaur', though true of nothing, will commonly be learned by description of its purported objects. Also of course it could be learned contextually. 'Sake' can be learned only contextually. 'Tile', which does refer to objects, may be learned either in isolation as a one-word sentence, or contextually, or by description. 'Molecule', which also (let us grant) refers to objects, will be learned both contextually and by description. Similarly for 'photon' and 'neutrino', except that the descriptive factor is less than in the case of 'molecule'. 'Class' and 'attribute', finally, whether or not we grant that they refer to objects, will pretty surely be learned in context only.

§ 5.   EVIDENCE

Words can be learned as parts of longer sentences, and some words can be learned as one-word sentences through direct ostension of their objects. In either event, words mean only as their use in sentences is conditioned to sensory stimuli, verbal and otherwise. Any realistic theory of evidence must be inseparable from the psychology of stimulus and response, applied to sentences.

The pattern of conditioning is complex and inconstant from person to person, but there are points of general congruence: combinations of questions and non-verbal stimulations which are pretty sure to elicit an affirmative answer from anyone fit to be numbered within the relevant speech community. Johnson struck such a combination, putting himself in the way of a stimulus that would trigger an affirmative response from any of us to the question whether a stone is there.

Calling a stone a stone at close quarters is an extreme case. Evidence is deliberately marshaled only when there is more nearly an equilibrium between the sensory conditioning of an affirmative response and the contrary conditioning, mediated by the interanimation of sentences. Thus the question under deliberation may be whether something glimpsed from a moving car was a stone. That it was a stone, and that it was a crumpled paper, are two ready responses; and the tendency to the former is inhibited by the tendency to the latter, via sentential interconnections at the level of common-sense physical theory. Then one "checks," or seeks overwhelming evidence, by returning to the spot to the best of his judgment and so putting himself in the way of stimulations more firmly and directly associated with the attribution of stonehood or paperhood.

If the thing was glimpsed rather from a moving train, the checking operation may be impracticable. In this event the question may be left frankly unresolved "for lack of evidence," or, if one cares a lot, tentatively resolved in the light of any available "circumstantial evidence." Thus if the region next traversed looks boulder-strewn, and signs of man are scarce, we may guess that the thing was stone rather than paper. What we are doing when we amass and use circumstantial evidence is to let ourselves be actuated as sensitively as possible by chain stimulations as they reverberate through our theory, from present sensory stimulations, via the interanimation of sentences.

Dr. Johnson's affirmative was firmly enough conditioned to the given stimuli, among others, to withstand any contrary pull via the interanimation of sentences; but in the general case evidence is a question of center of gravity. Commonly we have to be governed by a delicate balancing of varied forces transmitted across the fabric of sentences from remotely relevant stimuli. Sometimes this is because, as in the train, strong stimuli such as Johnson's are inaccessible, or because some fairly strong one is countered by the combined pull of many lesser forces from across the fabric. And often it is because the sentence at stake is one that is understood solely through a conditioning of it to other sentences.

Prediction combines what the car example illustrates with what the train example illustrates. Thus we may reach a verdict of stonehood by the indirect method of the train example, and still return to the spot to check. Our prediction is that the ensuing close-range stimulations will be of the sort that vigorously elicit verdicts of stonehood. Prediction is in effect the conjectural anticipation of further sensory evidence for a foregone conclusion. When a prediction comes out wrong, what we have is a divergent and troublesome sensory stimulation that tends to inhibit that once foregone conclusion, and so to extinguish the sentence-to-sentence conditionings that led to the prediction. Thus it is that theories wither when their predictions fail.

In an extreme case, the theory may consist in such firmly conditioned connections between sentences that it withstands the failure of a prediction or two. We find ourselves excusing the failure of prediction as a mistake in observation or a result of unexplained interference. The tail thus comes, in an extremity, to wag the dog.

The sifting of evidence would seem from recent remarks to be a strangely passive affair, apart from the effort to intercept helpful stimuli: we just try to be as sensitively responsive as possible to the ensuing interplay of chain stimulations. What conscious policy does one follow, then, when not simply passive toward this inter-animation of sentences? Consciously the quest seems to be for the simplest story. Yet this supposed quality of simplicity is more easily sensed than described. Perhaps our vaunted sense of simplicity, or of likeliest explanation, is in many cases just a feeling of conviction attaching to the blind resultant of the interplay of chain stimulations in their various strengths.

At any rate, simplicity considerations in some sense may be said to determine even the least inquisitive observer's most casual acts of individual recognition. For he is continually having to decide, if only implicitly, whether to construe two particular encounters as repeated encounters with an identical physical object or as encounters with two distinct physical objects. And he decides in such a way as to minimize, to the best of his unconscious ability, such factors as multiplicity of objects, swiftness of interim change of quality and position, and, in general, irregularity of natural law.[1]

The deliberate scientist goes on in essentially the same way, if more adroitly; and a law of least action remains prominent among his guiding principles. Working standards of simplicity, however difficult still of formulation, figure ever more explicitly. It is part of the scientist's business to generalize or extrapolate from sample data, and so to arrive at laws covering more phenomena than have been checked; and simplicity, by his lights, is just what guides his extrapolation. Simplicity is of the essence of statistical inference. If his data are represented by points on a graph, and his law is to be represented by a curve through the points, he draws the smoothest, simplest such curve he can. He even forces the points a little bit to make it simpler, pleading inaccuracy of measurement. If he can get a still simpler curve by omitting a few of the plotted points altogether, he tries to account for them separately.

Simplicity is not a desideratum on a par with conformity to observation. Observation serves to test hypotheses after adoption; simplicity prompts their adoption for testing. Still, decisive ob-

---

[1] For a brilliant logical paradigm of this enterprise see Carnap's *Aufbau*, where he sketches what he calls the *dritte Stufe*.

servation is commonly long delayed or impossible; and, insofar at least, simplicity is final arbiter.

Whatever simplicity is, it is no casual hobby. As a guide of inference it is implicit in unconscious steps as well as half explicit in deliberate ones. The neurological mechanism of the drive for simplicity is undoubtedly fundamental though unknown, and its survival value overwhelming.

One incidental benefit of simplicity that can escape notice is that it tends to enhance a theory's scope—its richness in observable consequences. For, let θ be a theory, and let C be the class of all the testable consequences of θ. The theory θ will have been suggested to us by some set K of prior observations, a subclass of C. In general, the simpler θ is, the smaller the sample K of C that will have sufficed to suggest θ. To say this is just to repeat the earlier remark: that simplicity is what guides extrapolation. But the relationship can also be described in inverted form: given K, the simpler θ is, the more inclusive C will tend to be. Granted, subsequent checking on C may do away with θ; meanwhile the gain in scope is there.[2]

Simplicity also engenders good working conditions for the continued activity of the creative imagination; for, the simpler a theory, the more easily we can keep relevant considerations in mind. But another quality which is perhaps equally valuable on this score is familiarity of principle.

Familiarity of principle is what we are after when we contrive to "explain" new matters by old laws; e.g., when we devise a molecular hypothesis in order to bring the phenomena of heat, capillary attraction, and surface tension under the familiar old laws of mechanics. Familiarity of principle also figures when "unexpected observations" (i.e., ultimately, some undesirable conflict between sensory conditionings as mediated by the interanimation of sentences) prompt us to revise an old theory; the way in which familiarity of principle then figures is in favoring minimum revision.

The helpfulness of familiarity of principle for the continuing activity of the creative imagination is a sort of paradox. Conservatism, a favoring of the inherited or invented conceptual scheme of one's own previous work, is at once the counsel of laziness and a strategy of discovery. Note, though, the important normative difference between simplicity and conservatism. Whenever simplicity

[2] On the benefits of simplicity see further Kemeny, "The use of simplicity in induction."

and conservatism are known to counsel opposite courses, the verdict of conscious methodology is on the side of simplicity. Conservatism is nevertheless the preponderant force, but no wonder: it can still operate when stamina and imagination fail.

Yet another principle that may be said to figure as a tacit guide of science is that of sufficient reason. A lingering trace of this venerable principle seems recognizable, at any rate, in the scientist's shunning of gratuitous singularities.[3] If he arrives at laws of dynamics that favor no one frame of reference over others that are in motion with respect to it, he forthwith regards the notion of absolute rest and hence of absolute position as untenable. This rejection is not, as one is tempted to suppose, a rejection of the empirically undefinable; empirically unexceptionable definitions of rest are ready to hand, in the arbitrary adoption of any of various specifiable frames of reference. It is a rejection of the gratuitous. This principle may, however, plausibly be subsumed under the demand for simplicity, thanks to the looseness of the latter idea.

§ 6.   POSITS AND TRUTH

We may think of the physicist as interested in systematizing such general truths as can be said in common-sense terms about ordinary physical things. But within this medium the best he achieves is a combination θ of ill-connected theories about projectiles, temperature changes, capillary attraction, surface tension, etc. A sufficient reason for his positing extraordinary physical things, viz. molecules and subvisible groups of molecules, is that for the thus-supplemented universe he can devise a theory θ' which is simpler than θ and agrees with θ in its consequences for ordinary things. Its further consequences for his posited extraordinary things are incidental.

(As it happens, he does a bit better. Besides being simpler than θ, his θ' excels θ on the score of familiarity of underlying principles; cf. § 5. Moreover, even those of its consequences that can be stated in common-sense terms about ordinary things exceed those of θ, and apparently without including sentences that there is reason to deny.)

If by some oracle the physicist could identify outright all the truths that can be said in common-sense terms about ordinary things, still his separation of statements about molecules into true

[3] See Birkhoff, Lecture II.

and false would remain largely unsettled. We can imagine him partly settling that separation by what is vaguely called scientific method: by considerations of simplicity of the joint theory of ordinary things and molecules. But conceivably the truths about molecules are only partially determined by any ideal organon of scientific method *plus* all the truths that can be said in common-sense terms about ordinary things; for in general the simplest possible theory to a given purpose need not be unique.

Actually the truths that can be said even in common-sense terms about ordinary things are themselves, in turn, far in excess of any available data. The incompleteness of determination of molecular behavior by the behavior of ordinary things is hence only incidental to this more basic indeterminacy: *both* sorts of events are less than determined by our surface irritations. This remains true even if we include all past, present, and future irritations of all the far-flung surfaces of mankind, and probably even if we throw in an in fact unachieved ideal organon of scientific method besides.

Considered relative to our surface irritations, which exhaust our clues to an external world, the molecules and their extraordinary ilk are thus much on a par with the most ordinary physical objects. The positing of those extraordinary things is just a vivid analogue of the positing or acknowledging of ordinary things: vivid in that the physicist audibly posits them for recognized reasons, whereas the hypothesis of ordinary things is shrouded in prehistory. Though for the archaic and unconscious hypothesis of ordinary physical objects we can no more speak of a motive than of motives for being human or mammalian, yet in point of function and survival value it and the hypothesis of molecules are alike. So much the better, of course, for the molecules.

To call a posit a posit is not to patronize it. A posit can be unavoidable except at the cost of other no less artificial expedients. Everything to which we concede existence is a posit from the standpoint of a description of the theory-building process, and simultaneously real from the standpoint of the theory that is being built. Nor let us look down on the standpoint of the theory as make-believe; for we can never do better than occupy the standpoint of some theory or other, the best we can muster at the time.

What reality is like is the business of scientists, in the broadest sense, painstakingly to surmise; and what there is, what is real, is part of that question. The question how we know what there is is simply part of the question, so briefly contemplated in § 5, of the evidence for truth about the world. The last arbiter is so-called scientific method, however amorphous.

Scientific method was vaguely seen in § 5 as a matter of being guided by sensory stimuli, a taste for simplicity in some sense, and a taste for old things. From a study of the considerable literature on scientific method, a more detailed body of canons could be brought together; though it is customary to doubt that the thing can be done finally and definitively. At any rate scientific method, whatever its details, produces theory whose connection with all possible surface irritation consists solely in scientific method itself, unsupported by ulterior controls. This is the sense in which it is the last arbiter of truth.

Peirce was tempted to define truth outright in terms of scientific method, as the ideal theory which is approached as a limit when the (supposed) canons of scientific method are used unceasingly on continuing experience.[1] But there is a lot wrong with Peirce's notion, besides its assumption of a final organon of scientific method and its appeal to an infinite process. There is a faulty use of numerical analogy in speaking of a limit of theories, since the notion of limit depends on that of "nearer than," which is defined for numbers and not for theories. And even if we by-pass such troubles by identifying truth somewhat fancifully with the ideal result of applying scientific method outright to the whole future totality of surface irritations, still there is trouble in the imputation of uniqueness ("*the* ideal result"). For, as urged two pages back, we have no reason to suppose that man's surface irritations even unto eternity admit of any one systematization that is scientifically better or simpler than all possible others. It seems likelier, if only on account of symmetries or dualities, that countless alternative theories would be tied for first place. Scientific method is the way to truth, but it affords even in principle no unique definition of truth. Any so-called pragmatic definition of truth is doomed to failure equally.

After that reflection, there may be some consolation in the following one. If there were (contrary to what we just concluded) an unknown but unique best total systematization θ of science conformable to the past, present, and future nerve-hits of mankind, so that we might define the whole truth as that unknown θ, *still* we

---

[1] Peirce, vol. 5, paragraph 407.

should not thereby have defined truth for actual single sentences. We could not say, derivatively, that any single sentence S is true if it or a translation belongs to θ, for there is in general no sense in equating a sentence of a theory θ with a sentence S given apart from θ. Unless pretty firmly and directly conditioned to sensory stimulation, a sentence S is meaningless except relative to its own theory; meaningless intertheoretically.[2] This point, already pretty evident from § 3 and from the parable of neutrinos in § 4, will be developed in more detail in Chapter II.

It is rather when we turn back into the midst of an actually present theory, at least hypothetically accepted, that we can and do speak sensibly of this and that sentence as true. Where it makes sense to apply 'true' is to a sentence couched in the terms of a given theory and seen from within the theory, complete with its posited reality. Here there is no occasion to invoke even so much as the imaginary codification of scientific method. To say that the statement 'Brutus killed Caesar' is true, or that 'The atomic weight of sodium is 23' is true, is in effect simply to say that Brutus killed Caesar, or that the atomic weight of sodium is 23.[3] That the statements are about posited entities, are significant only in relation to a surrounding body of theory, and are justifiable only by supplementing observation with scientific method, no longer matters; for the truth attributions are made from the point of view of the same surrounding body of theory, and are in the same boat.

Have we now so far lowered our sights as to settle for a relativistic doctrine of truth—rating the statements of each theory as true for that theory, and brooking no higher criticism? Not so. The saving consideration is that we continue to take seriously our own particular aggregate science, our own particular world-theory or loose total fabric of quasi-theories, whatever it may be. Unlike Descartes, we own and use our beliefs of the moment, even in the

---

[2] Rynin, in "The dogma of logical pragmatism" (p. 390), has argued to the contrary as follows: "Unless the component statements themselves have truth-values, they can make no contributions to the truth-values of the system as a whole. . . . But if a statement is true, then it is verifiable; and if false, then falsifiable; and if either, then meaningful. . . . Not merely *could* an individual statement be meaningful outside the whole of science, but . . . it *must be* if it can function within a system of science." The middle step, on verifiability, is where my dissent comes.

[3] For the classic development of this theme see "The concept of truth" in the Tarski volume.

midst of philosophizing, until by what is vaguely called scientific method we change them here and there for the better. Within our own total evolving doctrine, we can judge truth as earnestly and absolutely as can be; subject to correction, but that goes without saying.

Translation and Meaning

§7. FIRST STEPS OF RADICAL TRANSLATION[1]

We have been reflecting in a general way on how surface irritations generate, through language, one's knowledge of the world. One is taught so to associate words with words and other stimulations that there emerges something recognizable as talk of things, and not to be distinguished from truth about the world. The voluminous and intricately structured talk that comes out bears little evident correspondence to the past and present barrage of non-verbal stimulation; yet it is to such stimulation that we must look for whatever empirical content there may be. In this chapter we shall consider how much of language can be made sense of in terms of its stimulus conditions, and what scope this leaves for empirically unconditioned variation in one's conceptual scheme.

A first uncritical way of picturing this scope for empirically unconditioned variation is as follows: two men could be just alike in all their dispositions to verbal behavior under all possible sensory stimulations, and yet the meanings or ideas expressed in their identically triggered and identically sounded utterances could diverge radically, for the two men, in a wide range of cases. To put the matter thus invites, however, the charge of meaninglessness: one may protest that a distinction of meaning unreflected in the totality of dispositions to verbal behavior is a distinction without a difference.

---

[1] An interim draft of Chapter II was published, with omissions, as "Meaning and translation." Half of that essay survives verbatim here, comprising a scattered third of this chapter.

Sense can be made of the point by recasting it as follows: the infinite totality of sentences of any given speaker's language can be so permuted, or mapped onto itself, that (*a*) the totality of the speaker's dispositions to verbal behavior remains invariant, and yet (*b*) the mapping is no mere correlation of sentences with *equivalent* sentences, in any plausible sense of equivalence however loose. Sentences without number can diverge drastically from their respective correlates, yet the divergences can systematically so offset one another that the overall pattern of associations of sentences with one another and with non-verbal stimulation is preserved. The firmer the direct links of a sentence with non-verbal stimulation, of course, the less that sentence can diverge from its correlate under any such mapping.

The same point can be put less abstractly and more realistically by switching to translation. The thesis is then this: manuals for translating one language into another can be set up in divergent ways, all compatible with the totality of speech dispositions, yet incompatible with one another. In countless places they will diverge in giving, as their respective translations of a sentence of the one language, sentences of the other language which stand to each other in no plausible sort of equivalence however loose. The firmer the direct links of a sentence with non-verbal stimulation, of course, the less drastically its translations can diverge from one another from manual to manual. It is in this last form, as a principle of indeterminacy of translation, that I shall try to make the point plausible in the course of this chapter. But the chapter will run longer than it would if various of the concepts and considerations ancillary to this theme did not seem worthy of treatment also on their own account.

We are concerned here with language as the complex of present dispositions to verbal behavior, in which speakers of the same language have perforce come to resemble one another; not with the processes of acquisition, whose variations from individual to individual it is to the interests of communication to efface (cf. § 2). The sentence 'That man shoots well', said while pointing to an unarmed man, has as present stimulation the glimpse of the marksman's familiar face. The contributory past stimulation includes past observations of the man's shooting, as well as remote episodes that trained the speaker in the use of the words. The past stimulation is thus commonly reckoned in part to the acquisition of language and in part to the acquisition of collateral information; however, this subsidiary dichotomy can await some indication of what it is good for and what general clues there are for it in observable verbal behavior. (Cf. §§ 9, 12, 14.) Meanwhile what is before us is the going concern of verbal behavior and its currently observable correlations with stimulation. Reckon a man's current language by his current dispositions to respond verbally to current stimulation, and you automatically refer all past stimulation to the learning phase. Not but that even this way of drawing a boundary between language in acquisition and language in use has its fluctuations, inasmuch as we can consult our convenience in what bound we set to the length of stimulations counted as current. This bound, a working standard of what to count as specious present, I call the *modulus* of stimulation.

The recovery of a man's current language from his currently observed responses is the task of the linguist who, unaided by an interpreter, is out to penetrate and translate a language hitherto unknown. All the objective data he has to go on are the forces that he sees impinging on the native's surfaces and the observable behavior, vocal and otherwise, of the native. Such data evince native "meanings" only of the most objectively empirical or stimulus-linked variety. And yet the linguist apparently ends up with native "meanings" in some quite unrestricted sense; purported translations, anyway, of all possible native sentences.

Translation between kindred languages, e.g., Frisian and English, is aided by resemblance of cognate word forms. Translation between unrelated languages, e.g., Hungarian and English, may be aided by traditional equations that have evolved in step with a shared culture. What is relevant rather to our purposes is *radical translation*, i.e., translation of the language of a hitherto untouched people. The task is one that is not in practice undertaken in its extreme form, since a chain of interpreters of a sort can be recruited of marginal persons across the darkest archipelago. But the problem is the more nearly approximated the poorer the hints available from interpreters; thus attention to techniques of utterly radical translation has not been wanting.[2] I shall imagine that all help of interpreters is excluded. Incidentally I shall here ignore phonematic analysis (§ 18), early though it would come in our field

[2] See Pike.

linguist's enterprise; for it does not affect the philosophical point I want to make.

The utterances first and most surely translated in such a case are ones keyed to present events that are conspicuous to the linguist and his informant. A rabbit scurries by, the native says 'Gavagai', and the linguist notes down the sentence 'Rabbit' (or 'Lo, a rabbit') as tentative translation, subject to testing in further cases. The linguist will at first refrain from putting words into his informant's mouth, if only for lack of words to put. When he can, though, the linguist has to supply native sentences for his informant's approval, despite the risk of slanting the data by suggestion. Otherwise he can do little with native terms that have references in common. For, suppose the native language includes sentences S_1, S_2, and S_3, really translatable respectively as 'Animal', 'White', and 'Rabbit'. Stimulus situations always differ, whether relevantly or not; and, just because volunteered responses come singly, the classes of situations under which the native happens to have volunteered S_1, S_2, and S_3, are of course mutually exclusive, despite the hidden actual meanings of the words. How then is the linguist to perceive that the native would have been willing to assent to S_1 in all the situations where he happened to volunteer S_3, and in some but perhaps not all of the situations where he happened to volunteer S_2? Only by taking the initiative and querying combinations of native sentences and stimulus situations so as to narrow down his guesses to his eventual satisfaction.

So we have the linguist asking 'Gavagai?' in each of various stimulatory situations, and noting each time whether the native assents, dissents, or neither. But how is he to recognize native assent and dissent when he sees or hears them? Gestures are not to be taken at face value; the Turks' are nearly the reverse of our own. What he must do is guess from observation and then see how well his guesses work. Thus suppose that in asking 'Gavagai?' and the like, in the conspicuous presence of rabbits and the like, he has elicited the responses 'Evet' and 'Yok' often enough to surmise that they may correspond to 'Yes' and 'No', but has no notion which is which. Then he tries the experiment of echoing the native's own volunteered pronouncements. If thereby he pretty regularly elicits 'Evet' rather than 'Yok', he is encouraged to take 'Evet' as 'Yes'. Also he tries responding with 'Evet' and 'Yok' to the native's remarks; the one that is the more serene in its effect is the better candidate for 'Yes'. However inconclusive these methods, they generate a working hypothesis. If extraordinary difficulties attend all his subsequent steps, the linguist may decide to discard that hypothesis and guess again.[3]

Let us then suppose the linguist has settled on what to treat as native signs of assent and dissent. He is thereupon in a position to accumulate inductive evidence for translating 'Gavagai' as the sentence 'Rabbit'. The general law for which he is assembling instances is roughly that the native will assent to 'Gavagai?' under just those stimulations under which we, if asked, would assent to 'Rabbit?'; and correspondingly for dissent.

But we can do somewhat more justice to what the linguist is after in such a case if, instead of speaking merely of stimulations under which the native will assent or dissent to the queried sentence, we speak in a more causal vein of stimulations that will *prompt* the native to assent or dissent to the queried sentence. For suppose the queried sentence were one rather to the effect that someone is away tracking a giraffe. All day long the native will assent to it whenever asked, under all manner of irrelevant attendant stimulations; and on another day he will dissent from it under the same irrelevant stimulations. It is important to know that in the case of 'Gavagai?' the rabbit-presenting stimulations actually prompt the assent, and that the others actually prompt the dissent.

In practice the linguist will usually settle these questions of causality, however tentatively, by intuitive judgment based on details of the native's behavior: his scanning movements, his sudden look of recognition, and the like. Also there are more formal considerations which, under favorable circumstances, can assure him of the prompting relation. If, just after the native has been asked S and has assented or dissented, the linguist springs stimulation σ on him, asks S again, and gets the opposite verdict, then he may conclude that σ did the prompting.

Note that to prompt, in our sense, is not to elicit. What elicits the native's 'Evet' or 'Yok' is a combination: the prompting stimulation plus the ensuing query 'Gavagai?'

[3] See Firth, *Elements of Social Organization*, p. 23, on the analogous matter of identifying a gesture of greeting.

§ 8.   STIMULATION AND STIMULUS MEANING

It is important to think of what prompts the native's assent to 'Gavagai?' as stimulations and not rabbits. Stimulation can remain the same though the rabbit be supplanted by a counterfeit. Conversely, stimulation can vary in its power to prompt assent to 'Gavagai' because of variations in angle, lighting, and color contrast, though the rabbit remain the same. In experimentally equating the uses of 'Gavagai' and 'Rabbit' it is stimulations that must be made to match, not animals.

A visual stimulation is perhaps best identified, for present purposes, with the pattern of chromatic irradiation of the eye. To look deep into the subject's head would be inappropriate even if feasible, for we want to keep clear of his idiosyncratic neural routings or private history of habit formation. We are after his socially inculcated linguistic usage, hence his responses to conditions normally subject to social assessment. (Cf. § 2.) Ocular irradiation *is* intersubjectively checked to some degree by society and linguist alike, by making allowances for the speaker's orientation and the relative disposition of objects.

In taking the visual stimulations as irradiation patterns we invest them with a fineness of detail beyond anything that our linguist can be called upon to check for. But this is all right. He can reasonably conjecture that the native would be prompted to assent to 'Gavagai' by the microscopically same irradiations that would prompt him, the linguist, to assent to 'Rabbit', even though this conjecture rests wholly on samples where the irradiations concerned can at best be hazarded merely to be pretty much alike.

It is not, however, adequate to think of the visual stimulations as momentary static irradiation patterns. To do so would obstruct examples which, unlike 'Rabbit', affirm movement. And it would make trouble even with examples like 'Rabbit', on another account: too much depends on what immediately precedes and follows a momentary irradiation. A momentary leporiform image flashed by some artifice in the midst of an otherwise rabbitless sequence might not prompt assent to 'Rabbit' even though the same image would have done so if ensconced in a more favorable sequence. The difficulty would thus arise that far from hoping to match the irradiation patterns favorable to 'Gavagai' with those favorable to 'Rabbit', we could not even say unequivocally of an irradiation pattern, of itself and without regard to those just before and after, that it is favorable to 'Rabbit' or that it is not.[1] Better, therefore, to take as the relevant stimulations not momentary irradiation patterns, but evolving irradiation patterns of all durations up to some convenient limit or *modulus*. Furthermore we may think of the ideal experimental situation as one in which the desired ocular exposure concerned is preceded and followed by a blindfold.

In general the ocular irradiation patterns are best conceived in their spatial entirety. For there are examples such as 'Fine weather' which, unlike 'Rabbit', are not keyed to any readily segregated fragments of the scene. Also there are all those rabbit-free patterns that are wanted as prompting dissent from 'Rabbit'. And as for the patterns wanted as prompting assent to 'Rabbit', whole scenes will still serve better than selected portions might; for the difference between center and periphery, which is such an important determinant of visual attention, is then automatically allowed for. Total ocular irradiation patterns that differ in centering differ also in limits, and so are simply different patterns. One that shows the rabbit too peripherally simply will not be one that prompts assent to 'Gavagai' or 'Rabbit'.

Certain sentences of the type of 'Gavagai' are the sentences with which our jungle linguist must begin, and for these we now have before us the makings of a crude concept of empirical meaning. For meaning, supposedly, is what a sentence shares with its translation; and translation at the present stage turns solely on correlations with non-verbal stimulation.

Let us make this concept of meaning more explicit and give it a neutrally technical name. We may begin by defining the *affirmative stimulus meaning* of a sentence such as 'Gavagai', for a given speaker, as the class of all the stimulations (hence evolving ocular irradiation patterns between properly timed blindfoldings) that would prompt his assent. More explicitly, in view of the end of § 7, a stimulation σ belongs to the affirmative stimulus meaning of a sentence S for a given speaker if and only if there is a stimulation σ' such that if the speaker were given σ', then were asked S, then were given σ, and then were asked S again, he would dissent the first time and assent the second. We may define the *negative* stimulus meaning similarly with 'assent' and 'dissent' interchanged, and then

---

[1] This difficulty was raised by Davidson.

define the *stimulus meaning* as the ordered pair of the two. We could refine the notion of stimulus meaning by distinguishing degrees of doubtfulness of assent and dissent, say by reaction time; but for the sake of fluent exposition let us forbear. The imagined equating of 'Gavagai' and 'Rabbit' can now be stated thus: they have the same stimulus meaning.

A stimulus meaning is the stimulus meaning of a sentence for a speaker at a date; for we must allow our speaker to change his ways. Also it varies with the modulus, or maximum duration recognized for stimulations. For, by increasing the modulus we supplement the stimulus meaning with some stimulations that were too long to count before. Fully ticketed, therefore, a stimulus meaning is the stimulus meaning *modulo n* seconds of sentence S for speaker *a* at time *t*.

The stimulations to be gathered into the stimulus meaning of a sentence have for vividness been thought of thus far as visual, unlike the queries that follow them. Actually, of course, we should bring the other senses in on a par with vision, identifying stimulations not with just ocular irradiation patterns but with these and the various barrages of other senses, separately and in all synchronous combinations. Perhaps we can pass over the detail of this.

The affirmative and negative stimulus meanings of a sentence (for a given speaker at a given time) are mutually exclusive. Granted, our subject might be prompted once by a given stimulation σ to assent to S, and later, by a recurrence of σ, to dissent from S; but then we would simply conclude that his meaning for S had changed. We would then reckon σ to his affirmative stimulus meaning of S as of the one date and to his negative stimulus meaning of S as of the other date.

Yet the affirmative and negative stimulus meanings do not determine each other; for many stimulations may be expected to belong to neither. In general, therefore, comparison of whole stimulus meanings can be a better basis for translations than comparison merely of affirmative stimulus meanings.

What now of that strong conditional, the 'would' in our definition of stimulus meaning? Its use here is no worse than its use when we explain '*x* is soluble in water' as meaning that *x* would dissolve if it were in water. What the strong conditional defines is a disposition, in this case a disposition to assent to or dissent from S when variously stimulated. The disposition may be presumed to be some

subtle structural condition, like an allergy and like solubility; like
an allergy, more particularly, in not being understood.   The ontological status of dispositions, or the philosophical status of talk of
dispositions, is a matter which I defer to § 46; but meanwhile we are
familiar enough in a general way with how one sets about guessing,
from judicious tests and samples and observed uniformities, whether
there is a disposition of a specified sort.

The stimulus meaning of a sentence for a subject sums up his
disposition to assent to or dissent from the sentence in response to
present stimulation. The stimulation is what activates the disposition, as opposed to what instills it (even though the stimulation
chance to contribute somehow to the instilling of some further
disposition).

Yet a stimulation must be conceived for these purposes not as a
dated particular event but as a universal, a repeatable event form.
We are to say not that two like stimulations have occurred, but that
the same stimulation has recurred.   Such an attitude is implied the
moment we speak of sameness of stimulus meaning for two speakers.
We could indeed overrule this consideration, if we liked, by read-
justing our terminology.   But there would be no point, for there
remains elsewhere a compelling reason for taking the stimulations
as universals; viz., the strong conditional in the definition of stimulus meaning.   For, consider again the affirmative stimulus meaning
of a sentence S: the class Σ of all those stimulations that *would*
prompt assent to S.   If the stimulations were taken as events rather
than event forms, then Σ would have to be a class of events which
largely did not and will not happen, but which would prompt assent
to S if they were to happen.   Whenever Σ contained one realized or
unrealized particular stimulatory event σ, it would have to contain
all other unrealized duplicates of σ; and how many are there of
these?   Certainly it is hopeless nonsense to talk thus of unrealized
particulars and try to assemble them into classes.   Unrealized entities have to be construed as universals.

We were impressed in § 3 with the interdependence of sentences.
We may well have begun then to wonder whether meanings even
of whole sentences (let alone shorter expressions) could reasonably be talked of at all, except relative to the other sentences of an
inclusive theory.   Such relativity would be awkward, since, conversely, the individual component sentences offer the only way into
the theory.   Now the notion of stimulus meaning partially resolves
the predicament.   It isolates a sort of net empirical import of each

of various single sentences without regard to the containing theory, even though without loss of what the sentence owes to that containing theory. It is a device, as far as it goes, for exploring the fabric of interlocking sentences, a sentence at a time.

Between the notion of stimulus meaning and Carnap's remarks on empirical semantics [2] there are connections and differences worth noting. He suggests exploring the meaning of a term by asking the subject whether he would apply it under various imaginary circumstances, to be described to him. That approach has the virtue of preserving contrasts between such terms as 'goblin' and 'unicorn' despite the non-existence of contrasting instances in the world. Stimulus meaning has the same virtue, since there are stimulation patterns that would prompt assent to 'Unicorn?' and not to 'Goblin?'. Carnap's approach presupposes some decision as to what descriptions of imaginary circumstances are admissible; e.g., 'unicorn' would be not wanted in descriptions used in probing the meaning of 'unicorn'. He hints of appropriate restrictions for the purpose, mentioning "size, shape, color"; and my notion of stimulus meaning itself amounts to a firmer definition in that same direction. There remains a significant contrast in the uses the two of us make of subjunctive conditionals: I limit them to my investigator's considered judgment of what the informant would do if stimulated; Carnap has his investigator putting such conditionals to the judgment of the informant. Certainly my investigator would in practice ask the same questions as Carnap's investigator, as a quick way of estimating stimulus meanings, if language for such questions happened to be available. But stimulus meaning can be explored also at the first stages of radical translation, where Carnap's type of questionnaire is unavailable. On this score it is important, as we shall see in § 12, that my theory has to do primarily with sentences of a sort and not, like Carnap's, with terms.

§ 9. OCCASION SENTENCES.
INTRUSIVE INFORMATION

Occasion sentences, as against *standing* sentences, are sentences such as 'Gavagai', 'Red', 'It hurts', 'His face is dirty', which command

---

[2] *Meaning and Necessity*, 2d ed., Suppl. D. See also Chisholm, *Perceiving*, pp. 175 ff., and his references.

assent or dissent only if queried after an appropriate prompting stimulation. Verdicts to standing sentences *can* be prompted too: stimulation implemented by an interferometer once prompted Michelson and Morley to dissent from the standing sentence 'There is ether drift', and a speaker's assent can be prompted yearly to 'The crocuses are out', daily to 'The *Times* has come'. But these standing sentences contrast with occasion sentences in that the subject may repeat his old assent or dissent unprompted by current stimulation when we ask him again on later occasions, whereas an occasion sentence commands assent or dissent only as prompted all over again by current stimulation. Standing sentences grade off toward occasion sentences as the interval between possible repromptings diminishes; and the occasion sentence is the extreme case where that interval is less than the modulus. Like the stimulus meanings themselves, the distinction between standing sentences and occasion sentences is relative to the modulus; an occasion sentence modulo n seconds can be a standing sentence modulo $n - 1$.

The stimulations belonging to neither the affirmative nor the negative stimulus meaning of an occasion sentence are just those that would inhibit a verdict on the queried sentence, whether through indecisiveness (as in the case of a poor glimpse) or through shocking the subject out of his wits. On the other hand the stimulations belonging to neither the affirmative nor the negative stimulus meaning of a standing sentence are of two sorts: besides the inhibitory ones there are the *irrelevant* ones, which neither prompt nor inhibit. Querying the sentence on the heels of such a stimulation would elicit a verdict, but always the one that the query would have elicited without the attendant stimulation; never a change of verdict.

The stimulus meaning is a full cross-section of the subject's evolving dispositions to assent to or dissent from a sentence, if the sentence is an occasion sentence; less so if it is a standing sentence. Standing sentences can differ among themselves in "meaning," by any intuitive account,[1] as freely as occasion sentences; but, the less susceptible they are to prompted assent and dissent, the fewer clues are present in stimulus meaning. The notion of stimulus meaning

---

[1] Twice I have been startled to find my use of 'intuitive' misconstrued as alluding to some special and mysterious avenue of knowledge. By an intuitive account I mean one in which terms are used in habitual ways, without reflecting on how they might be defined or what presuppositions they might conceal.

is thus most important for occasion sentences, and we shall limit our attention for a while to them.

Even for such favored occasion sentences as 'Gavagai' and 'Rabbit', actually, sameness of stimulus meaning has its shortcomings as a synonymy relation. The difficulty is that an informant's assent to or dissent from 'Gavagai?' can depend excessively on prior collateral information as a supplement to the present prompting stimulus. He may assent on the occasion of nothing better than an ill-glimpsed movement in the grass, because of his earlier observation, unknown to the linguist, of rabbits near the spot. Since the linguist would not on his own information be prompted by that same poor glimpse to assent to 'Rabbit?', we have here a discrepancy between the present stimulus meaning of 'Gavagai' for the informant and that of 'Rabbit' for the linguist.

More persistent discrepancies of the same type can be imagined, affecting not one native but all, and not once but regularly. There may be a local rabbit-fly,[2] unknown to the linguist, and recognizable some way off by its long wings and erratic movements; and seeing such a fly in the neighborhood of an ill-glimpsed animal could help a native to recognize the latter as a rabbit. Ocular irradiations combining poor glimpses of rabbits with good ones of rabbit-flies would belong to the stimulus meaning of 'Gavagai' for natives generally, and not to that of 'Rabbit' for the linguist.

And, to be less fanciful, there are all those stimulations that incorporate verbal hints from native kibitzers. Thus suppose that the stimulation on the heels of which the informant is asked 'Gavagai?' is a composite stimulation presenting a bystander pointing to an ill-glimpsed object and saying 'Gavagai'. This composite stimulation will probably turn out to belong to the affirmative stimulus meaning of 'Gavagai' for the informant, and not to the stimulus meaning of 'Rabbit' for most English speakers, on whom the force of the bystander's verbal intervention would be lost. Such cases would not fool our linguist, but they do count against defining synonymy as sameness of stimulus meaning. For we must remember that every sufficiently brief stimulation pattern, though it be one that never gets actualized or that the linguist would never use, still by definition belongs to the stimulus meaning of 'Gavagai' for a man at a given time if it is one that *would* prompt his assent at that time.

[2] Here I am indebted to Davidson.

Intuitively the ideal would be to accord to the affirmative meaning of 'Gavagai' just those stimulations that would prompt assent to 'Gavagai?' on the strength purely of an understanding of 'Gavagai', unaided by collateral information: unaided by recent observation of rabbits near the spot, unaided by knowledge of the nature and habits of the rabbit-fly, unaided by conversance with the kibitzer's language. On the face of it there is a difficulty in excluding this third aid, considering our continuing dependence on the subject's understanding of 'Gavagai'. But also the trouble is more widespread. It is precisely that we have made no general experimental sense of a distinction between what goes into a native's learning to apply an expression and what goes into his learning supplementary matters about the objects concerned. True, the linguist can press such a distinction part way; he can filter out such idiosyncratic bits of collateral matter as the informant's recent observation of rabbits near the spot, by varying his times and his informants and so isolating a more stable and more social stimulus meaning as common denominator. But any socially shared information, such as that about the rabbit-fly or the ability to understand a bystander's remark, will continue to affect even that common denominator. There is no evident criterion whereby to strip such effects away and leave just the meaning of 'Gavagai' properly so-called—whatever meaning properly so-called may be.

Thus, to depict the difficulty in more general terms, suppose it said that a particular class Σ comprises just those stimulations each of which suffices to prompt assent to a sentence S outright, without benefit of collateral information. Suppose it said that the stimulations comprised in a further class Σ', likewise sufficient to prompt assent to S, owe their efficacy rather to certain widely disseminated collateral information, C. Now couldn't we just as well have said, instead, that on acquiring C, men have found it convenient implicitly to change the very "meaning" of S, so that the members of Σ' now suffice outright like members of Σ? I suggest that we may say either; even historical clairvoyance would reveal no distinction, though it reveal all stages in the acquisition of C, since meaning can evolve *pari passu*. The distinction is illusory: as mistaken as the notion, scouted in § 4, that we can determine separately what to talk about and what to say about it. It is simply a question whether to call the transitivity shortcuts (§ 3) changes of meaning or condensations of proof; and in fact an unreal question. What we objectively have is just an evolving adjustment to nature, reflected in an evolving set of dispositions to be prompted by stimulations to assent to or dissent from sentences. These dispositions may be conceded to be impure in the sense of including worldly knowledge, but they contain it in a solution which there is no precipitating.

Incidentally, note that stimulus meanings as defined in § 8 can even suffer some discrepancies that are intuitively attributable neither to differences of meaning nor to differences of collateral information. Thus take shocked silence. To begin with, if the speaker is already stunned at time *t*, all stimulus meanings for him at *t* will be empty. This outcome of the definition of stimulus meaning is unnatural but harmless, since we can ignore stimulus meanings for stunned persons. But in the case of a speaker alert at *t* there are stimulations that *would* stun him at *t* and so *would* preclude any assent to or dissent from the ensuing 'Gavagai?'. These, by definition, belong to neither the affirmative nor the negative stimulus meaning of 'Gavagai' for him at *t*. Now where a discrepancy in stimulus meanings will ensue is where a stimulation is such as would stun one speaker and not another; for it could belong say to the negative stimulus meaning of 'Gavagai' or 'Rabbit' for the latter speaker and to neither the affirmative nor the negative stimulus meaning for the former speaker. This again is a discrepancy that would not puzzle the linguist, but that exists under our definition. Also there are interferences of less drastic sorts. The native may dissent from 'Gavagai' in plain sight of the rabbit's ears, because the rabbit is in no position for shooting;[3] he has misjudged the linguist's motive for asking 'Gavagai?'.

We have now seen that stimulus meaning as defined falls short in various ways of one's intuitive demands on "meaning" as undefined, and that sameness of stimulus meaning is too strict a relation to expect between a native occasion sentence and its translation—even in so benign a case as 'Gavagai' and 'Rabbit'. Yet stimulus meaning, by whatever name, may be properly looked upon still as the objective reality that the linguist has to probe when he undertakes radical translation. For the stimulus meaning of an occasion sentence is by definition the native's total battery of present dispositions to be prompted to assent to or to dissent from the sentence; and these dispositions are just what the linguist has to sample and estimate.

[3] Here I am indebted to Raymond Firth.

We do best to revise not the notion of stimulus meaning, but only what we represent the linguist as doing with stimulus meanings. The fact is that he translates not by identity of stimulus meanings, but by significant approximation of stimulus meanings.

If he translates 'Gavagai' as 'Rabbit' despite the discrepancies in stimulus meaning imagined above, he does so because the stimulus meanings seem to coincide to an overwhelming degree and the discrepancies, so far as he finds them, seem best explained away or dismissed as effects of unidentified interferences. Some discrepancies he may sift out, as lately suggested, by varying his times and informants. Some, involving poor glimpses or shock or verbal intrusions, he would not even bother to bring to fulfillment by a querying of the sentence. Some, such as those involving the rabbit-fly, he will dismiss as effects of unidentified interferences if he does not encounter them often. In taking this last rather high line, clearly he is much influenced by his natural expectation that any people in rabbit country would have *some* brief expression that could in the long run be best translated simply as 'Rabbit'. He conjectures that the now-unexplained discrepancies between 'Gavagai' and 'Rabbit' are ones that may eventually be reconciled with his translation, after he has somehow got deep enough into the native language to ask sophisticated questions.

In practice, of course, the natural expectation that the natives will have a brief expression for 'Rabbit' counts overwhelmingly. The linguist hears 'Gavagai' once, in a situation where a rabbit seems to be the object of concern. He will then try 'Gavagai' for assent or dissent in a couple of situations designed perhaps to eliminate 'White' and 'Animal' as alternative translations, and will forthwith settle upon 'Rabbit' as translation without further experiment—though always in readiness to discover through some unsought experience that a revision is in order. I made the linguist preternaturally circumspect, and maximized his bad luck in respect of discrepant observations, in order to consider what theoretical bearing a native's collateral information can have upon the linguist's in fact wholly facile opening translation.

§ 10. OBSERVATION SENTENCES

Some stimulus meanings are less susceptible than others to the influences of intrusive information. There is on this score a significant contrast between 'Red' and 'Rabbit' even when 'Red' is taken on a par with 'Rabbit' as announcing not a passing sense datum but an enduring objective trait of the physical object. True, there are extreme cases where we may be persuaded, by collateral information about odd lighting and juxtaposition, that something is really red that did not seem so or vice versa; but, despite such cases, there is less scope for collateral information in deciding whether a glimpsed thing is red than in deciding whether it is a rabbit. In the case of 'Red', therefore, sameness of stimulus meaning comes unusually close to what one intuitively expects of synonymy.

Color words are notoriously ill matched between remote languages, because of differences in customary grouping of shades. But this is no present problem; it means merely that there may well be no native occasion sentence, at least no reasonably simple one, with approximately the stimulus meaning of 'Red'. Again, even if there is one, there may still be a kind of trouble in equating it to 'Red', just because of the vagueness of color boundaries in both languages. But this again is no problem of collateral information; it is a difficulty that would remain even if a distinction between meaning and collateral information were successfully drawn. It can be coped with by a rough matching of statistical scatterings. The penumbra of vagueness of 'Red' consists of stimulations in respect of which the stimulus meanings of 'Red' tend to vary from speaker to speaker and from occasion to occasion; correspondingly for the penumbra of vagueness of the native sentence; and then 'Red' is a good translation to the extent that it resembles the native sentence umbra for umbra and penumbra for penumbra.

In terms of direct behavioral evidence, how do those fluctuations of stimulus meaning that are attributable to a penumbra of vagueness differ from those fluctuations of stimulus meaning (e.g. of 'Gavagai') that are laid to variations of collateral information from occasion to occasion? Partly in that the penumbral fluctuations increase rather smoothly as the stimulations grade off, while the fluctuations laid to collateral information are more irregular, suggesting intrusion of extraneous factors. But mainly in that each individual's assent or dissent tends to be marked by doubt and hesitation when the prompting stimulation belongs to the penumbra. If we were to complicate the notion of stimulus meaning to the extent of weighting each stimulation inversely according to reaction time (cf. § 8), then discrepancies in stimulus meaning from speaker to speaker would tend to count for little where due to vagueness, and for more where not.

If 'Red' is somewhat less susceptible than 'Rabbit' to the influences of intrusive information, there are other sentences that are vastly more so. An example is 'Bachelor'. An informant's assent to it is prompted genuinely enough by the sight of a face, yet it draws mainly on stored information and none on the prompting stimulation except as needed for recognizing the bachelor friend concerned. As one says in the uncritical jargon of meaning, the trouble with 'Bachelor' is that its meaning transcends the looks of the prompting faces and concerns matters that can be known only through other channels. 'Rabbit' is a little this way, as witness papier-mâché counterfeits; 'Bachelor' much more so. The stimulus meaning of 'Bachelor' cannot be treated as its "meaning" by any stretch of the imagination, unless perhaps accompanied by a stretch of the modulus.

A mark of the intrusion of collateral information, except when the information is generally shared as in the examples of the kibitzer and the rabbit-fly (§ 9), was discrepancy in stimulus meaning from speaker to speaker of the same language. In a case like 'Bachelor', therefore, we may expect the discrepancies to be overwhelming; and indeed they are. For any two speakers whose social contacts are not virtually identical, the stimulus meanings of 'Bachelor' will diverge far more than those of 'Rabbit'.

The less susceptible the stimulus meaning of an occasion sentence is to the influences of collateral information, the less absurdity there is in thinking of the stimulus meaning of the sentence as the meaning of the sentence. Occasion sentences whose stimulus meanings vary none under the influence of collateral information may naturally be called *observation sentences,* and their stimulus meanings may without fear of contradiction be said to do full justice to their meanings. These are the occasion sentences that wear their meanings on their sleeves. Or, better, we may speak of degrees of observationality; for even the stimulus meaning of 'Red' can, we noted, be made to fluctuate a little from occasion to occasion by collateral information on lighting conditions. What we have is a gradation of observationality from one extreme, at 'Red' or above, to the other extreme at 'Bachelor' or below.

In the foregoing paragraph we have wallowed most unfastidiously in the conceptual slough of meaning and collateral information. But now it is interesting to note that what we have dredged out, a notion of degree of observationality, is not beyond cleaning up and rendering respectable. For, in behavioral terms, an occasion sentence may be said to be the more observational the more nearly its stimulus meanings for different speakers tend to coincide. Granted, this definition fails to give demerit marks for the effects of generally shared information, such as that about the rabbit-fly. But, as argued in § 9, I suspect that no systematic experimental sense is to be made of a distinction between usage due to meaning and usage due to generally shared collateral information.

The notion of observationality is relative to the modulus of stimulation. This is not to be wondered at, since the notion of stimulus meaning was relative to the modulus (cf. § 8), and so is the very distinction between habit formation and habit formed (cf. § 7). Observationality increases with the modulus, in the following way. A typical case of discrepancy between the stimulus meanings of 'Gavagai', for two natives, is the case where one native and not the other has lately seen rabbits near the spot that they are now viewing. An ill-glimpsed movement would now prompt the one native and not the other to assent to 'Gavagai?'. But if we make the modulus long enough to include as part of the one native's present stimulation his recent observation of rabbits near the spot, then what had been a discrepancy between stimulus meanings is a mere difference of stimulations: the one stimulation is such as would prompt either native to assent, and the other neither. Increase the modulus sufficiently to take in extended periods of learning about friends and you even increase the observationality of 'Bachelor'. But let us forget moduli again for a while, thus keeping our variables down.

We have defined observationality for occasion sentences somewhat vaguely, as degree of constancy of stimulus meaning from speaker to speaker. It would not do to use this definition generally among standing sentences, since the stimulus meaning of a standing sentence can show fair constancy from speaker to speaker for the wrong reason: mere sparseness of member stimulations. Among standing sentences that are well over toward the occasion end (cf. § 9), however, the notion of observationality works quite as well as among occasion sentences, and is significant in the same way; viz., the higher the observationality, the better we can get on with translation by stimulus meaning. We could hope, e.g., to translate 'The tide is out' by a rough matching of stimulus meanings; not so 'There is a famous novelist on board'.

Viewing the graded notion of observationality as the primary one, we may still speak of sentences simply as observation sentences when they are high in observationality. In a narrow sense, just 'Red' would qualify; in a wider sense, also 'Rabbit' and 'The tide is out'. It is for observation sentences in some such sense that the notion of stimulus meaning constitutes a reasonable notion of meaning.

To philosophers 'observation sentence' suggests the datum sentences of science. On this score our version is not amiss; for the observation sentences as we have identified them are just the occasion sentences on which there is pretty sure to be firm agreement on the part of well-placed observers. Thus they are just the sentences on which a scientist will tend to fall back when pressed by doubting colleagues. Moreover, the philosophical doctrine of infallibility of observation sentences is sustained under our version. For there is scope for error and dispute only insofar as the connections with experience whereby sentences are appraised are multifarious and indirect, mediated through time by theory in conflicting ways; there is none insofar as verdicts to a sentence are directly keyed to present stimulation. (This immunity to error is, however, like observationality itself, for us a matter of degree.) Our version of observation sentences departs from a philosophical tradition in allowing the sentences to be about ordinary things instead of requiring them to report sense data, but this departure has not lacked proponents.[1]

In estimating the stimulus meaning of a sentence for a speaker at a given time, the linguist is helped by varying the time and speaker. In choosing a translation, he is helped by comparing native speakers and so eliminating idiosyncrasies of stimulus meaning. Still the notion of stimulus meaning itself, as defined, depends on no multi-

---

[1] For remarks on this matter and references see von Mises, *Positivism*, pp. 91–95, 379. To the main theme of this paragraph I sense harmony in Strawson, *Individuals*, p. 212: "If any facts deserve . . . to be called . . . atomic facts, it is the facts stated by those propositions which demonstratively indicate the incidence of a general feature." For the propositions alluded to seem, in the light of adjacent text, to correspond pretty well to what I have called occasion sentences.

plicity of speakers. Now the notion of observationality, in contrast, is social. The behavioral definition offered for it above turns on similarities of stimulus meanings over the community.

What makes an occasion sentence low on observationality is, by definition, wide intersubjective variability of stimulus meaning. Language as a socially inculcated set of dispositions is substantially uniform over the community, but it is uniform in different ways for different sentences. If a sentence is one that (like 'Red' and 'Rabbit') is inculcated mostly by something like direct ostension, the uniformity will lie at the surface and there will be little variation in stimulus meaning; the sentence will be highly observational. If it is one that (like 'Bachelor') is inculcated through connections with other sentences, linking up thus indirectly with past stimulations of other sorts than those that serve directly to prompt present assent to the sentence, then its stimulus meaning will vary with the speakers' pasts, and the sentence will count as very unobservational. The stimulus meaning of a very unobservational occasion sentence for a speaker is a product of two factors, a fairly standard set of sentence-to-sentence connections and a random personal history; hence the largely random character of the stimulus meaning from speaker to speaker.

Now this random character has the effect not only that the stimulus meaning of the sentence for one speaker will differ from the stimulus meaning of *that* sentence for other speakers. It will differ from the stimulus meaning also of any other discoverable sentence for other speakers, in the same language or any other. Granted, a great complex English sentence can be imagined whose stimulus meaning for one man matches, by sheer exhaustion of cases, another man's stimulus meaning of 'Bachelor'; but such a sentence would never be spotted, because nobody's stimulus meaning of 'Bachelor' would ever be suitably inventoried to begin with.

For, consider again how it was with 'Gavagai'. Here the stimulations belonging to the affirmative stimulus meaning share a distinctive trait that is salient, to us as well as to the native: the containing of rabbit glimpses. The trait is salient enough so that the linguist generalizes on it from samples: he expects the next glimpse of a rabbit to prompt assent to 'Gavagai' as past ones have. His generalization is repeatedly borne out, and he concludes with his conjecture that the native's whole stimulus meaning of 'Gavagai'— never experimentally exhausted, of course—will tend to match ours of 'Rabbit'. Now a similar effort with a non-observational native occasion sentence, of the type of our 'Bachelor', would have bogged down in its early stages. Sample stimulations belonging to the affirmative stimulus meaning of such a sentence, for the given native, would show no tempting common traits by which to conjecture further cases, or none but such as fail to hold up on further tries.

§ 11. INTRASUBJECTIVE SYNONYMY OF OCCASION SENTENCES

Stimulus meaning remains defined without regard to observationality. But when applied to non-observational sentences like 'Bachelor' it bears little resemblance to what might reasonably be called meaning. Translation of 'Soltero' as 'Bachelor' manifestly cannot be predicated on identity of stimulus meanings between speakers; nor can synonymy of 'Bachelor' and 'Unmarried man'.

But curiously enough the stimulus meanings of 'Bachelor' and 'Unmarried man' are, despite all this, identical for any one speaker.[1] An individual would at any one time be prompted by the same stimulations to assent to 'Bachelor' and 'Unmarried man'; and similarly for dissent. *Stimulus synonymy*, or sameness of stimulus meaning, is as good a standard of synonymy for non-observational occasion sentences as for observation sentences as long as we stick to one speaker. For each speaker, 'Bachelor' and 'Unmarried man' are stimulus-synonymous without having the same meaning in any acceptably defined sense of 'meaning' (for stimulus meaning is, in the case of 'Bachelor', nothing of the kind). Very well; here is a case where we may welcome the synonymy and let the meaning go.

The one-speaker restriction presents no obstacle to saying that 'Bachelor' and 'Unmarried man' are stimulus-synonymous for the whole community, in the sense of being thus for each member. A

[1] It can be argued that this much-used example of synonymy has certain imperfections having to do with ages, divorce, and bachelors of arts. Another example much used in philosophy, 'brother' and 'male sibling', may be held to bog down under certain church usages. An example that is perhaps unassailable is 'mother's father' and 'maternal grandfather' (poetic connotations not being here in point), or 'widower' and 'man who lost his wife' (Jakobson). However, with this much by way of caveat against quibbling, perhaps we can keep to our conventional example and overlook its divagations.

practical extension even to the two-language case is not far to seek if a bilingual speaker is at hand. 'Bachelor' and 'Soltero' will be stimulus-synonymous for him. Taking him as a sample, we may treat 'Bachelor' and 'Soltero' as synonymous for the translation purposes of the two whole linguistic communities that he represents. Whether he is a good enough sample would be checked by observing the fluency of his communication in both communities and by comparing other bilinguals.

Section 10 left the linguist unable to guess the trend of the stimulus meaning of a non-observational occasion sentence from sample cases. We now see a way, though costly, in which he can still accomplish radical translation of such sentences. He can settle down and learn the native language directly as an infant might.[2] Having thus become bilingual, he can translate the non-observational occasion sentences by introspected stimulus synonymy.

This step has the notable effect of initiating clear recognition of native falsehoods. As long as the linguist does no more than correlate the native's observation sentences with his own by stimulus meaning, he cannot discount any of the native's verdicts as false—unless *ad hoc*, most restrainedly, to simplify his correlations. But once he becomes bilingual and so transcends the observation sentences, he can bicker with the native as a brother.

Even short of going bilingual there is no difficulty in comparing two non-observational native sentences to see if they are intrasubjectively stimulus-synonymous for the native. The linguist can do this without having intuitively conjectured the trend of stimulus meaning of either sentence. He need merely query the sentences in parallel under random stimulations until he either hits a stimulation that prompts assent or dissent to one sentence and not to the other, or else is satisfied at last that he is not going to. A visiting Martian who never learns under what circumstances to apply 'Bachelor', or 'Unmarried man' either, can still find out by the above method that 'Bachelor' for one English speaker does not have the same stimulus meaning as 'Bachelor' for a different English speaker and that it has the same as 'Unmarried man' for the same speaker. He can, anyway, apart from one difficulty: there is no evident reason why it should occur to him thus blindly to try comparing 'Unmarried man' with 'Bachelor'. This difficulty makes the intrasubjec-

[2] See Chapter III for reflections on the infant's learning of our own language.

tive stimulus synonymy of non-observational occasion sentences less readily accessible to an alien linguist than the stimulus synonymy of observation sentences such as 'Gavagai' and 'Rabbit'. Still the linguist can examine for intrasubjective stimulus synonymy any pair of native occasion sentences that it occurs to him to wonder about; and we shall see in § 15 how indirect considerations can even suggest such pairs for examination.

Between the stimulus meaning of any sentence for one man and the stimulus meaning of the same or any other sentence for another man there are almost bound to be countless discrepancies in point of verbally contaminated stimulations, as long as one man understands a language that the other does not. The argument is that of the kibitzer case in § 9. The translating linguist had for this reason to discount verbally contaminated discrepancies. But intrasubjective comparisons are free of this trouble. Intrasubjectively we can even compare the occasion sentences 'Yes', 'Uh huh', and 'Quite' for stimulus synonymy, though the stimulations that enter into the stimulus meanings of these sentences are purely verbal in their relevant portions. A further advantage of the intrasubjective situation appears in the case of stimulations that would at a given time shock one speaker and not another into silence (cf. § 9); for clearly these will constitute no discrepancies intrasubjectively. Altogether the equating of stimulus meanings works out far better intrasubjectively than between subjects: it goes beyond observation sentences, it absorbs shock, and it better accommodates verbal stimulations.

Verbal stimulations can plague even the intrasubjective comparisons when they are stimulations of "second intention"—i.e., when besides consisting of words they are about words. Second-intention examples are the bane of theoretical linguistics, also apart from synonymy studies. Thus take the linguist engaged in distinguishing between those sequences of sounds or phonemes that can occur in English speech and those that cannot: all his excluded forms can return to confound him in second-intention English, as between quotation marks. Now some second-intention stimulations that could prompt a subject to assent to one of the queries 'Bachelor?' and 'Unmarried man?' to the exclusion of the other are as follows: a stimulation presenting the spelling of 'bachelor'; a stimulation presenting the words 'rhymes with 'harried man''; a stimulation presenting a glimpse of a bachelor friend together with a plea to redefine 'bachelor'. It is not easy to find a behavioral criterion of second-intention whereby to screen such cases, especially the last.

Leaving that problem unsolved, we have still to note another and more humdrum restriction that needs to be observed in equating sentences by stimulus meanings: we should stick to short sentences. Otherwise subjects' mere incapacity to digest long questions can, under our definitions, issue in difference of stimulus meanings between long and short sentences which we should prefer to find synonymous. A stimulation may prompt assent to the short sentence and not to the long one just because of the opacity of the long one; yet we should then like to say not that the subject has shown the meaning of the long sentence to be different, but merely that he has failed to encompass it. Still a concept of synonymy initially significant only for short sentences can be extended to long sentences by analogy, e.g. as follows. By a *construction*, linguistically speaking, let us understand any fixed way of building a composite expression from arbitrary components of appropriate sort, one or more at a time. (What is fixed may include certain additive words, as well as the way of arranging the unfixed components.) Now two sentence-forming constructions may be so related that whenever applied to the same components they yield mutually synonymous results, as long as the results are short enough to be compared for synonymy. In this event it is natural, by extension, to count also as mutually synonymous any results of applying those constructions to identical components however long. But to simplify ensuing considerations let us continue to reason without reference to this refinement where we can.

Our success with 'Bachelor' and 'Unmarried man' has been sufficient, despite the impasse at second intention, to tempt us to overestimate how well intrasubjective stimulus synonymy withstands collateral information. By way of corrective, consider the Himalayan explorer who has learned to apply 'Everest' to a distant mountain seen from Tibet and 'Gaurisanker' to one seen from Nepal. As occasion sentences these words have mutually exclusive stimulus meanings for him until his explorations reveal, to the surprise of all concerned, that the peaks are identical. His discovery is painfully empirical, not lexicographic; nevertheless the stimulus meanings of 'Everest' and 'Gaurisanker' coincide for him thenceforward.[3]

---

[3] I am indebted to Davidson for this point and to Schrödinger, *What Is Life?*, for the example. I am told that the example is wrong geographically.

Or again consider the occasion sentences 'Indian nickel' and 'Buffalo nickel'. These have distinct stimulus meanings for a boy for his first minute or two of passive acquaintance with these coins, and when he gets to turning them over the stimulus meanings tend to fuse.

Do they fully fuse? The question whether 'Indian nickel' and 'Buffalo nickel' have the same stimulus meaning for a given subject is the question whether any sequence of ocular irradiations or other stimulation (within the modulus), realized or not, *would* now prompt the subject to assent to or dissent from 'Indian nickel' and not 'Buffalo nickel' or vice versa. Among such stimulations are those that present, to all appearances, a coin whose obverse is like that of an Indian nickel but whose reverse bears some device other than the buffalo. Such stimulations can with a little felony even be realized. After a modulus-long examination of such a hybrid coin, a novice might conclude with surprise that there are after all two kinds of Indian nickel, while an expert, sure of his numismatics, might conclude that the coin must be fraudulent. For the expert, 'Indian nickel' and 'Buffalo nickel' are stimulus-synonymous; for the novice not.

The novice does believe and continues to believe, as the expert does, that all Indian nickels are buffalo nickels and vice versa; for the novice has not been and will not be actually subjected to the surprising stimulation described. But the mere fact that there is such a stimulation pattern and that the novice *would* now thus respond to it (whether we know it or not) is what, by definition, makes the stimulus meanings of 'Indian nickel' and 'Buffalo nickel' differ for the novice even as of now.

To keep our example pertinent we must abstract from what may be called the conniving mode of speech: the mode in which we knowingly speak of Olivier as Macbeth, of a statue of a horse as a horse, of a false nickel as a nickel. Even the expert would in practice speak of the prepared coin as "that Indian nickel with the whoozis on the back," adding that it was phony. Here we have a broader usage of 'nickel', under which nobody would seriously maintain even that all Indian nickels are in point of fact buffalo nickels and vice versa; whereas our purpose in the example is to examine two supposedly coextensive terms for sameness of stimulus meaning. In the example, therefore, read 'Indian nickel' and 'buffalo nickel' as 'real Indian nickel', 'real buffalo nickel'.

From the example we see that two terms can in fact be coextensive, or true of the same things, without being intrasubjectively stimulus-synonymous as occasion sentences. They can be believed coextensive without being, even for the believer, stimulus-synonymous as occasion sentences; witness 'Indian nickel' and 'Buffalo nickel' for the novice. But when as in the expert's case the belief is so firm that no pattern of stimulation (within the modulus) would suffice to dislodge it, they are stimulus-synonymous as occasion sentences.

So it is apparent that intrasubjective stimulus synonymy remains open to criticism, from intuitive preconceptions, for relating occasion sentences whose stimulus meanings coincide on account of collateral information. Now there is still a way of cutting out the effects of idiosyncratic information: we can hold out for virtual constancy over the community. In this social sense of stimulus synonymy, 'Indian nickel' and 'Buffalo nickel' would cease to count as stimulus-synonymous, because of such speakers as our novice; whereas 'Bachelors' and 'Unmarried man' might still rate as stimulus-synonymous even socially, as being intrasubjectively stimulus-synonymous for nearly everybody. There is still no screen against the effects of collateral information common to the community; but, as urged in § 9, I think that at that point the ideal becomes illusory.

§ 12. SYNONYMY OF TERMS

In starting our consideration of meaning with sentences we have hewn the line of §§ 3 and 4, where it was stressed that words are learned only by abstraction from their roles in learned sentences. But there are one-word sentences, such as 'Red' and 'Rabbit'. Insofar as the concept of stimulus meaning may be said to constitute in some strained sense a meaning concept for these, it would seem to constitute a meaning concept for general terms like 'red' and 'rabbit'. This, however, is a mistake. Stimulus synonymy of the occasion sentences 'Gavagai' and 'Rabbit' does not even guarantee that 'gavagai' and 'rabbit' are coextensive terms, terms true of the same things.

For, consider 'gavagai'. Who knows but what the objects to which this term applies are not rabbits after all, but mere stages, or brief temporal segments, of rabbits? In either event the stimulus situations that prompt assent to 'Gavagai' would be the same as for 'Rabbit'. Or perhaps the objects to which 'gavagai' applies are all and sundry undetached parts of rabbits; again the stimulus meaning would register no difference. When from the sameness of stimulus meanings of 'Gavagai' and 'Rabbit' the linguist leaps to the conclusion that a gavagai is a whole enduring rabbit, he is just taking for granted that the native is enough like us to have a brief general term for rabbits and no brief general term for rabbit stages or parts.

A further alternative likewise compatible with the same old stimulus meaning is to take 'gavagai' as a singular term naming the fusion, in Goodman's sense, of all rabbits: that single though discontinuous portion of the spatiotemporal world that consists of rabbits. Thus even the distinction between general and singular terms is independent of stimulus meaning. The same point can be seen by considering, conversely, the singular term 'Bernard J. Ortcutt': it differs none in stimulus meaning from a general term true of each of the good dean's temporal segments, and none from a general term true of each of his spatial parts. And a still further alternative in the case of 'gavagai' is to take it as a singular term naming a recurring universal, rabbithood. The distinction between concrete and abstract object, as well as that between general and singular term, is independent of stimulus meaning.

Commonly we can translate something (e.g. 'for the sake of') into a given language though nothing in that language corresponds to certain of the component syllables. Just so the occasion sentence 'Gavagai' is translatable as saying that a rabbit is there, even if no part of 'Gavagai' nor anything at all in the native language quite corresponds to the term 'rabbit'. Synonymy of 'Gavagai' and 'Rabbit' as sentences turns on considerations of prompted assent; not so synonymy of them as terms. We are right to write 'Rabbit', instead of 'rabbit', as a signal that we are considering it in relation to what is synonymous with it as a sentence and not in relation to what is synonymous with it as a term.

Does it seem that the imagined indecision between rabbits, stages of rabbits, integral parts of rabbits, the rabbit fusion, and rabbithood must be due merely to some special fault in our formulation of stimulus meaning, and that it should be resoluble by a little supplementary pointing and questioning? Consider, then, how. Point to a rabbit and you have pointed to a stage of a rabbit, to an integral part of a rabbit, to the rabbit fusion, and to where rabbithood is manifested. Point to an integral part of a rabbit and you have pointed again to the remaining four sorts of things; and so on around. Nothing not distinguished in stimulus meaning itself is to be distinguished by pointing, unless the pointing is accompanied by questions of identity and diversity: 'Is this the same gavagai as that?', 'Do we have here one gavagai or two?'. Such questioning requires of the linguist a command of the native language far beyond anything that we have as yet seen how to account for. We cannot even say what native locutions to count as analogues of terms as we know them, much less equate them with ours term for term, except as we have also decided what native devices to view as doing in their devious ways the work of our own various auxiliaries to objective reference: our articles and pronouns, our singular and plural, our copula, our identity predicate.[1] The whole apparatus is interdependent, and the very notion of term is as provincial to our culture as are those associated devices. The native may achieve the same net effects through linguistic structures so different that any eventual construing of our devices in the native language and vice versa can prove unnatural and largely arbitrary. (Cf. § 15.) Yet the net effects, the occasion sentences and not the terms, can match up in point of stimulus meanings as well as ever for all that. Occasion sentences and stimulus meaning are general coin; terms and reference are local to our conceptual scheme.[2]

It will perhaps be countered that there is no essential difficulty in spotting judgments of identity on the part of the jungle native, or even of a speechless animal. This is true enough for qualitative identity, better called resemblance. In an organism's susceptibility to the conditioning of responses we have plentiful criteria for his standards of resemblance of stimulations. (Cf. § 17.) But what is relevant to the preceding reflections is numerical identity. Two pointings may be pointings to a numerically identical rabbit, to numerically distinct rabbit parts, and to numerically distinct rabbit stages; the inscrutability lies not in resemblance, but in the anatomy

[1] Strawson is making this point when he writes that "feature-placing sentences do not introduce particulars into our discourse" ("Particular and general," p. 244). See below, § 45, for a link with Brentano's thesis.

[2] Russell conceived of what he called "object words" as in effect occasion sentences (*Inquiry*, Ch. IV), but, like Carnap (see end of § 8, above), he failed to note the present point: that the use of a word as an occasion sentence, however determinate, does not fix the extension of the word as a term.

of sentences. We could equate a native expression with any of the disparate English terms 'rabbit', 'rabbit stage', 'undetached rabbit part', etc., and still, by compensatorily juggling the translation of numerical identity and associated particles, preserve conformity to stimulus meanings of occasion sentences.[3]

Intrasubjective stimulus synonymy, for all its advantages over the two-speaker case, is similarly powerless to equate terms. Our Martian of § 11 can find as he did that 'Bachelor' and 'Unmarried man' are synonymous occasion sentences for the English speaker, but still either *term* to the exclusion of the other might, so far as he knows, apply not to men but to their stages or parts or even to a scattered concrete totality or an abstract attribute.

We saw in § 11 that coextensiveness of terms, or even believed coextensiveness, is not sufficient for their stimulus synonymy as occasion sentences. We now see also that it is not necessary. Where other languages than our own are involved, coextensiveness of terms is not a manifestly clearer notion than synonymy or translation itself; it is no clearer than the considerations, whatever they are (§§ 15 and 16), that make for contextual translation of the identity predicate, the copula, and related particles.

Yet surely the main interest of the synonymy of 'Bachelor' and 'Unmarried man' as occasion sentences was the line it seemed to give on the synonymy of 'bachelor' and 'unmarried man' as terms. Now within English the situation is not beyond saving. To get synonymy of terms from synonymy of the corresponding occasion sentences we need only add a condition that will screen out such pairs as 'bachelor' and 'part of a bachelor'; and this we can do by requiring that the subject be prepared to assent to the standing sentence 'All Fs are Gs and vice versa', thinking of 'F' and 'G' as the terms in question. The definition becomes this: 'F' and 'G' are stimulus-synonymous as terms for a speaker at t if and only if as occasion sentences they have the same stimulus meaning for him at t and he would assent to 'All Fs are Gs and vice versa' if asked at t. But we can simplify this definition, by strengthening the latter part to make it assure the former part. Instead of just saying he would assent to 'All Fs are Gs and vice versa' as things stand at t, we can say he would still assent to it, if to anything, following any stimulation that might be imposed at t. (The 'if to anything' accommo-

---

[3] On this theme see further §§ 15, 16, 19, 20, 24.

dates shock.) This strengthened condition assures that 'F' and 'G'
will also agree in stimulus meaning as occasion sentences; for, if
each stimulation would leave the subject prepared to assent to 'All
Fs are Gs and vice versa' if to anything, then none would prompt
him to assent to or dissent from one of 'F' and 'G' and not the
other.[4]

For reasons evident in § 14, I call a sentence *stimulus-analytic*
for a subject if he would assent to it, or nothing, after every stimulation (within the modulus). Our condition of stimulus synonymy
of 'F' and 'G' as general terms then reduces to stimulus analyticity
of 'All Fs are Gs and vice versa'. This condition has its parallel for
singular terms, represented by 'a' and 'b'; viz., stimulus-analyticity
of '$a = b$'. But note that our formulations apply only to English and
to languages whose translations of 'all', 'are', and '=' are somehow
settled in advance. This limitation is to be expected in notions relating to terms.

Our simplification of the definition of term synonymy extends it
to all terms, regardless of whether their objects are such that we
could reasonably use the terms as occasion sentences. We must
not conclude, from seeming appropriateness of the definition as
applied to terms like 'rabbit', 'bachelor', and 'buffalo nickel', that it
is as appropriate to the wider domain. However, let us leave that
question and think further about the narrower domain.

Our version of synonymy makes the terms 'Indian nickel' and
'buffalo nickel' synonymous for the expert of § 11, and not for the
novice. It is open to criticism, from intuitive preconceptions, for its
equating of terms whose coextensiveness the subject has learned by
exploration and experiment and not merely by encompassing their
"meanings." Such, then, is the concept of stimulus synonymy of
terms that comes out of stimulus synonymy of occasion sentences for
individual speakers. We can still socialize the concept and so cut
out the effects of idiosyncratic information, as we did for occasion
sentences at the end of § 11: we can count just those terms as
socially stimulus-synonymous that come out stimulus-synonymous
for each individual speaker almost without exception. Socially,
'bachelor' and 'unmarried man' remain stimulus-synonymous while
'Indian nickel' and 'buffalo nickel' do not.

---

[4] Incoherent behavior is possible, but there is a limit to the bizarreness of
exceptions worth allowing for in these behavioral formulations.

We welcome this consequence of socializing our concept of stimulus synonymy because our intuitive semantics [5] rates 'bachelor' and 'unmarried man' as synonymous, and probably 'Indian nickel' and 'buffalo nickel' not. But now what can have been the cause of those intuitive ratings themselves? Not, I think, any close analogue, however unconscious, of our present construction: not an implicit sociological guess that under extraordinary stimulation most people would hold 'bachelor' and 'unmarried man' coextensive while many would let 'Indian nickel' and 'buffalo nickel' diverge. A likelier place to seek the cause is in the difference between how we whose mother tongue is English learn 'bachelor' and how we learn 'Indian nickel'. We learn 'bachelor' by learning appropriate associations of words with words, and 'Indian nickel' by learning directly to associate the term with sample objects.[6] It is the difference, so central to Russell's philosophy, between description and acquaintance. It is kept before us in synchronic behavior as a difference between the non-observational occasion sentences, with their random variation in stimulus meaning from speaker to speaker, and observation sentences with their socially uniform stimulus meanings. (Cf. § 10.) One looks to 'unmarried man' as semantically anchoring 'bachelor' because there is no socially constant stimulus meaning to govern the use of the word; sever its tie with 'unmarried man' and you leave it no very evident social determination, hence no utility in communication.

'Brother', in its synonymy with 'male sibling', is essentially like 'bachelor' in its synonymy with 'unmarried man'. We learn 'brother' (in its accurate adult use) only by verbal connections with sentences about childbirth, and 'sibling' by verbal connections with 'brother' and 'sister'. The occasion sentences 'Brother' and 'Sibling' are non-observational: their stimulus meanings vary over society in as random a fashion as that of 'Bachelor', and it is only the few verbal links that give the terms the fixity needed in communication.

Many terms of systematic theoretical science are of a third sort. They are like 'bachelor' and 'brother' in having no socially constant stimulus meanings to govern their use; indeed such a term is commonly useless in the role of occasion sentence, so that there is no

[5] See § 9, note 1.

[6] To be precise about the example, we learn 'nickel' and 'Indian' in direct association with sample objects or likenesses, and then 'Indian nickel' is self-explanatory once we see one.

question of stimulus meaning. Yet they are unlike 'bachelor' and 'brother' in having a more complex network of verbal connections, so that no one tie seems crucial to communication. Thus it is that in theoretical science, unless as recast by semantics enthusiasts, distinctions between synonymies and "factual" equivalences are seldom sensed or claimed. Even the identity historically introduced into mechanics by defining 'momentum' as 'mass times velocity' takes its place in the network of connections on a par with the rest; if a physicist subsequently so revises mechanics that momentum fails to be proportional to velocity, the change will probably be seen as a change of theory and not peculiarly of meaning.[7] Synonymy intuitions do not emerge here, just because the terms are linked to the rest of language in more ways than words like 'bachelor' are.[8]

§ 13. TRANSLATING LOGICAL CONNECTIVES

In §§ 7 through 11 we accounted for radical translation of occasion sentences, by approximate identification of stimulus meanings. Now there is also a decidedly different domain that lends itself directly to radical translation: that of *truth functions* such as negation, logical conjunction, and alternation. For this purpose the sentences put to the native for assent or dissent may be occasion sentences and standing sentences indifferently. Those that are occasion sentences will have to be accompanied by a prompting stimulation, if assent or dissent is to be elicited; the standing sentences, on the other hand, can be put without props. Now by reference to assent and dissent we can state semantic criteria for truth functions; i.e., criteria for determining whether a given native idiom is to be construed as expressing the truth function in question. The semantic criterion of negation is that it turns any short sentence to which one will assent into a sentence from which one will dissent, and vice versa. That of conjunction is that it produces compounds to which (so long as the component sentences are short)

---

[7] See the last section of my "Carnap and logical truth."

[8] Putnam in "The analytic and the synthetic" has offered an illuminating account of the synonymy intuition in terms of a contrast between terms that connote clusters of traits and terms that do not. My account fits with his and perhaps adds to the explanation. His cases of clustering correspond to my observational terms such as 'Indian nickel' and theoretical terms such as 'momentum', as against 'bachelor'.

one is prepared to assent always and only when one is prepared to assent to each component. That of alternation is similar with assent changed twice to dissent.

The point about short components is merely, as in § 11, that when they are long the subject may get mixed up. Identification of a native idiom as negation, or conjunction, or alternation, is not to be ruled out in view of a subject's deviation from our semantic criteria when the deviation is due merely to confusion. No limit is imposed on the lengths of the component sentences to which negation, conjunction, or alternation may be applied; it is just that the test cases for first spotting such constructions in a strange language are cases with short components.

When we find that a native construction fulfills one or another of these three semantic criteria, we can ask no more toward an understanding of it. Incidentally we can then translate the idiom into English as 'not', 'and', or 'or' as the case may be, but only subject to sundry humdrum provisos; for it is well known that these three English words do not represent negation, conjunction, and alternation exactly and unambiguously.

Any construction for compounding sentences from sentences is counted in logic as expressing a truth function if it fulfills this condition: the compound has a unique truth value (truth or falsity) for each assignment of truth values to the components. Semantic criteria can obviously be stated for all truth functions along the lines already followed for negation, conjunction, and alternation.

This approach ill accords with a doctrine of "prelogical mentality." To take the extreme case, let us suppose that certain natives are said to accept as true certain sentences translatable in the form 'p and not p'. Now this claim is absurd under our semantic criteria. And, not to be dogmatic about them, what criteria might one prefer? Wanton translation can make natives sound as queer as one pleases. Better translation imposes our logic upon them, and would beg the question of prelogicality if there were a question to beg.[1]

---

[1] Malinowski, pp. 68 ff., spared his islanders the imputation of prelogicality by so varying his translations of terms, from occurrence to occurrence, as to sidestep contradiction. Leach, p. 130, protested; but no clear criterion emerged. It is understandable that the further alternative of blaming the translation of conjunctions, copulas, or other logical particles is nowhere considered; for any considerable complexity on the part of the English correlates of such words would of course present the working translator with forbidding practical

Consider, for that matter, the Spaniard with his 'No hay nada.' Lovers of paradox may represent him as flouting the law of double negation. Soberer translators may reckon 'no' and 'nada', in this context, as halves of one negative.

That fair translation preserves logical laws is implicit in practice even where, to speak paradoxically, no foreign language is involved. Thus when to our querying of an English sentence an English speaker answers 'Yes and no', we assume that the queried sentence is meant differently in the affirmation and negation; this rather than that he would be so silly as to affirm and deny the same thing. Again, when someone espouses a logic whose laws are ostensibly contrary to our own, we are ready to speculate that he is just giving some familiar old vocables ('and', 'or', 'not', 'all', etc.) new meanings. This talk of meaning is intuitive, uncritical, and undefined, but it is a piece with translation; what it registers is our reluctance under such circumstances to "translate" the speaker's English into our English by the normal tacit method of homophonic translation.

Or consider the familiar remark that even the most audacious system-builder is bound by the law of contradiction. How is he really bound? If he were to accept contradiction, he would so readjust his logical laws as to insure distinctions of some sort; for the classical laws yield all sentences as consequences of any contradiction. But then we would proceed to reconstrue his heroically novel logic as a non-contradictory logic, perhaps even as familiar logic, in perverse notation.

The maxim of translation underlying all this is that assertions startlingly false on the face of them are likely to turn on hidden differences of language. This maxim is strong enough in all of us to swerve us even from the homophonic method that is so fundamental to the very acquisition and use of one's mother tongue.

The common sense behind the maxim is that one's interlocutor's silliness, beyond a certain point, is less likely than bad translation— or, in the domestic case, linguistic divergence.[2] Another account of the matter, as it touches logical laws in the domestic case, is as fol-

difficulties. —Eventually Levy-Bruhl, pp. 130 f., gave up his original doctrine of prelogical mentality; but the considerations that operated are not easy to relate to the present ones.

[2] Cf. Wilson's principle of charity: "We select as designatum that individual which will make the largest possible number of . . . statements true" (Wilson, "Substances without subtrata").

lows. The logical particles 'and', 'all', etc. are learned only from sentential contexts. Dropping a logical law means a devastatingly widespread unfixing of truth values of contexts of the particles concerned, leaving no fixity to rely on in using those particles. In short, their meanings are gone; new ones may be supplied. What prompts a sense of meaning-involvement here is thus at bottom the same as in the case of 'bachelor' and 'unmarried man' (§ 12).

Let us now resume our reflections on logic under radical translation. We have settled a people's logical laws completely, so far as the truth-functional part of logic goes, once we have fixed our translations by the above semantic criteria. Truths of this part of logic are called *tautologies*: the truth-functional compounds that are true by truth-functional structure alone. There is a familiar tabular routine for determining, for sentences in which the truth functions are however immoderately iterated and superimposed, just what assignments of truth values to the ultimate component sentences will make the whole compound true; and the tautologies are the compounds that come out true under all assignments.

But the truth functions and tautologies are only the simplest of the logical functions and logical truths. Can we perhaps do better? The logical functions that most naturally next suggest themselves are the categoricals, traditionally designated A, E, I, and O, and commonly construed in English by the constructions 'all are' ('All rabbits are timid'), 'none are', 'some are', 'some are not'. A semantic criterion for A perhaps suggests itself as follows: the compound commands assent (from a given speaker) if and only if the affirmative stimulus meaning (for him) of the first component is a subclass of the affirmative stimulus meaning of the second component and the negative stimulus meanings are conversely related. How to vary this for E, I, and O is obvious enough, except that the whole idea is wrong in view of § 12. Thus take A. All Indian nickels are buffalo nickels, and even are believed by the novice of § 12 to be buffalo nickels, but still the affirmative stimulus meaning of 'Indian nickel', for our novice anyway, has stimulus patterns in it that are not in the affirmative stimulus meaning of 'Buffalo nickel'. On this score the suggested semantic criterion is at odds with 'All Fs are Gs' in that it goes beyond extension. And it has a yet more serious failing of the opposite kind; for, whereas rabbit stages are not rabbits, we saw in § 12 that in point of stimulus meaning there is no distinction.

The difficulty is fundamental. The categoricals depend for their truth on the objects, however external and however inferential, of which the component terms are true; and what those objects are is not uniquely determined by stimulus meanings. Indeed the categoricals, like plural endings and identity, are part of our own special apparatus of objective reference, whereas stimulus meaning is, to repeat § 12, common coin. Of what we think of as logic, the truth-functional part is the only part the recognition of which, in a foreign language, we seem to be able to pin down to behavioral criteria.

The condition that was seen to be inadequate as a semantic condition for the A copula does still determine a copula. Let me write 'pars' for this copula. Its usage is to be such that a compound of the form '... pars ...', formed of two occasion sentences S_1 and S_2 in that order, is a standing sentence and is to command assent of just the speakers for whom the affirmative stimulus meaning of S_1 is a subclass of that of S_2 and conversely for the negative. Thus, if we think of S_1 and S_2 as general terms—a detail of translation left open by stimulus meaning—then 'F pars G' says approximately that every F is part of the fusion (§ 12) of the Gs; and if we think of S_1 and S_2 as singular terms, 'a pars b' says approximately that a is part of b. The theory of the part relation, called mereology by Leśniewski and the calculus of individuals by Goodman and Leonard,[3] is thus more amenable to radical semantic criteria than is the logic of the syllogism. But we must give full weight to the word 'approximately', twice used just now; the correspondence is rather poor, because, as remarked two paragraphs back, our semantic criterion makes demands beyond extension.

§ 14. SYNONYMOUS AND ANALYTIC SENTENCES

By its etymology, 'synonymous' applies to names. Though in use the term is intended simply to impute sameness of meaning, an effect of its etymology is seen in a tendency to invoke some other word, 'equivalent' or 'equipollent', for cases where both of the compared expressions are (unlike 'bachelor') verbally complex. My use of 'synonymous' is not thus restricted; I intend the word to carry the full generality of 'same in meaning', whatever that is. Indeed I

[3] See Goodman, *Structure of Appearance*, pp. 42 ff., and further references therein.

have made no essential use of a distinction between word and phrase. Even the first object of translation, say 'Gavagai', may or may not in the end be parsed as a string of several words, depending on one's eventual choice of analytical hypotheses (§§ 15, 16).

Taking this minor liberalization hereafter for granted, we still must distinguish between a broad and a narrow type of synonymy, or sameness of meaning, as applied to sentences. The broad one may be formulated in intuitive terms thus: the two sentences command assent concomitantly and dissent concomitantly, and this concomitance is due strictly to word usage rather than to how things happen in the world. One usually hears the matter described in terms rather of truth values than of assent and dissent; but I warp it over to the latter terms in order to maximize chances of making sense of the relation on the basis of verbal behavior.

For some purposes a narrower sort of synonymy of sentences is wanted, such as what Carnap calls intensional isomorphism, involving certain part-by-part correspondences of the sentences concerned. (Cf. § 42.) But such variant versions can be defined on the basis of the broader one. Synonymy of parts is defined by appeal to analogy of roles in synonymous wholes; then synonymy in the narrower sense is defined for the wholes by appeal to synonymy of homologous parts. So let us concentrate on the broader and more basic notion of sentence synonymy.

By talking in terms of assent and dissent here instead of in terms of truth values we introduce this difficulty: assent and dissent can be influenced by confusion due to a sentence's length and complexity. But this difficulty can be accommodated in the way sketched in § 11. Also it would be automatically taken care of under the program, just now mentioned, of deriving a relation of synonymy of sentence fragments and thence constructing a reformed synonymy relation for wholes. Let us pass over these points, for there is a more basic problem.

When the sentences are occasion sentences, the envisaged notion of synonymy is pretty well realized in intrasubjective stimulus synonymy, especially as socialized. For we can argue that only verbal habit can plausibly account for concomitant variation of two occasion sentences, in point of assent and dissent, over the whole gamut of possible stimulations. There are still the unscreened effects of community-wide collateral information, but there is no evident reason not to count such information simply as a determinant of the verbal habit (§ 9). When the sentences are standing sentences which, like 'The *Times* has come', closely resemble occasion sentences in the variability of assent and dissent, stimulus synonymy still does pretty well.

But the less variable the standing sentences are in point of assent and dissent, the sparser their stimulus meanings will be and hence the more poorly stimulus synonymy will approximate to synonymy of the envisaged sort. For, however sparse its stimulus meaning, a sentence retains its connections with other sentences and plays its distinctive part in theories. The sparseness of its stimulus meaning is no sparseness of meaning intuitively speaking, but has the effect that stimulus meaning fails to do the sentence much justice.

By lengthening the modulus of stimulation we can enrich the stimulus meanings and so tighten the relation of stimulus synonymy; for, the longer the stimulations the better their chance of influencing assent and dissent. However, matters get out of hand when the modulus is excessive. Thus consider stimulus synonymy modulo a month. To say that two sentences are now so related is to say that any and every pattern of month-long stimulation, if begun now and terminated next month with a querying of the two sentences, would elicit the same verdict on both. The trouble is that there is no telling what to expect under fairly fantastic stimulation sequences of such duration. The subject might revise his theories in unforeseeable ways that would be claimed to change meanings of words. There is no reason to expect the concomitances of sentences under such circumstances to reflect present sameness of meaning in any intuitively plausible sense. Lengthening the modulus enriches stimulus meanings and tightens stimulus synonymy only as it diminishes scrutability of stimulus synonyms.

Stimulus synonymy, on an optimum modulus, is an approximation to what philosophers loosely call sameness of confirming experiences and of disconfirming experiences. It is an approximation to what it might mean "to speak of two statements as standing in the same germaneness-relation to the same particular experiences." [1] Where standing sentences are of highly unoccasional type, the inadequacy of stimulus synonymy to synonymy intuitively so-called is shared by the vaguer formulations just now noted. And it is shared by the proposal of Perkins and Singer, viz., that we com-

[1] Grice and Strawson, p. 156.

pare sentences for synonymy by putting them to our informant for verification and seeing whether he proceeds similarly in both cases.[2] The trouble lies in the interconnections of sentences. If the business of a sentence can be exhausted by an account of the experiences that would confirm or disconfirm it as an isolated sentence in its own right, then the sentence is substantially an occasion sentence. The significant trait of other sentences is that experience is relevant to them largely in indirect ways, through the mediation of associated sentences. Alternatives emerge: experiences call for changing a theory, but do not indicate just where and how. Any of various systematic changes can accommodate the recalcitrant datum, and all the sentences affected by any of those possible alternative readjustments would evidently have to count as disconfirmed by that datum indiscriminately or not at all. Yet the sentences can be quite unlike with respect to content, intuitively speaking, or role in the containing theory.

Grice and Strawson try (*loc. cit.*) to meet this difficulty by defining S_1 and S_2 as synonymous when, for every assumption as to the truth values of other sentences, the same experiences confirm (and disconfirm) S_1 on that assumption as confirm (and disconfirm) S_2 on that assumption. Now instead of 'every assumption as to the truth values of other sentences' we can as well say simply 'every sentence S'; for S can be the logical conjunction of those "other sentences" in question or their negations. So S_1 and S_2 are defined to be synonymous when, for every S, the same experiences confirm (and disconfirm) S_1 on the hypothesis S as confirm (and disconfirm) S_2 on S. The notion of confirmatory and disconfirmatory experiences had a behavioral approximation in our notion of stimulus meaning; but can we relativize it thus to a hypothesis S? I think we can; for confirmation or disconfirmation of S_1 on S is presumably confirmation or disconfirmation of the conditional sentence consisting of S as antecedent and S_1 as consequent. Then the proposed definition of synonymy becomes: S_1 and S_2 are synonymous if for every S the conditional compound of S and S_1 and that of S and S_2 are stimulus-synonymous. But now it is apparent that the definition fails to provide a tighter relation between S_1 and S_2 than stimulus synonymy. For, if S_1 and S_2 are stimulus-synonymous than *a fortiori* the conditionals are too.

---

[2] See Perkins and Singer. It is significant that their examples are occasion sentences.

A variant suggestion would be to define S_1 and S_2 as synonymous when, for every S, the logical conjunction of S and S_1 and that of S and S_2 are stimulus-synonymous. But this is yet more readily seen not to provide a tighter relation.

If either of these ventures had succeeded, the synonymy yielded would still have been strictly intralinguistic; for the auxiliary S, belonging to one language, gets joined to both S_1 and S_2. But the language would not have to be our own. For, by § 13, conjunction is translatable; and so is the conditional, if we take it in the material sense 'Not (p and not q)'.

The general relation of intrasubjective sentence synonymy thus unsuccessfully sought is interdefinable with another elusive notion of intuitive philosophical semantics: that of an *analytic* sentence. Here the intuitive notion is that the sentence is true purely by meaning and independently of collateral information: thus 'No bachelor is married', 'Pigs are pigs', and, by some accounts, '$2 + 2 = 4$'.[3] The interdefinitions run thus: sentences are synonymous if and only if their biconditional (formed by joining them with 'if and only if') is analytic, and a sentence is analytic if and only if synonymous with self-conditionals ('If p then p').

As synonymy of sentences is related to analyticity, so stimulus synonymy of sentences is related to stimulus analyticity (§ 12).

[3] There is a small confusion that I should like to take this opportunity to resolve, though it lies aside from the main course of the present reflections. Those who talk confidently of analyticity have been known to disagree on the analyticity of the truths of arithmetic, but are about unanimous on that of the truths of logic. We who are less clear on the notion of analyticity may therefore seize upon the generally conceded analyticity of the truths of logic as a partial extensional clarification of analyticity; but to do this is not to embrace the analyticity of the truths of logic as an antecedently intelligible doctrine. I have been misunderstood on this score by Gewirth, p. 406 n., and others. Contrast my "Truth by convention." Not that all criticisms of my remarks on truths of logic turn on this misunderstanding. Pap's criticism in *Semantics and Necessary Truth*, p. 237 n., is another matter, and was answered anticipatorily in my "Carnap and logical truth," end of § IX (to which he had no access). Strawson's criticism in "Propositions, concepts, and logical truths" is another still, and an interesting one, which I cannot claim to have answered anywhere. — Speaking of "Truth by convention," I would remark that my much-cited definition of logical truth therein was meant only as an improved exposition of a long-current idea. So I was not taken aback at Bar-Hillel's finding the idea in Bolzano; I was, though, at recently uncovering an anticipation of my specific exposition, in Ajdukiewicz.

Philosophical tradition hints of three nested categories of firm truths: the analytic, the *a priori,* and the necessary. Whether the first exhausts the second, and the second the third, are traditional matters of disagreement, though none of the three has traditionally been defined in terms of detectable features of verbal behavior. Pressed nowadays for such a clarification, some who are content to take the three as identical have responded in this vein: the analytic sentences are those that we are prepared to affirm come what may. This comes to naught unless we independently circumscribe the 'what may'. Thus one may object that we would not adhere to 'No bachelor is married' if we found a married bachelor; and how are we to disallow his example without appealing to the very notion of analyticity we are trying to define? One way is to take 'come what may' as 'come what stimulation (§ 8) may'; and this gives virtually the definition (§ 12) of stimulus analyticity.[4]

We improved stimulus synonymy a bit by socializing it. We can do the same for analyticity, calling socially stimulus-analytic just the sentences that are stimulus-analytic for almost everybody. But analyticity in even this improved sense will apply as well to 'There have been black dogs' as to '2 + 2 = 4' and 'No bachelor is married'. Let us face it: our socialized stimulus synonymy and stimulus analyticity are still not behavioristic reconstructions of intuitive semantics, but only a behavioristic ersatz.

At the end of § 12 we speculated on what makes for the intuition of synonymy of terms. Similar considerations apply to intuitions of sentence synonymy and analyticity. Such an intuition figures in the case of analyticity despite the technical sound of the word; sentences like 'No unmarried man is married', 'No bachelor is married', and '2 + 2 = 4' have a feel that everyone appreciates. Moreover the notion of "assent come what may" gives no fair hint of the intuition involved. One's reaction to denials of sentences typically felt as analytic has more in it of one's reaction to ungrasped foreign sentences.[5] Where the sentence concerned is a law of logic, something of the ground of this reaction was discerned in § 13: dropping a logical law disrupts a pattern on which the communicative use of

---

[4] I am indebted to Davidson for the concept of stimulus analyticity, as well as for this observation concerning it. Mates also may be said to have taken a step in somewhat this direction, in his proposal of contrary-to-fact questionnaires ("Analytic sentences," p. 532).

[5] Cf. Grice and Strawson, pp. 150 f.

a logical particle heavily depends. Much the same applies to '2 + 2 = 4', and even to 'The parts of the parts of a thing are parts of the thing'. The key words here have countless further contexts to anchor their usage, but somehow we feel that if our interlocutor will not agree with us on these platitudes there is no depending on him in most of the further contexts containing the terms in question.

Examples like 'No bachelor is married' rate as analytic both directly on the vague count just now conjectured and by virtue of coming from logical truths by synonymy substitution.

If the mechanism of analyticity intuitions is substantially as I have vaguely suggested, they will in general tend to set in where bewilderment sets in as to what the man who denies the sentence can be talking about. This effect can be gradual and also cumulative.[6] The intuitions are blameless in their way, but it would be a mistake to look to them for a sweeping epistemological dichotomy between analytic truths as by-products of language and synthetic truths as reports on the world. I suspect that the notion of such a dichotomy only encourages confused impressions of how language relates to the world.[7] Stimulus analyticity, our strictly vegetarian imitation, is of course not here in question.

[6] Apostel and his associates have explored this matter experimentally by asking subjects to classify chosen sentences, with and without the guidance of prior headings. Their findings suggest a gradualism of intuitive analyticity. For earlier experimentation on synonymy intuitions see Naess. On gradualism see also Goodman, "On likeness of meaning," and White, "The analytic and the synthetic."

[7] The notion, reminiscent of Kant, is often uncritically assumed in modern epistemological writing. Sometimes it has been given a semblance of foundation in terms of "semantical rules" or "meaning postulates" (Carnap, *Meaning and Necessity*, especially 2d ed.), but these devices only assume the notion in a disguised form. (See my "Two dogmas of empiricism" and "Carnap and logical truth.") The notion has long had its doubters; Duhem's views in 1906, pp. 303, 328, 347 f., are scarcely congenial to it, and idealists have expressly scouted it. (See Gewirth, p. 399, for references.) My misgivings over the notion came out in a limited way in "Truth by convention" (1936), and figured increasingly in my lectures at Harvard. Tarski and I long argued the point with Carnap there in 1939–40. Soon White was pursuing the matter with Goodman and me in triangular correspondence. Essays questioning the distinction issued from a number of pens, sometimes independently of the Harvard discussions; for instance Reid, 1943. Carnap and White mentioned my position in their 1950 papers, but my published allusions to it were slight (1940, p. 55; 1943, p. 120; 1944, Intro.; 1947, pp. 44 f.) until in 1950 I was invited to address the American Philosophical Association on the issue, and so wrote

§ 15. ANALYTICAL HYPOTHESES

We have had our linguist observing native utterances and their circumstances passively, to begin with, and then selectively querying native sentences for assent and dissent under varying circumstances. Let us sum up the possible yield of such methods. (1) Observation sentences can be translated. There is uncertainty, but the situation is the normal inductive one. (2) Truth functions can be translated. (3) Stimulus-analytic sentences can be recognized. So can the sentences of the opposite type, the "stimulus-contradictory" sentences, which command irreversible dissent. (4) Questions of intrasubjective stimulus synonymy of native occasion sentences even of non-observational kind can be settled if raised, but the sentences cannot be translated.

And how does the linguist pass these bounds? In broad outline as follows. He segments heard utterances into conveniently short recurrent parts, and thus compiles a list of native "words." Various of these he hypothetically equates to English words and phrases, in such a way as to conform to (1)–(4). Such are his *analytical hypotheses*, as I call them. Their conformity to (1)–(4) is ideally as follows. The sentence translations derivable from the analytical hypotheses are to include those already established under (1); they are to fit the prior translation of truth functions, as of (2); they are to carry sentences that are stimulus-analytic or stimulus-contradictory, according to (3), into English sentences that are likewise stimulus-analytic or stimulus-contradictory; and they are to carry sentence pairs that are stimulus-synonymous, according to (4), into English sentences that are likewise stimulus-synonymous.

The analytical hypotheses are begun, however tentatively, long before the work of (1)–(4) is finished, and they help guide the choice of examples for investigation under (1)–(4). This point is essential to (4), since without indirect hints through analytical hypotheses there is virtually no telling what pairs of non-observational sentences to try for intrasubjective stimulus synonymy.

"Two dogmas." The ensuing controversy has run to many articles and several books. Besides items mentioned in notes of this section and §§ 12, 42, 43, see particularly Pasch (Part I), White (*Toward Reunion in Philosophy*, pp. 133–163), and Bennett. The title of "Two dogmas," by the way, has proved unfortunate in its unintended but very real suggestion that there is no empiricism without the dogmas in question; cf. e.g. Hofstadter, pp. 410, 413.

Our recipe is overschematic. If the analytical hypotheses give some English platitude as translation of some native standing sentence, there would be encouragement in finding that the latter also commands general and unreflective assent among natives, even if neither is quite stimulus-analytic. Degrees of approximation to stimulus-analyticity, as well as degrees of observationality, would be allowed for in a truer account. And anyway the analytical hypotheses are not strictly required to conform to (1)–(4) with respect to quite every example; the neater the analytical hypotheses, the more tolerance.

Tolerance is bound to have been exercised if a native sentence, believed by the whole community with a firmness that no stimulus pattern of reasonable duration would suffice to shake, is translated as 'All rabbits are men reincarnate'. To translate a stimulus-analytic native sentence thus into an English sentence that is not stimulus-analytic is to invoke translator's license. I think this account gives such a translation quite the proper air: that of a bold departure, to be adopted only if its avoidance would seem to call for much more complicated analytical hypotheses. For certainly, the more absurd or exotic the beliefs imputed to a people, the more suspicious we are entitled to be of the translations; the myth of the prelogical people marks only the extreme.[1] For translation theory, banal messages are the breath of life.

It may occur to the reader to try to derive from stimulus analyticity a finer analyticity concept by screening out sentences such as the native one about reincarnation, using this criterion: through indirect considerations they get translated into sentences of another language that are not stimulus-analytic. However, this criterion is illusory because of its relativity to analytical hypotheses, which, as stressed in succeeding pages, are not determinate functions of linguistic behavior.

Let us now get back to the analytical hypotheses for a more leisurely consideration of their form and content. They are not in general held to equational form. There is no need to insist that the native word be equated outright to any one English word or phrase. Certain contexts may be specified in which the word is to be translated one way and others in which the word is to be translated in another way. The equational form may be overlaid with

---

[1] See § 13 on this myth and the principle of charity.

supplementary semantical instructions *ad libitum.* Since there is no general positional correspondence between the words and phrases of one language and their translations in another, some analytical hypotheses will be needed also to explain syntactical constructions. These are usually described with help of auxiliary terms for various classes of native words and phrases. Taken together, the analytical hypotheses and auxiliary definitions constitute the linguist's jungle-to-English dictionary and grammar. The form they are given is immaterial because their purpose is not translation of words or constructions but translation of coherent discourse; single words and constructions come up for attention only as means to that end.

Nevertheless there is reason to draw particular attention to the simple form of analytical hypothesis which equates a native word or construction to a hypothetical English equivalent. For hypotheses need thinking up, and the typical case of thinking up is the case where the linguist apprehends a parallelism in function between some component fragment of a translated whole native sentence and some component word of the translation of the sentence. Only in some such way can we account for anyone's ever thinking to translate a native locution radically into English as a plural ending, or as the identity predicate '=', or as a categorical copula, or as any other part of our domestic apparatus of objective reference. It is only by such outright projection of prior linguistic habits that the linguist can find general terms in the native language at all, or, having found them, match them with his own; stimulus meanings never suffice to determine even what words are terms, if any, much less what terms are coextensive.

The method of analytical hypotheses is a way of catapulting oneself into the jungle language by the momentum of the home language. It is a way of grafting exotic shoots on to the old familiar bush—to recur to the concluding metaphor of § 2—until only the exotic meets the eye. From the point of view of a theory of translational meaning the most notable thing about the analytical hypotheses is that they exceed anything implicit in any native's dispositions to speech behavior. By bringing out analogies between sentences that have yielded to translation and others they extend the working limits of translation beyond where independent evidence can exist.

Not that (1)–(4) themselves cover all available evidence. For remember that we stated those only with reference to a linguist whose gathering of data proceeded by querying native sentences for assent and dissent under varying circumstances. A linguist can broaden his base, as remarked in § 11, by becoming bilingual. Point (1) is thereupon extended to this: (1') All occasion sentences can be translated. Point (4) drops as superfluous. But even our bilingual, when he brings off translations not allowed for under (1')–(3), must do so by essentially the method of analytical hypotheses, however unconscious. Thus suppose, unrealistically to begin with, that in learning the native language he had been able to simulate the infantile situation to the extent of keeping his past knowledge of languages out of account. Then, when as a bilingual he finally turns to his project of a jungle-to-English manual, he will have to project analytical hypotheses much as if his English personality were the linguist and his jungle personality the informant; the differences are just that he can introspect his experiments instead of staging them, that he has his notable inside track on non-observational occasion sentences, and that he will tend to feel his analytical hypotheses as obvious analogies when he is aware of them at all. Now of course the truth is that he would not have strictly simulated the infantile situation in learning the native language, but would have helped himself with analytical hypotheses all along the way; thus the elements of the situation would in practice be pretty inextricably scrambled. What with this circumstance and the fugitive nature of introspective method, we have been better off theorizing about meaning from the more primitive paradigm: that of the linguist who deals observably with the native informant as live collaborator rather than first ingesting him.

Whatever the details of its expository devices of word translation and syntactical paradigm, the linguist's finished jungle-to-English manual has as its net yield an infinite *semantic correlation* of sentences: the implicit specification of an English sentence, or various roughly interchangeable English sentences, for every one of the infinitely many possible jungle sentences. Most of the semantic correlation is supported only by analytical hypotheses, in their extension beyond the zone where independent evidence for translation is possible. That those unverifiable translations proceed without mishap must not be taken as pragmatic evidence of good lexicography, for mishap is impossible.

Thus let us recall § 12, where we saw that stimulus meaning was incapable of deciding among 'rabbit', 'rabbit stage', and various other terms as translations of 'gavagai'. If by analytical hypothesis we take 'are the same' as translation of some construction in the jungle language, we may proceed on that basis to question our informant about sameness of gavagais from occasion to occasion and so conclude that gavagais are rabbits and not stages. But if instead we take 'are stages of the same animal' as translation of that jungle construction, we will conclude from the same subsequent questioning of our informant that gavagais are rabbit stages. Both analytical hypotheses may be presumed possible. Both could doubtless be accommodated by compensatory variations in analytical hypotheses concerning other locutions, so as to conform equally to all independently discoverable translations of whole sentences and indeed all speech dispositions of all speakers concerned. And yet countless native sentences admitting no independent check, not falling under (1')–(3), may be expected to receive radically unlike and incompatible English renderings under the two systems.

There is an obstacle to offering an actual example of two such rival systems of analytical hypotheses. Known languages are known through unique systems of analytical hypotheses established in tradition or painfully arrived at by unique skilled linguists. To devise a contrasting system would require an entire duplicate enterprise of translation, unaided even by the usual hints from interpreters. Yet one has only to reflect on the nature of possible data and methods to appreciate the indeterminacy. Sentences translatable outright, translatable by independent evidence of stimulatory occasions, are sparse and must woefully under-determine the analytical hypotheses on which the translation of all further sentences depends. To project such hypotheses beyond the independently translatable sentences at all is in effect to impute our sense of linguistic analogy unverifiably to the native mind. Nor would the dictates even of our own sense of analogy tend to any intrinsic uniqueness; using what first comes to mind engenders an air of determinacy though freedom reign. There can be no doubt that rival systems of analytical hypotheses can fit the totality of speech behavior to perfection, and can fit the totality of dispositions to speech behavior as well, and still specify mutually incompatible translations of countless sentences insusceptible of independent control.

§ 16.   ON FAILURE TO PERCEIVE THE INDETERMINACY

Thus the analytical hypotheses, and the grand synthetic one that they add up to, are only in an incomplete sense hypotheses. Contrast the case of translation of the occasion sentence 'Gavagai' by similarity of stimulus meaning. This is a genuine hypothesis from sample observations, though possibly wrong. 'Gavagai' and 'There's a rabbit' have stimulus meanings for the two speakers, and these are roughly the same or significantly different, whether we guess right or not. On the other hand no such sense is made of the typical analytical hypothesis. The point is not that we cannot be sure whether the analytical hypothesis is right, but that there is not even, as there was in the case of 'Gavagai', an objective matter to be right or wrong about.

There are at least seven causes of failure to appreciate this point. One is that analytical hypotheses are confirmed in the field. Now this simply means that supplementary cases of the sorts summed up under (1)–(4) or (1')–(3) of § 15 are gathered after the analytical hypotheses have been framed. The unverifiable consequences I mean are translations not covered by (1)–(4) or even (1')–(3). They can be defended only through the analytical hypotheses, now and forever.

Another of the causes of failure to appreciate the point is confusion of it with the more superficial reflection that uniqueness of grammatical systematization is not to be expected. Obviously the grammatical theories can differ in word segmentations, in parts of speech, in constructions, and perforce then in dictionaries of translation, and still have identical net outputs in the way of whole sentences and even of English sentence translations. But I am talking of difference in net output.

A third cause of failure to appreciate the point is confusion of it with the platitude that uniqueness of translation is absurd. The indeterminacy that I mean is more radical. It is that rival systems of analytical hypotheses can conform to all speech dispositions within each of the languages concerned and yet dictate, in countless cases, utterly disparate translations; not mere mutual paraphrases, but translations each of which would be excluded by the other system of translation. Two such translations might even be patently contrary in truth value, provided there is no stimulation that would encourage assent to either.

A fourth and major cause of failure to appreciate the point is a stubborn feeling that a true bilingual surely is in a position to make uniquely right correlations of sentences generally between his languages. This feeling is fostered by an uncritical mentalistic theory of ideas: each sentence and its admissible translations express an identical idea in the bilingual's mind. The feeling can also survive rejection of the ideas: one can protest still that the sentence and its translations all correspond to some identical even though unknown neural condition in the bilingual. Now let us grant that; it is only to say that the bilingual has his own private semantic correlation— in effect his private implicit system of analytical hypotheses—and that it is somehow in his nerves. My point remains; for my point is then that another bilingual could have a semantic correlation incompatible with the first bilingual's without deviating from the first bilingual in his speech dispositions within either language, except in his dispositions to translate.

A fifth cause is that linguists adhere to implicit supplementary canons that help to limit their choice of analytical hypotheses. For example, if a question were to arise over equating a short native locution to 'rabbit' and a long one to 'rabbit part' or vice versa (§ 12), they would favor the former course, arguing that the more conspicuously segregated wholes are likelier to bear the simpler terms. Such an implicit canon is all very well, unless mistaken for a substantive law of speech behavior.

A sixth cause is that a few early analytical hypotheses carry the linguist so far. Once he has hypotheses covering identity, the copula, and associated particles, he can translate terms by stimulus synonymy of sentences. A few further hypotheses can create a medium in which to challenge native statements and elicit argument, or even to ask about intuitive synonymy. Abundant new structural data are then forthcoming, and one fails to note the free prior decisions to which these data owe their significance.

A seventh cause is that in framing his analytical hypotheses the linguist is subject to practical constraints. For he is not, in his finitude, free to assign English sentences to the infinitude of jungle ones in just any way whatever that will fit his supporting evidence; he has to assign them in some way that is manageably systematic with respect to a manageably limited set of repeatable speech segments. Once he has cut the segments, begun his analytical hypotheses, and devised an auxiliary apparatus of word classes for his formulations, his freedom of subsequent choice is narrowed further still.

The linguist's working segmentation does yet more than narrow the possibilities of analytical hypotheses. It even contributes to setting, for him or the rest of us, the ends of translation. For a premium is put on structural parallels: on correspondence between the parts of the native sentence, as segmented, and the parts of the English translation. Other things being equal, the more literal translation is seen as more literally a translation.[1] A tendency to literal translation is assured anyway, since the purpose of segmentation is to make long translations constructible from short correspondences; but one goes farther and makes of this tendency an objective—and an objective that even varies in detail with the practical segmentation adopted.

Complete radical translation goes on, and analytical hypotheses are indispensable. Nor are they capricious; we have seen in outline how they are supported. May we not then say that in those very ways of thinking up and supporting the analytical hypotheses a sense *is* after all given to sameness of meaning of the expressions which those hypotheses equate? No. We could claim this only if no two conflicting sets of analytical hypotheses could be tied for first place on all theoretically accessible evidence. The indefinability of synonymy by reference to the methodology of analytical hypotheses is formally the same as the indefinability of truth by reference to scientific method (§ 5). Also the consequences are parallel. Just as we may meaningfully speak of the truth of a sentence only within the terms of some theory or conceptual scheme (cf. § 5), so on the whole we may meaningfully speak of interlinguistic synonymy only within the terms of some particular system of analytical hypotheses.

May we conclude that translational synonymy at its worst is no worse off than truth in physics? To be thus reassured is to misjudge the parallel. In being able to speak of the truth of a sentence only within a more inclusive theory, one is not much hampered; for one is always working within some comfortably inclusive theory, however tentative. Truth is even overtly relative to

---

[1] Hence Lewis's concept of analytic meaning, and Carnap's of intensional isomorphism. See below, § 42.

language, in that e.g. the form of words 'Brutus killed Caesar' could by coincidence have unrelated uses in two languages; yet this again little hampers one's talk of truth, for one works within some language. In short, the parameters of truth stay conveniently fixed most of the time. Not so the analytical hypotheses that constitute the parameter of translation. We are always ready to wonder about the meaning of a foreigner's remark without reference to any one set of analytical hypotheses, indeed even in the absence of any; yet two sets of analytical hypotheses equally compatible with all linguistic behavior can give contrary answers, unless the remark is of one of the limited sorts that can be translated without recourse to analytical hypotheses.

Something of the true situation verges on visibility when the sentences concerned are extremely theoretical. Thus who would undertake to translate 'Neutrinos lack mass' into the jungle language? If anyone does, we may expect him to coin words or distort the usage of old ones. We may expect him to plead in extenuation that the natives lack the requisite concepts; also that they know too little physics. And he is right, except for the hint of there being some free-floating, linguistically neutral meaning which we capture, in 'Neutrinos lack mass', and the native cannot.

Containment in the Low German continuum facilitated translation of Frisian into English (§ 7), and containment in a continuum of cultural evolution facilitated translation of Hungarian into English. In facilitating translation these continuities encourage an illusion of subject matter: an illusion that our so readily intertranslatable sentences are diverse verbal embodiments of some intercultural proposition or meaning, when they are better seen as the merest variants of one and the same intracultural verbalism. The discontinuity of radical translation tries our meanings: really sets them over against their verbal embodiments, or, more typically, finds nothing there.

Observation sentences peel nicely; their meanings, stimulus meanings, emerge absolute and free of residual verbal taint. Similarly for occasion sentences more generally, since the linguist can go native. Theoretical sentences such as 'Neutrinos lack mass', or the law of entropy, or the constancy of the speed of light, are at the other extreme. It is of such sentences above all that Wittgenstein's dictum holds true: "Understanding a sentence means understanding

a language." [2] Such sentences, and countless ones that lie intermediate between the two extremes, lack linguistically neutral meaning.

There is no telling how much of one's success with analytical
hypotheses is due to real kinship of outlook on the part of the natives
and ourselves, and how much of it is due to linguistic ingenuity
or lucky coincidence. I am not sure that it even makes sense to
ask. We may alternately wonder at the inscrutability of the native
mind and wonder at how very much like us the native is, where in
the one case we have merely muffed the best translation and in the
other case we have done a more thorough job of reading our own
provincial modes into the native's speech.

Thus consider, in contrast, a simple instance where cultural difference does objectively manifest itself in language without intervention of analytical hypotheses. Certain islanders are said to
speak of pelicans as their half-brothers. [3] One is not of course put
off by this obvious shorthand translation of a native word as 'half-
brother' rather than in some such more inclusive fashion as 'half-
brother or totem associate'. There remains an objective cultural
difference apart from that, and it is linguistically reflected as follows: the islanders have a short occasion sentence that commands
an islander's assent indiscriminately on presentation of any of his
half-brothers or any pelican, and presumably no comparably short
one for the case of half-brothers exclusively, whereas English is oppositely endowed. Such contrasts, between peoples' basic or
short-sentence partitionings of stimulations, are genuine cultural
contrasts objectively describable by reference to stimulus meanings. [4] Where cultural contrasts begin to be threatened with meaninglessness is rather where they depend on analytical hypotheses.

One frequently hears it urged [5] that deep differences of language carry with them ultimate differences in the way one thinks,
or looks upon the world. I would urge that what is most generally

[2] *Blue and Brown Books*, p. 5. Perhaps the doctrine of indeterminacy of
translation will have little air of paradox for readers familiar with Wittgenstein's
latter-day remarks on meaning.

[3] The example is from Lienhardt, p. 97. His discussion of it accords somewhat with mine.

[4] A striking example is the comparison of color words in Lenneberg and
Roberts, pp. 23–30.

[5] Thus Cassirer, D. D. Lee, Sapir (Ch. X), Whorf. See further Bedau's
review.

involved is indeterminacy of correlation. There is less basis of comparison—less sense in saying what is good translation and what is bad—the farther we get away from sentences with visibly direct conditioning to non-verbal stimuli and the farther we get off home ground.

Our advantage with a compatriot is that with little deviation the automatic or homophonic (§ 13) hypothesis of translation fills the bill. If we were perverse and ingenious we could scorn that hypothesis and devise other analytical hypotheses that would attribute unimagined views to our compatriot, while conforming to all his dispositions to verbal response to all possible stimulations. Thinking in terms of radical translation of exotic languages has helped make factors vivid, but the main lesson to be derived concerns the empirical slack in our own beliefs. For our own views could be revised into those attributed to the compatriot in the impractical joke imagined; no conflicts with experience could ever supervene, except such as would attend our present sensible views as well. To the same degree that the radical translation of sentences is under-determined by the totality of dispositions to verbal behavior, our own theories and beliefs in general are under-determined by the totality of possible sensory evidence time without end.

It may be protested that when two theories agree thus in point of all possible sensory determinants they are in an important sense not two but one. Certainly such theories are, as wholes, empirically equivalent. If something is affirmed in the one theory and denied in the other, one may argue that the particular form of words affirmed and denied is itself unlike in meaning in the two cases but that the containing theories as wholes have the same net meaning still. Similarly one may protest that two systems of analytical hypotheses are, as wholes, equivalent so long as no verbal behavior makes any difference between them; and, if they offer seemingly discrepant English translations, one may again argue that the apparent conflict is a conflict only of parts seen out of context. Now this account is fair enough, apart from its glibness on the topic of meaning; and it helps to make the principle of indeterminacy of translation less surprising. When two systems of analytical hypotheses fit the totality of verbal dispositions to perfection and yet conflict in their translations of certain sentences, the conflict is precisely a conflict of parts seen without the wholes. The principle of indeterminacy of translation requires notice just because translation proceeds little by little and sentences are thought of as conveying meanings severally.   That it requires notice is plainly illustrated by the almost universal belief that the objective references of terms in radically different languages can be objectively compared.

The indeterminacy of translation has been less generally appreciated than its somewhat protean domestic analogue.   In mentalistic philosophy there is the familiar predicament of private worlds.   In speculative neurology there is the circumstance that different neural hookups can account for identical verbal behavior.   In language learning there is the multiplicity of individual histories capable of issuing in identical verbal behavior.   Still one is ready to say of the domestic situation in all positivistic reasonableness that if two speakers match in all dispositions to verbal behavior there is no sense in imagining semantic differences between them.   It is ironic that the interlinguistic case is less noticed, for it is just here that the semantic indeterminacy makes clear empirical sense.

CHAPTER THREE

The Ontogenesis of Reference

§ 17. WORDS AND QUALITIES

We saw that the specific objective reference of foreign terms is in-scrutable by stimulus meanings or other current speech dispositions. When in English we decide whether a term is meant to refer to a single inclusive object or to each of various of its parts, our decision is bound up with a provincial apparatus of articles, copulas, and plurals that is untranslatable into foreign languages save in tra-ditional or arbitrary ways undetermined by speech dispositions. Toward understanding the workings of this apparatus, the most we can do is examine its component devices in relation to one another and in the perspective of the development of the individual or the race. In this chapter we shall ponder the accreting of those devices to the speech habits of the child of our culture. The phylogenetic aspect will be neglected, except in a few speculative remarks to-ward the end of the chapter; and in what I shall have to say even of the ontogenetic aspect I shall venture no psychological details as to actual order of acquisition. As remarked, the language now con-cerned is specifically English; this parochialism becomes increas-ingly marked from § 19 onward.

An oddity of our garrulous species is the babbling period of late infancy. This random vocal behavior affords parents continual opportunities for reinforcing such chance utterances as they see fit; and so the rudiments of speech are handed down. The babbling is a case of what Skinner [1] calls *operant behavior*, "emitted rather

[1] Skinner, *Science and Human Behavior*, pp. 107 f. See also his *Verbal Behavior*, pp. 20 f., 203 ff., and Langer, pp. 124 f.

than elicited." Operant behavior can be selectively reinforced, in people and other animals, by quick reward. The creature tends to repeat the rewarded act when stimuli recur that chanced to be present at the original performance. What had been stimulation accidentally attending the act becomes transmuted, by the reward, into a stimulus *for* the act.

The operant act may be the random babbling of something like 'Mama' at some moment when, by coincidence, the mother's face is looming. The mother, pleased at being named, rewards this random act, and so in the future the approach of the mother's face succeeds as a stimulus for further utterances of 'Mama'. The child has learned an occasion sentence.

That original utterance of 'Mama' will have occurred in the midst of sundry stimulations, certainly; the mother's face will not have been all. There was simultaneously, we may imagine, a sudden breeze. Also there was the sound 'Mama' itself, heard by the child from his own lips.[2] Hence the effect of the reward will be to make him tend to say 'Mama' in the future not only on seeing the approaching face, but likewise on feeling a breeze or hearing 'Mama'. The tendency so to respond to subsequent breezes will die out for lack of further reward on later occasions; the tendency so to respond to the heard word 'Mama', however, will continue to be rewarded, for everyone will applaud the child's seeming mimicry. So really the stimuli to saying 'Mama' which continue to be reinforced are of two very different kinds: the seen face and the heard word. The beginnings of mimicry are thus in the very beginnings of word learning; and so is ambiguity, or homonymy, as between use and mention of words.

In learning words we have to learn to send and to receive. We have imagined a child learning to send 'Mama', and also learning to parrot the word on hearing it, but we have not considered intelligent hearing. What would count as an intelligent response to the heard word 'Mama', and be observable enough for onlookers to appreciate and reinforce? Prompted assent (§ 7) is no game for such small children. Perhaps rather something like this: the child hears 'Mama' (say from the father) while sensing the mother in the periphery of his visual field, and then turns visibly on the mother. This

---

[2] This circumstance is indeed concurrent with the utterance, rather than prior; but it still admits of reinforcement. Cf. Osgood and Sebeok, p. 21.

turning response to the heard word could be learned before or after the speaking response to the face. It is in the same old pattern of reinforcement, only this time the child's initial act is that of turning rather than babbling. Turning toward the mother while happening to hear 'Mama', the child is applauded and so is confirmed in the routine. But learning thus to face a named object does not have to await the whims of operant behavior; for the child can be directed.

Eventually the child becomes amenable to suggestion also in the initial utterance of new words. Mimicry, which we already saw foreshadowed within the mechanism of reinforced operant behavior, develops to the point where any new utterance from someone else becomes a direct stimulus for a duplicate. Once the child reaches this stage, his further learning of language becomes independent of operant behavior even on the speaking side; and then, with little or no deliberate encouragement on the part of his elders, he proceeds to amass language hand over fist.

Skinner, whose ideas the foregoing sketch is meant to follow in essential respects, is not without his critics.[3] But at worst we may suppose that the description, besides being conveniently definite, is substantially true of a good part of what goes into the first learning of words. Room remains for further forces. Thus 'Mama' may issue, as is often said, from anticipatory feeding movements; nor would Skinner object, for operant behavior is not supposed to be uncaused. Again some basic predilection for conformity, rather than merely ulterior values such as communication and praise, may figure in the rewarding of good speech and the discouraging of poor;[4] but this again is congenial enough to Skinner's scheme, for he does not enumerate the rewards. Such a predilection may be needed to account fully for mimicry, despite the entering wedge observed above.

It remains clear in any event that the child's early learning of a verbal response depends on society's reinforcement of the response in association with the stimulations that merit the response, from society's point of view, and society's discouragement of it otherwise. This is true whatever the cause of the child's first venturing of the response; and it is true even when society's reinforcement

[3] E.g., Chomsky.
[4] I owe this suggestion to G. A. Miller.

consists in no more than corroborative usage, whose resemblance to the child's effort is the sole reward.

There is no reason to suppose that the stimulations for which the child thus eventually learns his uniform verbal response were originally unified for him under any one idea, whatever that might mean. If the child is to be amenable to such training, however, what he must have is a prior tendency to weight qualitative differences unequally. He must, so to speak, sense more resemblance between some stimulations than between others. Otherwise a dozen reinforcements of his response 'Red', on occasions where red things were presented, would no more encourage the same response to a thirteenth red thing than to a blue one; and a dozen reinforcements of his response 'Mama', on occasions dominated by the mother's face at various angles, would be just as inconsequential.

In effect therefore we must credit the child with a sort of prelinguistic quality space. We may estimate relative distances in his quality space by observing how he learns. If we reinforce his response of 'Red' in the presence of crimson and discourage it in the presence of yellow, and then find that he makes the response to pink and not to orange, we can infer that the shades of crimson and pink used are nearer each other, in his quality space, than the crimson and orange. Supplementary clues to spacing are available in the child's hesitation, or reaction time.

The finest distinctions that the child can be got to make under such reinforcement and extinction tests are called his discrimination thresholds, or just-noticeable differences. But by indirect reasoning from these minimum discriminations we can get smaller intervals still. We find that the child discriminates qualities A and C from each other but not from B; so we count B different from A and C in the child's quality space, even though less than noticeably different.

In thus elaborately exploring and plotting a child's prelinguistic quality space we could, indeed, be systematically deceiving ourselves. For perhaps the space thus reconstructed corresponds only minimally to his initial dispositions, and was molded mainly by the progressive effects on the child of our tests themselves.[5] This possibility could be dismissed if we found some fair uniformity of quality spaces from child to child, under permutation of the se-

[5] This caveat is due to Davidson.

quence of tests.   Note, however, that such a criterion can never attest to prelinguistic quality spaces except as they are uniform from child to child.   Psychology, like other sciences, favors the uniformity of nature in the very criteria of its concepts.

If we suppose it settled that the child has a fairly substantial prelinguistic quality space, then interesting questions arise regarding the structure of the space.   Do the just-noticeable differences always add up in such a way as to agree with our other distance comparisons?   For example, are there more just-noticeable differences between the crimson and orange of our recent example than between the crimson and pink?

Connexity is bound to fail: no chain of subliminal differences will reach from sounds to colors.   We shall need a separate quality space for each of the senses.[6]   Worse, subsidiary spaces may have to be distinguished within a single sense.   For example, we may seem to discover, by watching the child learn 'Ball', that a red ball, a yellow ball, and a green ball are less distant from one another in his quality space than from a red kerchief; and yet we may also seem to discover, by watching him learn 'Red', that the red ball, the red kerchief, and a red block are less distant from one another than from the green and yellow balls.   A simple distance concept even within the sense of sight may thus break down, giving way to distances in sundry "respects."   But enough; there is no cause to speculate further on the quality spaces in these pages.

In § 8 a partial substitute for talk of sense qualities was seen in talk of stimulations.   Much the same substitution is in order here—conspicuously so when we are concerned with subliminal differences.   For consider again the case where the child discriminates A and C from each other and not from B.   It is by our knowledge of the physical arrangements that we know that it was indeed B twice over (not A and C) that was tested respectively against A and C.   Substantial sameness of stimulations is what we work from. The denizens of what we have been calling the child's quality space are, we can as well say, the stimulations; what needs to have been peculiarly "within" the child is just the spacing of them.   Yet we need not disclaim, for all that, the insight into the child's immediate experience that our probing of his qualitative spacing of the stimu-

[6] Cf. Carnap, *Der logische Aufbau der Welt*.   For more on the construction of quality spaces see Goodman, *The Structure of Appearance*.   For early experiments see Anrep; Bass and Hull; Hovland.

lations affords us. Reference to immediate experience is at its best just here, as an intermediate theoretical chapter within a going theory of physical objects, human and otherwise.

§ 18.   PHONETIC NORMS

Vagueness is of the essence of the first phase of word learning. Stimulations eliciting a verbal response, say 'red', are best depicted as forming not a neatly bounded class but a distribution about a central *norm*. The nearer in quality space a stimulation lies to those for which the response 'red' was directly reinforced, the more probably or firmly it will elicit the response. Such a norm will not be a mere point in quality space; it will sprawl freely, rather, in the dimensions that do not matter to redness. Thus, if we think of one's quality space as a qualitative spacing of stimulations, the norm of red will be a class of stimulations that differ from one another in visual shape as well as in brightness. In hue, however, the stimulations belonging to the norm may be thought of as held to red at its reddest. Other stimulations, then, deviating in hue from these, grade off in their tendency to elicit 'red'.

For full justice to the situation, this account needs complicating in several respects. For one thing, volunteered verbal responses to non-verbal stimuli are too scarce to define norms by; thus it was that in § 7 we had to lay on a routine of query and assent. For another thing, norms are warped on occasion by contrasts; thus a stimulation will elicit 'red' the more readily in contrast with a green irradiation. Comparison of more and less red might thus be said to be more basic to learning than the norm of red; however, each determines the other.

Moreover, the pattern of a clustering about a norm is not peculiar to the stimulus side of word learning. There is a similar pattern on the response side; for what the red presentations elicit is not an unvarying response 'red'. The effect of society's rewards and penalties is a phonetic clustering about a phonetic norm 'red' on the part of the subject's responses to stimulations clustering about a chromatic norm of redness. Like the norm of red, that of 'red' extends freely in some dimensions: thus pitch and volume of utterance are indifferent to whether an utterance is an utterance of 'red'. But the norm may be thought of as arbitrarily narrow in respect of certain acoustical qualities, determined by details of oral articulation.

Other utterances, deviating in point of these latter qualities, will grade off in their capacity to pass for utterances of 'red'. Factors of environmental contrast enter here too to complicate the picture, as green did in the case of red.

The phonetic norms have a curiously nagging quality that the chromatic ones have not. A color that is markedly off center relative to every color word can still be a color to prize and to try to match; but ab-norm-al speech is simply poor performance, like singing off key. Such is the importance of phonetic norms that we may do well to dwell on the topic for a few pages, though no use will be made of these reflections in subsequent sections.

Norms are a means of reconciling continuity and discreteness. When we listen to bad singing we grasp the intended melody by assigning each sour note to one of the twelve norms of the diatonic scale. All gradations of pitch are thus acceptable in a sense, but also in a sense not: for the performance is taken only as a sour rendering of a diatonic tune, and not as a faithful rendering of something else. Similarly there are continuous phonetic gradations from 'red' to 'raid', and from 'raid' to 'rate'; and all these gradations belong to English in a way, and in a way not. They belong in that they may occur in English speech, and they fail to belong in that they are proxies for the three norms 'red', 'raid', and 'rate'. Utterances falling between norms are treated as utterances of the nearest norm, or allocated by guess and by context.

The contrary attitude, of counting each slight imprecision as a full miss, would impose inconveniently high standards on singers and speakers. Indeed it would be inapplicable in principle, since a miss can be ever so slight; we could never recognize a hit. The policy of allocating misses to the nearest norms is, in contrast, easy and practical. Trouble arises only in those cases where, because of bad performance or noisy background, the reception falls just about midway between two norms, and there happen furthermore to be no clues in the context. Such cases are minimized in speech in three ways: systematically by a generous spacing of norms; unsystematically by moderately careful enunciation, well away from the midpoints; and unsystematically by wilful pleonasm, calculated to create contextual aids. When contextual aids are at hand, enunciation gratefully sags.

Our linguistic norms probably engender no outright breaks in the continuum of linguistically admissible sounds; for even a sound just midway between two norms can occur unambiguously in some contexts, viz., in those where only one of the two norms would make sense. But the norms do engender near-breaks: the sounds nearly midway between norms will tend to occur less frequently than others, because it is there in general that the safeguards against ambiguity are least.

We have seen why it is far better to accept continuous gradations, and interpret them in terms of discrete norms, than to accept just those discrete values and scorn all approximations. But what now of a continuous symbolic medium in its own right, without norms? For instance we might work out a continuous hummed vocabulary for the reporting of color, as follows. The continuum of pitches, over some arbitrary octave, might be used to represent the continuum of hues over the spectrum. Loudness might be used to represent brightness. Time order in the vocalization might be used to represent spatial order within the object talked about, say a variegated ribbon. Here, then, is a symbolism that knows no norms; none in the sounds that are its vehicle, and none in the colors that are its subject matter. A second example can be got by reversing this one, thus using the ribbon as a notation for a tune. A third example is cartoon in pantomime, as a medium for rudimentary narration. But all three lack the versatility of genuine languages. (Cartooning differs in this from conventional picture-writing, which has norms.) Their subject matter is limited to selected traits—color, tone, position—which mirror the continuity of the symbols.

Suppose there were a discontinuity of subject matter; suppose e.g. that the pitches up only to middle C were to represent hues, and higher pitches something else. At middle C, then, there would be a drastic ambiguity. Indiscriminable pitches in that neighborhood would differ sharply in reference, rather than just indiscernibly as elsewhere. Consequently communicators would tend to shun middle C, as if it were a midpoint between norms. Allow many discontinuities of subject matter and you create many of these points of scarcity in the continuum of pitches, until what remains is a range flecked with norms as points of condensation.

In the access of power which norms make possible there is an air of paradox, since we impoverish our continuum of symbols when we condense it about a finite array of norms. But the explanation lies in the resources of combination. Thus, consider again the tones. We may do away with not only the systematic reference of pitch to hue, but also the systematic reference of temporal succession to spatial contiguity. Thenceforward we are free to make such symbolic use as we please not only of the relatively few selected norms of pitch, but of the infinite fund of distinguishable finite sequences that can be formed from them. Such also is the efficacy of the alphabet.

An incidental boon of norms is the possibility of indefinitely prolonged relay. A message can be transmitted verbatim from mouth to mouth across a linguistic community and down the generations, provided merely that at each transmission the sounds heard be recognizably near the then-intended norms. Each man rectifies his predecessor's inaccuracies before substituting inaccuracies of his own, and error is thus not accumulated.[1]

Here then we have another paradox: painstaking mimicry at each stage of transmission would have hastened the loss of the message by causing small distortions to accumulate. When there are no norms, e.g. in a man's effort to imitate bird calls, prolonged relay is bound to eventuate in something unrecognizable.

Oral relay, if unaided by notes, must depend also on memory between transmissions. Here again the norms operate: a message, if remembered verbatim at all, will be remembered with reference somehow to the phonetic norms; other details, if remembered, are extra. Memory indeed is relay of a sort from self to self.[2] Written records diminish our dependence on relay, but admit in turn of relaying: a text can be recopied indefinitely and rejuvenated each time, because there are notational norms to which to rectify.

The task of learning what will pass for an utterance of one word or another would be forbidding indeed were it not for pervasive part-identities among the norms of different words. Once the child has been inducted by reinforcement and extinction into the right phonetic habits for 'mama', so that his utterances of this word come to cluster about the orthodox norm, he has a head start on 'marble' and to a less degree on 'milk'. By the time he has learned to say a few dozen words, there will be no further word in the language that

---

[1] A further aid to such rectification is redundancy, and not only in the form of wilful pleonasm. See Shannon and Weaver; also Mandelbrot.

[2] We noticed in § 1 another aspect of this relay mechanism, in the dependence of memory on conceptualization.

has not already been anticipated in its entirety, albeit piecemeal. Thus it is that the child reaches the point of being able to divine the norm of any new word or phrase from hearing just one passable utterance of it. This vast saving of labor hinges on the following law of phonetic norms: *The norms of segments of an utterance are segments of the norm of the utterance.* The law is inaccurate, for the sounds in a stream of speech are normally tempered rather to the sounds before and after them;[3] still the departures from the law are not so considerable as to deprive the child of his labor-saving shortcut.

Linguists handle the phonetic norms with help of their concept of *phoneme.* The phonemes of a language are to speech in that language what letters are to writing. Indeed the invention of the alphabet was a first primitive step toward phonematic analysis, though conventional spelling usually falls short of mirroring the phonemes. The phonemes of a language can be viewed as short segments of the norms of utterances in that language. Linguists choose them short enough so that they can keep their number down and still represent every longer norm as a string of them. Talking of phonemes enables linguists to abstract from all phonetic minutiae not germane to the grammar and lexicography of the language; for each phoneme is just the norm, as against the innumerable more or less passable deviations from that norm.

The law of phonetic norms gives substance to the phonematic approach, assuring us that any utterance has as its norm the sequence of those phonemes approximated in the utterance. But note that that law affords no basis for any particular snipping of phonemes to length. Whether to treat 'cheer' as segmented merely into two syllables 'chee' and 'er', or into a consonant 'ch', a vowel 'ee', and a vowel 'er', or into a consonant 't', a consonant 'sh', a vowel 'ee', a glide 'y', and a vowel 'er', is indifferent to our law of phonetic norms and to the child's learning of language as well. The language has its utterances and its norms, and then the linguist imposes a technical segmentation upon the norms to implement his business of specifying the lot.

Phonemes are sometimes construed as the classes of their approximations. In representing them rather as segments of norms I stress the qualitative clustering about statistical norms, and minimize

[3] Cf. Joos; also Zipf, pp. 85–121.

the suggestion of an enclosing boundary. But we can still think of each norm as the class of the events that are occurrences of it.[4]

§ 19. DIVIDED REFERENCE[1]

If a term admits the definite and indefinite article and the plural ending, then normally under our perfected adult usage it is a general term. Its singular and plural forms are most conveniently looked on not as two kindred terms, but as ways in which one and the same term turns up in varying contexts. The '-s' of 'apples' is to be reckoned thus merely as an outlying particle comparable to the 'an' of 'an apple'. We shall see later (§§ 24, 36) that by certain standardizations of phrasing the contexts that call for plurals can in principle be paraphrased away altogether. But the dichotomy between *singular terms* and *general terms,* inconveniently similar in nomenclature to the grammatical one between singular and plural, is less superficial.[2] A singular term, e.g. 'mama', admits only the singular grammatical form and no article. Semantically the distinction between singular and general terms is vaguely that a singular term names or purports to name just one object, though as complex or diffuse an object as you please, while a general term is true of

[4] For more on the nature of phonemes see Bloomfield, Ch. V, and Jakobson and Halle, pp. 7–37. On anticipations in ancient India see Brough, "Theories of general linguistics."

[1] Half of this section is taken from pp. 9–11 of "Speaking of objects," with permission of the American Philosophical Association. In that address I called terms with divided reference individuative, and in my Harvard and Oxford lectures of previous years I vacillated between 'individuative' and 'articulative', both of which suffer from unintended associations. Both of these designations are preserved in Strawson's "Particular and general," pp. 238, 254 n., but his regular designation in that work is 'substance-name', which gives way in his new book to 'sortal universal' (*Individuals,* pp. 168 ff., 205 ff.). Woodger's term, p. 17, is 'shared name'. Martin, in *Truth and Denotation,* Ch. IV, speaks of divided reference as multiple denotation. I applaud that use of 'denote', having so used the word myself until deflected to 'true of' by readers' misunderstanding; and Martin's 'multiple' obviates the misunderstanding. I hope my 'divided reference' may be felt as casual enough not to count as further proliferation of terminology. Its stress on division, as against multiplication, seems best suited to what I here want to bring out.

[2] "The distinction . . . between *general* . . . and . . . *singular* . . . is fundamental," Mill wrote, "and may be considered as the first grand division of names" (Bk. I, Ch. II, § 3).

each, severally, of any number of objects. The distinction will become sharper in § 20.

It is in full-fledged general terms like 'apple', or 'rabbit', that peculiarities of reference emerge which call for distinctions not implicit in the mere stimulatory occasions of occasion sentences. To learn 'apple' it is not sufficient to learn how much of what goes on counts as apple; we must learn how much counts as *an* apple, and how much as another. Such terms possess built-in modes, however arbitrary, of dividing their reference.

The contrast lies in the terms and not in the stuff they name. It is not a question of scatter. Water is scattered in discrete pools and glassfuls, and red in discrete objects; still it is just 'pool', 'glassful', and 'object', not 'water' or 'red', that divide their reference. Or, consider 'shoe', 'pair of shoes', and 'footwear': all three range over exactly the same scattered stuff, and differ from one another solely in that two of them divide their reference differently and the third not at all.

So-called *mass* terms like 'water', 'footwear', and 'red' have the semantical property of referring cumulatively: any sum of parts which are water is water.[3] Grammatically they are like singular terms in resisting pluralization and articles. Semantically they are like singular terms in not dividing their reference (or not much; cf. § 20). But semantically they do not go along with singular terms (or not obviously; cf. § 20) in purporting to name a unique object each. More will be said of their status in § 20, as the reader will have divined. Meanwhile note that full-fledged general terms like 'apple' are also commonly made to double as mass terms. We may say 'Put some apple in the salad', not meaning 'some apple or other'. Likewise we may say 'Mary had a little lamb' in either of two senses. Conversely, as readers more contentious than yourself

---

[3] A term with this semantic trait is what Goodman (*Structure of Appearance*, p. 49) calls *collective*. I should indeed prefer 'collective term' to 'mass term' for words like 'water' and the like, were it not too apt to suggest such unintended cases as 'flock', 'army', etc. 'Partitive' is inviting, but it connotes a wrong principle, since some parts of furniture and even of water are not furniture or water. Strawson's term in "Particular and general" (p. 238) is 'material-name'. In 'mass term' I follow Jespersen, whose 'mass word' seems fairly intrenched in linguistics in the sense required. In "Speaking of objects" I used 'bulk term', which is more nearly the *mot juste;* but I shall not persist in thus multiplying alternatives.

have been clamoring to say for ten lines running, 'water' has a special use that admits the plural.

From the point of view of infantile learning, as from the point of view of the first steps of radical translation (Ch. II), we do best to look upon 'Mama', 'Red', 'Water', and the rest simply as occasion sentences. All the linguist can claim for his first radical translations is agreement in stimulus meanings, and all the baby learns is to say his word when appropriately irritated and not otherwise. It is in relation rather to the going concern of general terms with divided reference that it first becomes pertinent to ask with regard to an occasion sentence ('Mama', 'Red', 'Water', 'Apple', 'Apples') whether it is a singular term sententially used or a general term sententially used. If infantile occasion sentences are to be seen as incipient terms, the category of mass terms is perhaps the most inviting one to identify them with, just because of its indecisiveness in relation to the sophisticated dichotomy between singular and general.[4]

We in our maturity have come to look upon the child's mother as an integral body who, in an irregular closed orbit, revisits the child from time to time; and to look upon red in a radically different way, viz., as scattered about. Water, for us, is rather like red, but not quite; things are red, stuff alone is water. But the mother, red, and water are for the infant all of a type; each is just a history of sporadic encounter, a scattered portion of what goes on. His first learning of the three words is uniformly a matter of learning how much of what goes on about him counts as the mother, or as red, or as water. It is not for the child to say in the first case 'Hello! mama again', in the second case 'Hello! another red thing', and in the third case 'Hello! more water'. They are all on a par: Hello! more mama, more red, more water.

The child can learn 'mama', 'red', and 'water' quite well before he ever has mastered the ins and outs of our adult conceptual scheme of mobile enduring physical objects, identical from time to time and place to place. In principle he might do the same for 'apple', as a mass term for sporadic uncut apple stuff. But he can never fully master 'apple' in its divisive use, except as he gets on with the scheme of enduring and recurrent physical objects. He may come somewhat to grips with the divisive use of 'apple' before quite mastering the comprehensive physical outlook, but his usage will be

[4] See § 12, particularly note 1.

marred by misidentifications of distinct apples over time, or misdiscriminations of identical ones.

He has really got on to divided reference, one is tempted to suppose, once he responds with the plural 'apples' to a heap of apples. But not so. He may at that point have learned 'apples' as another mass term, applicable to just so much apple as is taken up in apple heaps. 'Apples', for him, would be subordinated to 'apple' as is 'warm water' to 'water', and 'bright red' to 'red'.

The child might proceed to acquire 'block' and 'blocks', 'ball' and 'balls', as mass terms in the same fashion. By the force of analogy among such pairs he might even come to apply the plural '-s' with seeming appropriateness to new words, and to drop it with seeming appropriateness from words first learned only with it. We might well not detect, for a while, his misconception: that '-s' just turns mass terms into more specialized mass terms connoting clumpiness.

A plausible variant misconception is this: 'apple' masswise might cover not apples generally, but just the lone ones, while 'apples' still figures as last suggested. Then apples and apple would be mutually exclusive rather than subordinate the one to the other. This variant misconception could likewise be projected systematically to 'block' and 'blocks', 'ball' and 'balls', and long escape exposure.

How can we ever tell, then, whether the child has really got the trick of general terms? Only by engaging him in sophisticated discourse of 'that apple', 'not that apple', 'an apple', 'same apple', 'another apple', 'these apples'. It is only at this level that a palpable difference emerges between the genuinely divided reference of general terms and the counterfeits lately imagined. (Cf. § 12.)

Doubtless the child gets the swing of these peculiar adjectives 'same', 'another', 'an', 'that', 'not that', contextually: first he becomes attuned to various longer phrases or sentences that contain them, and then gradually he develops appropriate habits in relation to the component words as common parts and residues of those longer forms (cf. § 4). His tentative acquisition of the plural '-s', lately speculated on, is itself a first primitive step of the kind. The contextual learning of these various particles goes on simultaneously, we may suppose, so that they are gradually adjusted to one another and a coherent pattern of usage is evolved matching that of society. The child scrambles up an intellectual chimney, supporting himself against each side by pressure against the others.

That these matters are not reflected in stimulus meaning is why the child has to scramble for them by a method of simultaneous learning, and why the linguist has to resort to analytical hypotheses to translate them. Let us pursue the parallel. The notable point about the analytical hypotheses was that two independent Martians could acquire perfect and indistinguishable English through unlike and even incompatible systems of English-to-Martian analytical hypotheses. The corresponding point about English children is that two of them may attain to an identical command of English through very dissimilar processes of tentative association and adjustment of the various interdependent adjectives and particles on which the trick of divided reference depends. Or, to revert to the hypothesis of neural hookups (§ 16, "fourth cause"), the children's identical command of English may be the outward manifestation of very dissimilar patterns of neural interconnection. The identical elephantine form may, in the figure of § 2, overlie very unlike configurations of twigs and branches.

My remarks on how the child gradually acquires and coordinates the various locutions needed to implement divided reference have been both slight and metaphorical. I might do well now to illustrate one conceivable phase of the process, however unrealistically, just by way of suggesting the type of accomplishment wanted. The child has learned 'Mama' and 'Daddy', let us suppose, in the essentially ostensive way of § 17. Then suppose, and here is the unrealistic part, that by a similar but binary process of ostension he learns 'Same-person'. This term goes with simultaneous or closely consecutive presentations in pairs. It proves to apply whenever both presentations are appropriate to 'Mama' and whenever both are appropriate to 'Daddy', but never when one is appropriate to 'Mama' and the other to 'Daddy'. Once the child has ascended in a behavioral way to this higher-level generalization, he may perhaps be said to be in a fair way to appreciating what it is for Mama and Daddy to be persons and not the same one—though it will take a third-level abstraction from this generalization and others like it to bring off any such separation of 'same' from 'person'. On the side of radical translation, a similar series of generalizations could underlie a Martian's eventual analytical hypotheses regarding our apparatus of divided reference.

Once the child has mastered the divided reference of general terms, he has mastered the scheme of enduring and recurring physical objects. For our commonest general terms are over-whelmingly terms which, like 'apple' and 'river', divide their reference according to conservation or continuity of change of substance, and conservation or continuity of change of position in objective space. To what extent the child may be said to have grasped identity of physical objects (and not just similarity of stimulation) ahead of divided reference, one can scarcely say without becoming clearer on criteria.

Be that as it may, the child who has general terms and identity of physical objects in hand is then prepared to reassess prior terms. 'Mama', in particular, gets set up retroactively as the name of a broad and recurrent but withal individual object, and thus as a singular term *par excellence*. Occasions eliciting 'mama' being just as discontinuous as those eliciting 'water', the two terms had been on a par; but now the mother becomes integrated into a cohesive spatiotemporal convexity, while water remains scattered even in space-time. The two terms thus part company.

The mastery of divided reference seems scarcely to affect people's attitude toward 'water'. For 'water', 'sugar', and the like the category of mass terms remains, a survival perhaps of the undifferentiated occasion sentence, ill fitting the dichotomy into general and singular. Further terms even are added to this archaic category, after divided reference is at hand; witness 'furniture', 'footwear'. Also genuine general terms may retain a mass use, as lately observed of 'lamb' and 'apple'.

§ 20. PREDICATION

The distinction between general and singular terms may seem overrated. After all, it may be objected, the singular term differs from general terms only in that the number of objects of which it is true is one rather than some other number. Why pick the number one for separate attention? But actually the difference between being true of many objects and being true of just one is not what matters to the distinction between general and singular. This point is evident once we get to derived terms such as 'Pegasus', which are learned by description (§ 23), or such as 'natural satellite of the earth', which are compounded of learned parts. For 'Pegasus' counts as a singular term though true of nothing, and 'natural satellite of the earth' counts as a general term though true of just one object. As one vaguely says, 'Pegasus' is singular in that it *purports* to refer to just one object, and 'natural satellite of the earth' is general in that its singularity of reference is not something *purported* in the term. Such talk of purport is only a picturesque way of alluding to distinctive grammatical roles that singular and general terms play in sentences. It is by grammatical role that general and singular terms are properly to be distinguished.

The basic combination in which general and singular terms find their contrasting roles is that of *predication:* 'Mama is a woman', or schematically '*a* is an *F*' where '*a*' represents a singular term and '*F*' a general term. Predication joins a general term and a singular term to form a sentence that is true or false according as the general term is true or false of the object, if any, to which the singular term refers.

Because of our concern in this book with the mechanisms of reference, it is natural that predication and the associated grammatical contrast between general and singular terms should loom large for us. The case is otherwise with the grammatical contrasts among substantive, adjective, and verb. These again are contrasts in grammatical role, with associated distinctions in word form; but it happens that the separation of roles into those that call for the substantival form, those that call for the adjectival, and those that call for the verbal has little bearing on questions of reference. Our study can consequently be simplified by viewing substantive, adjective, and verb merely as variant forms given to a general term.

Thus we may best picture predication in the neutral logical schematism '*Fa*', understood as representing not only '*a* is an *F*' (where '*F*' represents a substantive) but also '*a* is *F*' (where '*F*' represents an adjective) and '*a Fs*' (where '*F*' represents an intransitive verb).[1] Predication is illustrated indifferently by 'Mama is a woman', 'Mama is big', and 'Mama sings'. The general term is what is predicated, or occupies what grammarians call predicative position; and it can as well have the form of an adjective or verb as that of a substantive. For predication the verb may even be looked on as the fundamental form, in that it enters the predication without the auxiliary apparatus 'is' or 'is an'.

---

[1] In many writings on logic, my own included, '*Fa*' is used rather to represent any sort of sentence involving '*a*', regardless of whether the portions other than '*a*' are drawn together into a general term. But such will not be my usage in this book, except where I say so.

The copula 'is' or 'is an' can accordingly be explained simply as a prefix serving to convert a general term from adjectival or substantival form to verbal form for predicative position. 'Sings', 'is singing', and 'is a singer' thus all emerge as verbs, and interchangeable ones apart from some subtleties (§ 36) of English idiom. Conversely '-ing' and '-er' are suffixes serving to convert a general term from verbal form to adjectival or substantival form, to suit various positions other than predicative (§§ 21–23); and 'thing' and '-ish' are suffixes for converting adjectives into substantives and vice versa.[2]

Adjectives in English bear a formal resemblance to mass substantives in that we cannot apply 'an' to them, nor the plural ending. Adjectives that are cumulative in reference (§ 19) even double as mass substantives—as when we say 'Red is a color' or 'Add a little more red'. In such cases English agrees with us in making light of the distinction between substantive and adjective. But in general we must note which substantive it is that an adjective does not need to be distinguished from. The substantives to be thus equated to 'red', 'wooden', and 'spherical' are 'red', 'wood', and 'sphere', not 'redness', 'woodenness', and 'sphericity'. These latter are quite another matter: abstract singular terms (§ 25). In general a faithful substantival rendering of a term, if not the briefest, can be got from the adjective by appending 'thing' or 'stuff'.

Now let us get back to the dichotomy between general and singular terms, as clarified by the roles in predication. The ambivalence of mass terms with respect to that dichotomy is strikingly seen in predication. For the mass term is found to enter predication sometimes after 'is', like a general term in adjectival form, and sometimes before 'is', like a singular term. The simplest plan seems to be to treat it accordingly: as a general term in its occurrences after 'is', and as a singular term in its occurrences before 'is'.

Examples showing mass terms after 'is' are 'That puddle is water', 'The white part is sugar', 'The rest of the cargo is furniture'. Let us not pause over the compound singular terms 'that puddle', 'the white part', 'the rest of the cargo'; they are business for the next section. The present point is rather the predicative use of the mass terms. We can view the mass terms in these contexts as general terms, reading 'is water', 'is sugar', 'is furniture' in effect as

---

[2] This theme has been developed by Peano in papers of 1912 and 1930. See his *Opere Scelte,* vol. 2, pp. 458 ff., 503 ff.

'is a bit of water', 'is a bit of sugar', 'is a batch of furniture'. In general a mass term in predicative position may be viewed as a general term which is true of each portion of the stuff in question, excluding only the parts too small to count. Thus 'water' and 'sugar', in the role of general terms, are true of each part of the world's water or sugar, down to single molecules but not to atoms; and 'furniture', in the role of general term, is true of each part of the world's furniture down to single chairs but not to legs and spindles.

In 'Water is a fluid', on the other hand, and 'Water is fluid', and 'Water flows', the mass term is much on a par with the singular term of 'Mama is big' or 'Agnes is a lamb'. A mass term used thus in subject position differs none from such singular terms as 'mama' and 'Agnes', unless the scattered stuff that it names be denied the status of a single sprawling object. Doubtless a child's first glimmering of the mechanism of general and singular terms does depend on the conspicuous unity of something seen against a contrasting background, but in time he masters less visibly bounded entities; certainly for us adults, retrospectively describing the behavior of terms, there is no reason to boggle at water as a single though scattered object, the aqueous part of the world. Even the tightest object, short of an elementary particle, has a scattered substructure when the physical facts are in. We can treat 'water' in this sophisticated way without imputing any reflective semantics to the user; it suffices that his use of 'water' in subject position be enough like his use of 'mama' and 'Agnes' to make our thoughtful semantics come out right.

Similarly the mass substantive 'red' in subject position may be conceived as a singular term naming the scattered totality of red substance. 'Color' becomes a general term true of each of various such scattered totalities.

Let it not be imagined that in sanctioning scattered concrete objects we facilely reduce all multiplicities to unities, all generalities to particulars. This is not the point.[3] There remain, besides the world's water as a total scattered object, sundry parts which are lakes, pools, drops, and molecules; and in singling out such sorts of parts for express mention we still need general terms as usual—

---

[3] On the efficacy and limitations of the device as a means of reducing universals to particulars see Goodman, *Structure of Appearance*, pp. 155 f., 203 ff., and my *From a Logical Point of View*, pp. 68–77.

'lake', 'pool', 'drop', 'water molecule'. Treating 'water' as a name of a single scattered object is not intended to enable us to dispense with general terms and plurality of reference. Scatter is in fact an inconsequential detail. General terms are needed as much for distinguishing parts (arms, legs, fingers, cells) of an unscattered object (mama) as for distinguishing parts of the scattered object water. Scatter is one thing, multiplicity of reference another. Recognition of a scattered object as a single object reduces the category of mass terms to that of singular terms, but leaves the cleavage between singular terms and general terms intact.

Mass terms before the copula having been assimilated to singular terms thus by appeal to scattered objects, the idea suggests itself of carrying the artificiality a step farther and treating mass terms thus as singular terms equally after the copula. It may seem that this can be done by reconstruing 'is' in such contexts as 'is a part of'. But this version fails, because there are parts of water, sugar, and furniture too small to count as water, sugar, furniture.[4] Moreover, what is too small to count as furniture is not too small to count as water or sugar; so the limitation needed cannot be worked into any general adaptation of 'is' or 'is a part of', but must be left rather as the separate reference-dividing business of the several mass terms, conceived as general terms. We shall do best to acquiesce in a certain protean character on the part of mass terms, treating them as singular in the subject and general in the predicate.[5]

The protean character indeed goes farther. We already noted in § 19 that even an ordinary general term such as 'apple' or 'lamb' could double as a mass term. In all, thus, 'lamb' figures not in two ways but three. In 'Lamb is scarce' it figures as a mass term used as a singular term to name that scattered object which is the world's lamb meat. In 'Agnes is a lamb' it figures as a general term true of each young specimen of *Ovis aries*. In 'The brown part is lamb', finally, it figures as a mass term used as a general term true of each portion or scattered quantity of lamb meat. The constancy in form of the word 'lamb', amid these three functions, is a reminder

---

[4] Cf. Goodman, *Structure of Appearance*, p. 48. The terms are not, in his terminology, *dissective*.

[5] Here I follow Lewis, "Modes of meaning," p. 239, only in part.

of the state of the child before he learns to deal with the divided reference of general terms. Revolutionary though his learning about divided reference is, language before and language after are continuous; and thus it is that prior words survive with branching uses. Moreover, such being the pattern, even a word subsequently acquired will by analogy bear a constant form in three functions. But the distinction of functions in question matters much to us, however poorly reflected in word forms. We need not hesitate to draw distinctions, where they clarify our concerns, though they have no vivid reflections in English idiom; nor to waive distinctions indifferent to our concerns, though English idiom exalt them.

§ 21. DEMONSTRATIVES. ATTRIBUTIVES

Much of the utility of general terms lies in their yield of demonstrative singular terms. These are got from general terms by prefixing demonstrative particles, 'this' and 'that'. The economy of effort afforded is enormous. For one thing, we are saved the burden of knowing names. We can get by with 'this river', 'this woman', without knowing what names the things actually bear. Second, we are enabled to refer singly to objects that simply have no proper names: this apple. Third, we are aided in the teaching of proper names. Say we want to teach the name 'Nile'. The hard way would consist in protracted training similar to what went into 'mama' and 'water'. We might expose our pupil to bits and stretches of the Nile from Kenya to the sea, schooling him in the proper applications of the word and discouraging its abuse, until satisfied that he was prepared to apply the term throughout the intended portion of the world and not beyond. Given his mastery of the general term 'river', on the other hand, and of the device of deriving singular terms, we have only to stand with him on the quay at Cairo and say once, pointing, 'This river is the Nile'.

A general term imposes a division of reference which, once mastered, can be thus exploited in no end of particular cases to fix the intended ranges of application of singular terms. 'This is the Nile', with accompanying gesture but without the general term 'river', might be misconstrued as identifying a bend in the river; 'This is Nadejda' might be misconstrued as identifying the material of the faithful creature's rude garment; but 'This river is the Nile', 'This woman is Nadejda', settle matters.

Often 'this' serves as a singular term by itself. If the object indicated contrasts with its surroundings, the intended limits of reference within present space will be evident without help of a general term; and even the intended limits of reference backward and forward in time can commonly be inferred well enough. And an isolated 'this' would usually suffice for the Nile or Nadejda because of what one knows of human interest: rivers and women are likelier objects of identification than bends and fabrics.

Also we can use 'this' with a mass term: 'this water', 'this sugar'. After 'this', as after 'is', we do best to view a bulk term as a general term. 'Water' so used amounts to the general term 'body of water', conceived as applying equally to a river, a puddle, and the contents of a glass.

A notable trait of 'this', 'this river', 'this water', and similar terms is their transiency of reference, in contrast to tenacious singular terms like 'mama', 'water', 'Nile', 'Nadejda'. Such is the effect not only of the two demonstrative particles, but of the *indicator words* generally: 'this', 'that', 'I', 'you', 'he', 'now', 'here', 'then', 'there', 'today', 'tomorrow'. The child's learning of 'mama' and 'water' depended on fixity of reference; he was trained, by reinforcement and extinction on multiple occasions of utterance, to adjust to norms or boundaries of reference which were held fast for him. In learning the indicator words he learns a higher-level technique: how to switch the reference of a term according to systematic cues of context or environment. Demonstrative singular terms thus gained have the convenience of flexibility and the drawback of instability; and it is just when this drawback begins to count that we introduce a proper name to carry the reference for good: 'This river is the Nile', 'This woman is Nadejda'.[1]

The demonstrative singular terms preserve the mechanism of *ostension*—direct experiential association with the object of refer-

---

[1] For more concerning indicator words see Goodman, *Structure of Appearance*, pp. 290 ff., or his dissertation, Harvard, 1940, pp. 594 ff.; Russell, *Inquiry into Meaning and Truth*, Ch. VII; Reichenbach, § 50. The term is Goodman's; Jespersen (*Language*) called them shifters, Russell called them egocentric particulars, and Reichenbach called them token-reflexive. Peirce called them indices, but he applied this term also more broadly; see vol. 2, paragraphs 248, 265, 283 ff., 305.

ence—at the same time that they by-pass the training process which attended the ostensive teaching of 'mama' and 'water'. General terms are what make that shortcut possible. The general terms thus exploited do have first to be learned, and the learning of them is, as observed (§ 19), a more elaborate affair than the learning of words like 'mama' and 'water'. But, once got, they make for high-speed ostensive introduction of singulars, both temporary ('this river', 'this woman') and permanent ('the Nile', 'Nadejda'). Such derived singulars, moreover, facilitate ostensive introduction in turn of further general terms. Thus, having the general term 'round (thing)', and thence the singular term 'that round thing', we may proceed to explain 'pomegranate' in the fashion 'That round thing is a pomegranate'. Our pupil may need several such lessons in order to learn the allowable range of variation from pomegranate to pomegranate. But the other factor in learning a general term, viz. the dividing of reference, is in this case taken care of in advance; for we give him each example as 'that round thing', exploiting thus a prior general term whose dividing of reference he has already mastered.

We have seen that not only are general terms useful for their yield of demonstrative singular terms, but also demonstrative singular terms are useful in getting further general terms. Now this last is an understatement. Demonstrative singular terms figure even in the child's first acquisition of general terms: he has to learn of *this* apple and *that* apple, when to identify and when to distinguish. (Cf. § 19.) Demonstrative singular terms, though formed of general terms, are thus needed in getting on to the trick of general terms. The general term and the demonstrative singular are, along with identity (§ 24), interdependent devices, that the child of our culture must master all in one mad scramble.

Often the general term that follows 'this' or 'that' suffices, along with the circumstances of the utterance, to direct attention to the intended object without a gesture. In such cases 'this' and 'that' tend to be weakened to 'the': thus 'the river'. Such degenerate demonstrative singular terms are called *singular descriptions,* though the phrase becomes more apt when we come to where the general terms available as components can themselves be composite.

Often the object is so patently intended that even the general term can be omitted. Then, since 'the' (unlike 'this' and 'that') is never substantival, a *pro forma* substantive is supplied: thus 'the

man', 'the woman', 'the thing'. These minimum descriptions are
abbreviated as 'he', 'she', 'it'. Such a pronoun may be seen thus as
a short singular description, while its grammatical antecedent is
another singular term referring to the same object (if any) at a
time when more particulars are needed for its identification.

We turn now to a further method of forming composite terms.
This one is not, like the method of demonstrative singular terms, presupposed in what it presupposes; the child can learn it serenely after
his scrambling is done. It is the joining of adjective to substantive
in what grammarians call *attributive position*. 'Red' has attributive
position in 'red house', as against its predicative position in 'Eliot
House is red'. A composite general term thus formed is true of
just the things of which the components are both true.

Substantives also commonly occur in what seems like attributive
position, but for the most part the compounds thus formed are best
seen rather as irrelevantly similar condensations of multifarious
phrases. For whereas red houses and red wine are red, water wings
are not water; nor are water meters, water rights, water rats. There
is even a kind of solecism (viz., syllepsis) in saying 'water wings,
meters, rights, and rats'; 'water' needs repeating because its bearing
on each of the adjoined terms is different. It is only in occasional
cases such as 'student prince', 'lady cop', and 'iron bar' that we find
substantives in truly attributive use, functionally speaking; whereas
such use of adjectives is usual.

In the case of adjectives also there are exceptions. A mere child
is not something that is mere and a child. Similarly for dubious
honors, feigned affection, real money, and expectant mothers. Such
an adjective invites the old philosophical word *syncategorematic*.
For such an adjective is not a term (in my sense) marking out a
category of objects in its own right; it makes sense only with (*syn*)
such a term, e.g. 'mother', as part of a further such term, e.g. 'expectant mother'. Even when a syncategorematic adjective appears
alone in the predicate, as in 'The honor is dubious', 'The money is
real', its dependence on its host term remains; an appropriate
genuine predication (§ 20) would be rather 'The thing is a dubious honor', 'The stuff is real money'. The syncategorematic imita-
tions of the attributive and predicative use of adjectives belong to
a more sophisticated phase in the learning of language than now
concerns us; let us now further examine the truly attributive use
of adjectives that are genuinely terms.

In predicative use the adjective is to be taken, we know, as a general term: the 'F' of 'Fa'. Likewise in attributive use, next to a general term, the adjective is to be taken as a general term; for it is only thus that we can reckon the compound a general term true of the things of which the two components are jointly true. But in attributive position next to a mass term the adjective must be treated as a mass term: thus 'red' in 'red wine'. The two mass terms unite to form a compound mass term. When we think of the two component mass terms as singular terms naming two scattered portions of the world, the compound becomes a singular term naming that smaller scattered portion of the world which is just the common part of the two. Red wine is that part of the world's wine which is also part of the world's red stuff. When the compound mass term occurs rather as a general term, as in 'That puddle is red wine' (cf. § 20), its parts likewise figure as general terms; they amount in such contexts to 'red thing' and 'bit (or batch) of wine', and then the compound is true of each of the things of which the two components are jointly true.

The formal resemblance noted in § 20 between adjectives and mass substantives must not be allowed to obscure the fact that many adjectives, such as 'spherical', divide their reference as insistently as any substantive. Such adjectives are not cumulative in reference, not mass terms; the reason they can manage without articles and plural endings is only that we attach those accessories rather to the substantive which, predicatively or attributively, the adjective accompanies. But now what is to be said of such adjectives, under our precept that an adjective in attributive position next to a mass term be treated as a mass term? It is reassuring to note that adjectives not cumulative in reference simply tend not to occur next to mass terms ('spherical wine', 'square water'). Such adjectives serve as general terms only. On the other hand adjectives which can function as mass terms will, as seen, normally function both as singular terms ('red' in 'red wine') and, in three situations, as general terms ('red' in 'Eliot House is red', in 'red house', and sometimes in 'red wine').

But 'red' as general term so far diverges from 'red' as singular term as to be true of things that are not even parts of the total red substance of the world. Red houses and red apples overlap the red substance of the world in only the most superficial sort of way, being red only outside. It is thus borne in on us that the distinction between a word as singular term and the same word as general term is no mere pedantic distinction in modes of reference; even the concerned regions of the world can diverge. Yet both uses of 'red' are natural descendants of that single primeval one which alone is accessible to the child before he gets on to divided reference and the notion of physical object. For at that early phase no distinction can be drawn between 'red' said of an apple and 'red' said only of its skin. The child can see the uncut apple as red, and can see a subsequently exposed cross-section of it as white, but the white is no newly exposed cross-section of a formerly uncut red apple save in terms of a sophisticated physical identification across time.

Closely related to the attributive joining of terms is the joining of terms by 'and' or 'or'. When these conjunctive particles are used, both component terms are substantival in form or both adjectival. Used as in '*a* is *F* and *G*', the 'and' compound has the force of the compound formed in the attributive way; viz., it is true of just the objects that both components are true of. When pluralized, however, as in '*F*s and *G*s are *H*', the 'and' compound commonly functions rather as a term true of all objects that one or both components are true of. This force is reserved rather to the 'or' compound when the plural is not used.

§ 22. RELATIVE TERMS.
FOUR PHASES OF REFERENCE

What I have thus far been calling general terms are, more expressly, *absolute* general terms. For there are in addition the *relative* ones,[1] such as 'part of', 'bigger than', 'brother of', and 'exceeds'. Whereas an absolute general term is simply true of an object x, and of an object y, and so on, a relative term is true rather of x with respect to some object z (same or different), and of y with respect to w, and so on. Thus 'part of' is true of Roxbury with respect to Boston. 'Bigger than' and 'exceeds' are true of Boston with respect to Roxbury. 'Brother of' is true of Cain with respect to Abel and vice versa; true also of Sir Osbert Sitwell with respect to Dame Edith, but not vice versa.

Just as an absolute general term may take the form indifferently of substantive, adjective, or intransitive verb, so a relative term may

---

[1] This terminology comes to us through Mill, Bk. I, Ch. II, along with 'general' and 'singular', 'concrete' and 'abstract' (§ 25 below).

take the form indifferently of substantive plus preposition ('brother of'), adjective plus preposition or conjunction ('part of', 'bigger than', 'same as'), or transitive verb. Also a relative term may take the form of a lone preposition: 'in', 'under', 'like'.

Parallel to the form of predication 'Fa' for absolute terms there is, for relative terms, the form of predication 'Fab': 'a is F to b', or 'a Fs b'.

Relative terms are, as we might say, true of objects pairwise. But we must also recognize relative terms in an extended sense—triadic ones—that are true of objects in sequences of three; also tetradic ones and higher. 'Gives to', as in 'a gives b to c', is a triadic relative term; 'pays to for' is tetradic. Predication of such terms may be represented as '$Fabc$', '$Fabcd$', etc. Mostly, though, in talking of relative terms I shall intend the dyadic case just as in talking of general terms I shall usually continue to intend the absolute case.

Often we can pair relative terms off as mutual *converses*: the one is true of anything x with respect to anything y if and only if the other is true of y with respect to x. Thus 'bigger than' and 'less than'; also 'parent of' and 'offspring of'. Often, as in the case of 'brother of', 'father of', and 'part of', there happens to be no pat English word for the converse. But when in particular the relative term has the form of a transitive verb, we have in English a general formula for forming the converse: switch to passive voice and add 'by'.

Commonly the key word of a relative term is used also *derelativized*, as an absolute term to this effect: it is true of anything x if and only if the relative term is true of x with respect to at least one thing. Thus anyone is a brother if and only if there is someone of whom he is a brother. Where the relative term is a transitive verb, the corresponding absolute term is the same verb used intransitively.

Relative terms also combine with singular terms by *application*, to give absolute general terms of a composite kind. Thus the relative term 'brother of' gives not only the absolute general term 'brother' but also the absolute general term 'brother of Abel'. Similarly the relative term 'loves' gives not only the absolute general term 'loves' (intransitive) but also the absolute general term 'loves Mabel'. Again the relative term 'at' gives the absolute general term 'at Macy's'.[2]

---

[2] The temporal 'at' is treated along different lines in § 36.

We have seen two basic methods of getting composite general terms. One is the adjoining of one general term attributively to another (§ 21); thus 'red house', 'iron bar'. The other, just illustrated by 'brother of Abel', 'loves Mabel', and 'at Macy's', is application of a relative general term to a singular term. These two operations can be combined to get more complex general terms; thus 'wicked brother of Abel', formed by joining 'wicked' attributively to 'brother of Abel', or again 'man at Macy's', formed by joining the composite adjectival general term 'at Macy's' attributively to 'man'. Compound general terms obtained by either or both devices can be useful in turn under 'this', 'that', and 'the' in the forming of further singular terms. To composite singular terms, conversely, we can apply relative terms to get further general terms; and so round and round. So succinct a term as 'his brother' may be seen as encapsulating a three-layer compound of the kind, for we can view it as short for 'the brother of him' where 'him' is short for 'the man' (cf. § 21). Singular description makes a notable stride as a result of this access to composite general terms, for a composite general term will frequently suffice to fix the object of reference uniquely without the aid of any supplementary determinants in the context or in other circumstances of the utterance. The traditional example from Russell is the composite general term 'author of *Waverley*'; add 'the' and you have a singular term whose reference is stable and independent of context and occasion. Most singular descriptions, of course, e.g. 'the man at Macy's' or 'the president of the United States', continue to depend for their uniqueness of reference upon context or occasion.

'Wicked brother of Abel', parsed above, invites a further reflection. 'Natural satellite of the earth' might be parsed similarly; or one might prefer to view 'natural satellite of' as the relative term, and to view 'natural' as syncategorematic (§ 21) therein. Certainly this is the necessary line on 'natural son of Charles the Bald'. If syncategorematic adjectives have not figured much in our survey of the compounding of terms, it is simply because they are not terms. There is this to say of them, and equally of adverbs: they are words for attaching to terms, whether relative ('son of', 'loves') or absolute ('mother', 'red', 'talks'), to form further such terms ('natural son of', 'loves dearly', 'expectant mother', 'deep red', 'talks fast').

Akin to the application of relative terms to singular terms, as in 'brother of Abel' and 'loves Mabel', there is also the application of relative terms to general terms. In this combination the subsidiary general term is given the plural form, thus 'benefactor of refugees', and the result is again a general term.

The forming of composite general terms by applying relative terms thus to further terms, singular or general, brings a new kind of referential power. Let us look back over the phases that we have already distinguished in the referential function of language, so as to see the significance of this new one in the proper setting.

In the first phase, terms like 'mama' and 'water' were learned which may be viewed retrospectively as names each of an observed spatiotemporal object. Each such term was learned by a process of reinforcement and extinction, whereby the spatiotemporal range of application of the term was gradually perfected. The object named is assuredly an observed one, in the sense that the reinforced stimuli proceeded pretty directly from it. Granted, this talk of name and object belongs to a later phase of language learning, even as does the talk of stimulation.

The second phase is marked by the advent of general terms and demonstrative singular terms; also, as degenerate cases of the latter, singular descriptions. The general terms are learned still by ostension, but they differ from their precursors in their divided reference. The division of reference is such as to give prominence to temporal continuities of substance and of objective position (§ 19). Already it may be possible to learn a general term such as 'unicorn' by ostension of pictures and be quite prepared to find that it refers to nothing; for one soon appreciates that terms are intended less commonly for pictures than for things they depict.[3] And in any event failures of reference of a sort become possible on the part of demonstrative singular terms and singular descriptions, as when 'this apple' or 'the apple' is used in connection with something that proves to lack its back half or to be a tomato. But despite the scope for failure of reference, the objects amenable to reference are still substantially the same old ones. They are the objects from which the reinforced stimuli proceeded in our ostensive learning of the general terms concerned, or objects enough like them to invite application of the same terms.

The third phase brings compound general terms, through the

[3] Here I am indebted to Davidson.

attributive joining of general terms. Here we are more clearly assured than before of cases of failure of reference on the part of general terms; we get compounds like 'square apple' and 'flying horse' that are not true of anything, because of non-duplication among the objects of which the component terms are true. The attributive joining of terms can also issue directly in singular terms that name nothing; viz., such compound mass terms as 'dry water'. Moreover, from attributively compounded general terms we can get demonstrative singular terms and singular descriptions whose failure of reference is categorically assured: 'this square apple', 'the flying horse'.

This third phase, for all the possibilities of failure of reference that it opens up, still provides no reference to new sorts of objects on the part of general terms. When there are things at all for the newly compounded general terms to be true of, they are just some among the same old things to which the component terms apply. The third phase brings mass production of general terms, far out-running the objects of reference; but those objects are the same old ones.

One may still ask whether the third phase does not open the way to new objects for singular terms. For the attributive compounding of mass terms yields a singular term that refers to just the common part of the two masses or scattered totalities named by the components. May it not happen that that common part is something that no previous singular term refers to and that none of the general terms at hand is true of either? Not so. Each of the components, being a mass term, has its predicative use as a general term (cf. § 20), and, so used, will already have been true of that common part among other things.

It is reserved rather to the fourth phase to give access to new objects. This is the phase ushered in just now by applying relative terms to singular or general terms to form general terms. This phase brings a new mode of understanding, by generating such compounds as 'smaller than that speck'. Such a compound is unlike 'square apple' in that it does not even purport to denote things to which we could point and give individual names if they came our way. The relative term 'smaller than' has enabled us to transcend the old domain, without a sense of having fallen into gibberish. The mechanism is of course analogy, and more specifically extrapolation (cf. § 4).

The positing of new objects is not the work only of this grammatical construction. Relative clauses (§ 23) afford admirably flexible means of formulating conditions for objects to fulfill, and indefinite singular terms (§ 23) enable us to be quite articulate about the existence of any objects we care to assume. Abstract objects insinuate themselves in other ways soon to be speculated upon (§ 25). But the special interest of the applying of relative terms to terms is that in the series of simple constructions thus far taken up, it is the first to widen our referential horizons.

§ 23. RELATIVE CLAUSES. INDEFINITE SINGULAR TERMS

The use of the word 'relative' in 'relative clause' has little to do with its use in 'relative term'. A relative clause is usually an absolute term. It has the form of a sentence except that a relative pronoun stands in it where a singular term would be needed to make a sentence, and often the word order is switched; thus 'which I bought'. A general term of this sort is true of just those things which, if named in the place of the relative pronoun, would yield a true sentence; thus 'which I bought' is true of just those things x such that x I bought, or, better, such that I bought x.

From this last broad rule we see in particular that a relative pronoun is in a way redundant when it occurs as subject. For example, 'who loves Mabel' is true of just the persons of whom 'loves Mabel' is true, and 'which is bigger than Roxbury' is true of just the things of which 'bigger than Roxbury' is true. But the redundant pronoun can serve a grammatical purpose: we switch from 'loves Mabel' to 'who loves Mabel' for attributive use as in 'brother who loves Mabel', just because relative clauses are adjectival and hence suited, unlike the verbal form 'loves Mabel', to attributive position. There is less purpose in 'which is bigger than Roxbury', since 'bigger than Roxbury' is adjectival already. The main use of a form like 'which is bigger than Roxbury' is after a comma as an unrestrictive clause; and we may pass over unrestrictive clauses, for they are only stylistic variants of coordinate sentences.

At any rate the peculiar genius of the relative clause is that it creates from a sentence '... x ...' a complex adjective summing up what that sentence says about x. Sometimes the same effect could be got by dropping 'x is', as in the last example, or by other expedients; thus, in the case of 'I bought x', 'bought by me' (formed by conversion and application) would serve as well as the relative clause 'which I bought'. But often, as in the case of 'the bell tolls for x', the relative clause is the most concise adjective available for the purpose.

We reflected in § 21 that some adjectives, such as 'spherical', cannot function as singular terms, while others, such as 'red', are free to behave both as general terms alongside general terms and as singular terms alongside singular terms. These remarks apply in particular to relative clauses. In 'Coffee from which extract is made is grown in the lowlands', the substantive 'coffee' and the adjective 'from which extract is made' are mass terms which stand as singular terms, each the name of a scattered portion of the world; and the compound formed of them, 'coffee from which extract is made', is a singular term naming that smaller scattered portion of the world which is the common part of the two.

'Which', 'who', and 'whom' are not the only relative pronouns to which all these reflections apply. 'That' is another, but I have avoided it because of its uses as demonstrative and conjunction. And there is the variant style of simply leaving the relative pronoun tacit, as in 'car I bought from you'.

A fruitful basis for singular descriptions is the general term of the form of a relative clause; thence 'the car [which] I bought from you'. Let us build this example from its elements. We have a triadic relative term 'bought from', which, applied predicatively to the singular terms 'I', 'x' (say), and 'you', gives a sentence form 'I bought x from you'. Putting a relative pronoun for the 'x' here and permuting, we get the relative clause 'which I bought from you'. This clause is a general term, adjectival in status. Combining it attributively with the general term 'car', we get the general term 'car which I bought from you'; and then 'the' yields the singular term.

The relative clause must be combined attributively with a substantive before 'the' is applied, since 'the' applies to substantives whereas relative clauses are adjectives. If there is no interest in the attached substantive beyond this grammatical requirement, a colorless 'thing' or 'object' or 'person' is used for the purpose; and then 'the object which' is shortened in turn to 'that which', or even 'what'. We thus come out with such singular descriptions as 'what the cat dragged in'. Note that this is a singular term, and a substantive, while 'which the cat dragged in' is a general term and an adjective.

The reason for permuting word order in forming relative clauses is to bring the relative pronoun out to the beginning or near it. The task can be exacting in complex cases, and is sometimes avoided by recourse to an alternative construction, the unlyrical 'such that'. This construction demands none of the tricks of word order demanded by 'which', because it divides the two responsibilities of 'which': the responsibility of standing in a singular-term position within the clause is delegated to 'it', and the responsibility of signaling the beginning of the clause is discharged by 'such that'. Thus 'which I bought' becomes 'such that I bought it'; 'for whom the bell tolls' becomes 'such that the bell tolls for him'.

The 'such that' construction is thus more flexible than the 'which' construction. But what is more striking is the power and flexibility of either of these constructions as contrasted with the earlier or "algebraic" ways of deriving general terms: such operations as attributive juxtaposition, application of relative terms, conversion to passive voice, derelativization ('brother' from 'brother of'), and the joining of terms by 'and' and 'or'. It is not obvious that any preassigned finite set of algebraic operations could suffice for the work of all relative clauses; though actually Schönfinkel's work, which marked the inception of combinatory logic, may be said to establish an affirmative answer to that question.

Much discourse depends on the *indefinite* singular terms, formed typically with help of 'an' in place of 'this' or 'that' or 'the'. In 'I saw the lion', the singular term 'the lion' is presumed to refer to some one lion, distinguished from its fellows for speaker and hearer by previous sentences or attendant circumstances. In 'I saw a lion', the singular term 'a lion' carries no such presumption; it is just a dummy singular term. 'I saw a lion' counts as true if at least one lion, no matter which, was seen by me on the occasion in question.

It is with the advent of indefinite singular terms that we find pure affirmations of existence. 'I saw a lion' is true if there is at least one object satisfying the conditions of being a lion and being seen by one on the occasion in question; otherwise false. Sentences like 'Mama sings' and 'I saw the lion', which contain definite singular terms, may indeed be said to depend for their truth on the existence of objects named by those terms, but the difference is that they do not clearly become false (and their negations true) failing such objects. Failing objects of reference for their definite singular terms, such sentences are likely to be looked upon as neither true nor false but simply as uncalled for.[1]

The difference between such indefinite singular terms and the ordinary or definite ones is accentuated when repetitions occur. In 'I saw the lion and you saw the lion', we are said to have seen the same lion; indeed 'it' or 'him' could just as well have been used in place of the second occurrence of 'the lion'. But in 'I saw a lion and you saw a lion' there is no such suggestion of identity. In this sentence we could put 'so did you' for the last four words, but we cannot put 'it' or 'him' for the last two without imputing an identity not originally intended. There is no one thing named by the indefinite singular term 'a lion'; no one thing even temporarily for the space of the single sentence. In this respect the indefinite singular term is somewhat like the relative pronoun 'which', which, though it occupies positions in relative clauses corresponding to positions of singular terms in sentences, can scarcely be said even temporarily to name anything.

On this score the ordinary pronouns 'he', 'she', and 'it' are altogether different. They are, as lately remarked, definite singular terms. How much better it is to view them thus, than as somehow "standing for" their grammatical antecedents, is incidentally pointed up by the failure of substitution noted in the preceding paragraph: 'it' cannot be supplanted by its grammatical antecedent when that is an indefinite singular term, simply because 'it' remains a definite singular term whether its antecedent is or not.

'He', 'she', and 'it' are definite singular terms on a par with 'that lion' and 'the lion'. Any of these may depend for its reference upon determinants in antecedent verbiage, and any of them may be used subject to no better than the false or dummy determinants provided by an indefinite singular term. The three compound sentences 'I saw a lion and you saw that lion', 'I saw a lion and you saw the lion', and 'I saw a lion and you saw it' are interchangeable. Such use of a definite singular term dependently upon an indefinite antecedent is a departure from the uses of definite singular terms considered in preceding pages, but it makes no distinction between a pronoun such as 'it' and a singular description such as 'the lion'.

[1] Cf. Frege, "On sense and reference."

The use of 'it', 'he', etc. in connection with 'such that' may seem more of a departure from the pattern of singular description. Yet even there 'the thing', 'the man', etc. can be substituted without violence. The fact is that 'such that' clauses usually drop into context in such a way that the pronoun associated with 'such that' is felt to have a definite or indefinite singular term as antecedent. In 'the car such that I bought it from you' or 'a car such that I bought it from you' we sense a routine use of 'it' with 'the car' or 'a car' as antecedent. Granted, this feeling cuts across our analysis, which counts the article 'the' or 'a' rather as governing a composite general term formed by adjoining the 'such that' clause attributively to 'car'. And our analysis is desirable on various counts; for instance, it makes 'the' cover as much as possible of what might contribute to the uniqueness of reference which that word imputes. This analysis does require viewing the function of pronouns in connection with 'such that' as a special one.

'An' is not the only particle used in forming indefinite singular terms. Another is 'every'. This differs from 'an' in the truth condition for sentences that contain it, but it is like 'an' in that it produces only a dummy singular term. There is no one thing, neither a lion nor a class nor anything else, that is named by 'every lion', any more than by 'a lion'. Moreover the example 'I saw a lion and you saw a lion', which helped bring out the oddity of indefinite singular terms, can be matched for 'every'. For, consider first 'This lion is African or this lion is Asiatic'. 'This lion' here is a definite singular term, and can as well be supplanted by 'he' or even deleted in its second occurrence. But 'every lion', in the false statement 'Every lion is African or every lion is Asiatic', cannot be so treated. To delete the second occurrence of 'every lion', or supplant it by 'he', would radically change our false sentence, turning it into a true one.

The particles 'an' and 'every' have variants, notably 'some', 'each', and 'any'. The interchangeabilities here are curiously erratic, as one sees by putting 'every', 'some', and 'any' for 'a' in the sentences 'John can outrun a member of the team' and 'John cannot outrun a member of the team' and comparing. (Cf. § 29.)

§ 24. IDENTITY

Identity is expressed in English by those uses of 'is' that one is prepared to expand into 'is the same object as'. The sign '=' may conveniently be thought of as annexed to English in this sense, enabling us as it does to be brief about the matter without ambiguity. But the notion of identity, however written, is fundamental indeed to our language and conceptual scheme.

The sign '=' of identity is a relative term; thus a transitive verb, we might say, not boggling at the spectacle of a direct object in the nominative. Like any such term it joins singular terms to make a sentence. The sentence thus formed is true if and only if those component terms refer to the same object.

Identity is intimately bound up with the dividing of reference. For the dividing of reference consists in settling conditions of identity: how far you have the same apple and when you are getting onto another. It was only when the child had mastered this talk of same and other to some degree that he could be said to know about general terms. Conversely, also, identity is pointless otherwise. We can perhaps imagine saying 'This is mama' or 'This is water' before general terms are in, and the 'is' here is '=', but only in retrospect. Except with a view to the eventual divided reference of general terms, 'This is mama' and 'This is water' are better thought of as 'Mama here', 'Water here'.

At that earliest phase of reference the one other conceivable case of identity is the case where instead of a demonstrative 'this' on one side and a stable term such as 'mama' on the other, we have terms of the latter sort on both sides. But such an identity would be true only if both terms were conditioned to the same range of stimulations for the same person; and if they were, which is unlikely, the identity would for that very reason convey no new information.

'Gaurisanker = Everest' is indeed informative, even though both of its singular terms are ostensively learned (in the case imagined in § 11). For they are learned not in the primeval manner of 'mama', but only after mastering general terms and the adult scheme of enduring physical objects. Even if our explorer learns each of the names by ostension on the part of natives incapable of supplying the auxiliary English demonstrative term 'that mountain', it will be much the same to the explorer as if they had supplied it: he is confident that both natives are naming from their respective points of view the enduring solid and not just a current phase or exposed side of it.

More typical still of the useful and informative identities are the cases where one or both terms are complex; thus 'Mama is the new treasurer', also 'The barn behind 21 Elm Street is the same barn as the one behind 16 High Street'.[1]

Though the notion of identity is so simple, confusion over it is not uncommon. One instance is suggested in the fragment from Heraclitus, according to which you cannot step into the same river twice, because of the flowing of the water. This difficulty is resolved by looking to the principle of division of reference belonging to the general term 'river'. One's being counted as stepping into the same river both times is typical of precisely what distinguishes rivers both from river stages and from water divided in substance-conserving ways.[2]

Other difficulties over identity form the background of this statement of Hume's: "We cannot, in any propriety of speech, say, that an object is the same with itself, unless we mean, that the object existent at one time is the same with itself existent at another."[3] It seems likely that his statement is prompted in part by what we noted three paragraphs back: that identity sentences joining simple terms are idle before the scheme of physical objects is grasped. But there is also another cause, clearly traceable in Hume's pages: if identity is taken strictly as the relation that every entity bears to itself only, he is at a loss to see what is relational about it, and how it differs from the mere attribute of existing.[4] Now the root of this trouble is confusion of sign and object. What makes identity a relation, and '=' a relative term, is that '=' goes between distinct occurrences of singular terms, same or distinct, and not that it relates distinct objects.

Similar confusion of sign and object is evident in Leibniz where he explains identity as a relation between the signs, rather than between the named object and itself: *"Eadem sunt quorum unum potest substitui alteri, salva veritate."*[5] Frege at one time took a

---

[1] After Lewis.

[2] For more on this theme see § 36 below; also *From a Logical Point of View*, pp. 65–70.

[3] Hume, p. 201.

[4] See Hume, p. 200.

[5] Leibniz, *Opera Philosophica* (ed. Erdmann), 1840, p. 94. On the other hand Aristotle had the matter straight: things are identical (ταὐτὰ) when "whatever is predicated of the one should be predicated of the other" (*Topics*, Bk. 7, Ch. I, 15). Aquinas says the same, *Summa Theologica*, Part I, question 40, art. I, 3. Cf. Peano, *Opere Scelte*, vol. 2, pp. 258, 417, whence these references.

similar line.[6] This confusion is curiously doubled in Korzybski, when he argues that '1 = 1' must be false because the two sides of the equation are spatially distinct.[7]

Identity evidently invites confusion between sign and object in men who would not make the confusion in other contexts. Those involved include most of the mathematicians who have liked to look upon equations as relating numbers that are somehow equal but distinct. Whitehead once defended the view, writing e.g. that "2 + 3 and 3 + 2 are not identical; the order of the symbols is different in the two combinations, and this difference of order directs different processes of thought." [8] It is debatable how much this defense depends on confusion of sign and object, and how much on a special doctrine that numbers are thought processes. Wittgenstein's mistake is more clearly recognizable, when he objects to the notion of identity that "to say of *two* things that they are identical is nonsense, and to say of *one* thing that it is identical with itself is to say nothing." [9] Actually of course the statements of identity that are true and not idle consist of unlike singular terms that refer to the same thing.

The device of identity combines with that of indefinite singular terms to produce the equivalents of a wealth of familiar and useful idioms. Thus take 'Mabel loves none but George'. This amounts to an identity having the definite singular term 'George' as one side and the indefinite singular term 'everyone whom Mabel loves' as its other side. This indefinite singular term is in turn formed by applying the indefinite particle 'every' to the general term 'one whom Mabel loves'. This general term is essentially just the relative clause 'whom Mabel loves'; the 'one' is a substantivizing particle, present for no other reason than that 'every' applies to general terms only in substantival and not in adjectival form.

Or take 'Mabel loves George and someone else'. This amounts to 'Mabel loves George and someone other than George'. The indefinite singular term 'someone other than George' is formed by applying the indefinite particle 'some' (or 'an') to the (substantivized form of the) general term 'other than George', which in its

---

[6] See "On sense and reference," opening remarks. Geach has more recently taken this line; see his pp. 540 f.

[7] Korzybski, p. 194.

[8] *Universal Algebra*, p. 6.

[9] *Tractatus*, 5.5303.

turn amounts to a relative clause 'who $\neq$ George', the negation of 'who = George'.

General terms of the form just remarked on, 'other than y', are of particular interest in that they enable us to analyze away the most distinctive use of the grammatical plural. Thus take 'I hear lions', meaning at least two. This amounts to 'I hear a lion other than a lion which I hear'—a paraphrase which, however unnatural, is both straightforward and devoid of plural endings. (The 'other than' in it may, as before, be rewritten 'which $\neq$'.) Extensions of the same method enable us to say specifically for each n that there are n objects of a given sort, that there are more than n, and that there are fewer, still without recourse to plural forms.[10]

The combination 'is an', which we have been treating as a single copula, can be reanalyzed as a composite of 'is' and 'an' now that 'an' is seen as a particle for the formation of indefinite singular terms. 'Agnes is a lamb' then ceases to be seen as 'Fa', and comes to be seen as '$a = b$' where 'b' represents an indefinite singular term of the form 'an F'. 'Agnes bleats' and 'Agnes is docile' retain the form 'Fa', and the 'is' of 'is docile' retains the status of a copula, or of a particle for converting adjectives to verbs; but the 'is' of 'is a lamb' becomes '='. In a way this treatment is juster to English, but it stresses an excessively local trait. In German and the Romance languages the pattern is simply 'a is F', as often as not, even when the general term is a substantive; thus '$Il\ est\ médecin$'. In Polish and Russian, articles do not exist at all. What is more to the point, our original treatment of 'a is an F' as 'Fa' meshes better with the logical developments of a later chapter. Not but that plenty of uses of 'is' still have to be construed as '='.

§ 25. ABSTRACT TERMS

At length there comes a phase at which a drastically new kind of posit sets in. This phase is marked by the advent of terms like 'roundness': abstract singular terms, purported names of qualities or attributes. Before speculating on the mechanism of this new move, let us see what it consists in. Let us see wherein such terms differ in function from 'round'.

[10] The required manners of extension, due to Frege, are easily devised in the light of pp. 211 and 231 f. of my *Methods of Logic*. On uses of the plural not concerned in the present remarks see below, §§ 25, 28.

We attached only superficial significance to the distinction between substantive, adjective, and verb; hence between 'round thing', 'round', and 'is round'. But we took the distinction between general and singular terms seriously; and such is the important distinction between 'round' and 'roundness'. The basic construction in which the distinction between general and singular figured was that of predication. Whereas 'round' and the like play the role of 'F' in 'Fa', 'roundness' and the like are suited rather to the role of 'a' or 'b' in 'Fa', 'Fab', etc. Now in order for this latter role to exist for abstract singular terms, there have to be some abstract general terms for the supporting role of 'F': some general terms predicable of abstract objects. Two such abstract general terms are 'virtue' and 'rare'; thus 'Fa' can be 'Humility is a virtue', or 'Humility is rare'. Again a relative term that is abstract at one end is 'has', as in 'a has humility', or 'a has roundness', which have the form 'Fab'. The move that ushers in abstract singular terms has to be one that simultaneously ushers in abstract general ones.

If the parsing of certain words as abstract terms, general and singular, were to depend simply on parsing their combinations as predications in certain ways, and vice versa, then decisions on either point would be pretty empty.[1] But the fact is that general and singular terms, abstract or concrete, are not to be known only by their role in predication. There is also the use of singular terms as antecedents of 'it', and the use of general terms after articles and under pluralization. Predication is but part of a pattern of interlocking uses wherein the status of a word as general or singular term consists. By the time we encounter abstract general terms in such contexts as 'He has a rare virtue', for instance, we are left with no very evident alternative to recognizing them as abstract general terms and recognizing the sentence even as affirming, outright, the existence of an abstract object.

For I deplore that facile line of thought according to which we may freely use abstract terms, in all the ways terms are used, without thereby acknowledging the existence of any abstract objects. According to this counsel, abstract turns of phrases are mere linguistic usage innocent of metaphysical commitment to a peculiar realm of entities. For anyone with scruples about what objects

[1] It was in part perhaps this sort of reflection that occasioned Lazerowitz's second chapter.

he assumes, such counsel should be no less unsettling than reassuring; for it drops the distinction between irresponsible reification and its opposite. And indeed anyone, interested in the question of abstract objects or not, is bound to be interested in some of the existential implications of some bodies of discourse; some at least of the ostensibly referential turns of phrase have therefore to be taken tentatively at face value, if only as a step toward drawing eventual boundaries between what to count at face value and what not. If idioms ostensibly about abstract objects are to be defended as linguistic conveniences, why not see this defense as a defense of the reifications in the only possible sense? One's privilege not to be interested in some of the ontic [2] implications of one's discourse is better exercised by ignoring them than by denying them. The matter is indeed not wholly simple; there is more to be said as to what uses of a term to regard as unequivocally affirming existence of its ostensible objects. But this is a topic that we can pursue more minutely when we get to Chapter VII.

We saw that the emergence of abstract singular terms is not to be separated from that of abstract general terms, and that neither is to be separated from the emergence of a systematic pattern of uses of such words in connection with pronouns, plural endings, articles, and the like. Still it may not be amiss to speculate on this development with special reference to the abstract singular. Now what can the mechanism have been?

One wedge is the mass term. Such terms can be learned at the very first phase, we saw, on a par with 'mama'. We saw them diverge from 'mama' at the second phase, simply on the score that the woman comes then to be appreciated as an integrated spatiotemporal thing while the world's water or red stuff ordinarily does not. For the child, thus, who is not on to the sophisticated idea of the scattered single object, the mass term already has an air of generality about it, comparable to the general term 'apple'; and still it is much like the singular term 'mama' in form and function, having even been learned or learnable at the first phase on a par with 'mama'. So the mass term already has rather the hybrid air of the abstract singular term. 'Water' might even be said to name (1) a

---

[2] Of the three evident advantages of 'ontic' over 'ontological', in the special sense of 'as to what there is', brevity is the least. In thus reforming my usage I follow Williams.

shared *attribute* of the sundry puddles and glassfuls rather than
(2) a scattered portion of the world *composed* of those puddles
and glassfuls; for the child of course adopts neither position. The
virtues of (2) as a retrospective assessment of mass terms are that
it preserves the kinship of terms learned or learnable at the first
phase, and it postpones the eventuality of abstract objects; but
surely the child, as unversed in the idea of a scattered concrete object as in that of an abstract one, is done quite as much justice by
(1) as by (2). The distinction is as irrelevant to infant speech as
it is to stimulus meaning (cf. § 12).

In the category of mass terms, then, that archaic survival of the
first phase of language learning, the child already has forerunners
of his eventual abstract singulars. Now further transition is facilitated by such an example as 'red'. This word is learnable at the
first phase, where, as noted (§ 21), the difference between 'red' said
of apples and 'red' said of their outsides is not yet significant. Thus
the child ends up with 'red' both as a mass term and as an adjective
true of things not even composed primarily of red stuff. Of course
he does not consciously distinguish the words as functionally two.
Result: 'red' comes in effect to name a shared attribute not only of
the puddles and blobs of homogeneous red stuff, but also of apples.
Now this abstract object cannot be put aside quite so easily as the
water attribute was put aside, viz. by letting (2) prevail over (1).
Even we, who in our sophistication recognize water as a concrete
scattered object and red (the red stuff of the world) as another,
are apt to admit in addition this abstract object—red*ness* (as we
may call it to stress the distinction). The analogy then spreads
beyond mass terms altogether, to terms with the most strictly
divided reference; thus roundness, sphericity. Each general term
delivers an abstract singular.

Much of the utility of abstract terms lies in abbreviated cross-
reference. For example, after an elaborate remark regarding
President Eisenhower, someone says 'The same holds for Churchill'.
Or, by way of supporting some botanical identification, one says
'Both plants have the following attribute in common' and proceeds
with a double-purpose description. In such cases a laborious
repetition is conveniently circumvented. Now the cross-reference in
such cases is just to a form of words. But we have a stubborn
tendency to reify the unrepeated matter by positing an attribute,

instead of just talking of words. Certainly there is an archaic precedent for such confusions of sign and object; cf., in the case of
'mama', the simultaneous reinforcement of the looming face and
the heard word (§ 17). So ingrained is this kind of confusion that
many unreflective persons will insist on the reality of attributes for
no other reason than that the two plants (or Eisenhower and
Churchill) "admittedly have something in common."

Insofar as the talk of attributes issues from such abbreviated
cross-reference, the supposed attributes are likely to correspond
not to simple abstract terms but to elaborate phrases; for, the more
elaborate the phrase, the greater the saving achieved by the cross-
reference. The ontology of attributes that thus develops allows an
attribute corresponding to any sentence, however elaborate, that
we can formulate about a thing. Complex singular terms for attributes commonly take the form of gerundive clauses (e.g., 'bearing
spines in clusters of five'), preceded or not by 'the attribute (or
quality or property) of'.

We have seen how the child might slip into the community's
ontology of attributes by easy stages, from mass terms onward.
We have also seen how talk of attributes will continue to be encouraged, in the child and the community, by a certain convenience
of cross-reference coupled with a confusion of sign and object.
We have in these reflections some materials for speculation regarding the early beginnings of an ontology of attributes in the childhood of the race. There is room, as well, for alternative or supplementary conjectures; e.g., that the attributes are vestiges of the
minor deities of some creed outworn.[3]

One might, with laudably scientific motives, resolve to sweep
these abstract objects aside. One might begin by explaining 'Humility is a virtue' and 'Redness is a sign of ripeness' away as perverse
ways of saying of humble concrete persons and red concrete fruits
that they are virtuous and ripe. But such a program cannot without difficulty be carried far. What of 'Humility is rare'? We may
for the sake of argument construe 'Humility is a virtue' and 'Humility
is rare' as 'Humble persons are virtuous' and 'Humble persons are
rare'; but the similarity is misleading. For whereas 'Humble persons
are virtuous' means in turn that each humble person is virtuous,
'Humble persons are rare' does not mean that each humble person

---

[3] Thus Cassirer, pp. 95 ff.

is rare; it means something rather about the class of humble persons, viz., how small a part it is of the class of persons. But these classes are abstract objects in turn—not to be distinguished from attributes, save on a certain technical point (§ 43). So 'Humble persons are rare', unlike 'Humble persons are virtuous', has only the appearance of concreteness; 'Humility is rare' is the more forthright rendering. Maybe this abstract reference can still be eliminated, but only in some pretty devious way.

Once we start admitting abstract objects, there is no end. Not all of them are attributes, at least not *prima facie;* there are or purport to be classes, numbers, functions, geometrical figures, units of measure, ideas, possibilities. Some of these categories are satisfactorily reducible to others, and some are best repudiated. Each such reform is an adjustment of the scientific scheme, comparable to the introduction or repudiation of some category of elementary physical particles. We shall come to grips with such issues to some extent in Chapter VII.

We speculated briefly on the disreputable origins of abstract discourse: how the individual and the race are abetted in this development by confusions over mass terms, confusions of sign and object, perhaps even a savage theology. In a general way such speculation is epistemologically relevant, as suggesting how organisms maturing and evolving in the physical environment we know might conceivably end up discoursing of abstract objects as we do. But the disreputability of origins is of itself no argument against preserving and prizing the abstract ontology. This conceptual scheme may well be, however accidental, a happy accident, just as the theory of electrons would be none the worse for having first occurred to its originator in the course of some absurd dream.

Devices conceived in error have had survival value, and are to be assessed on present utility. But we stand to increase our gains by clearing away confusions that continue to surround them; for clarity is more fruitful on the average than confusion, even though the fruits of neither are to be despised. Hence we do well to distinguish abstract singular terms from concrete general ones by faithful use of '-ness', '-hood', and '-ity', at least in contexts of philosophical analysis, despite the fact that the inception of abstract singular terms probably depended on the absence of a distinctive mark.

The interlocked conceptual scheme of physical objects, identity, and divided reference is part of the ship which, in Neurath's figure, we cannot remodel save as we stay afloat in it. The ontology of abstract objects is part of the ship too, if only a less fundamental part. The ship may owe its structure partly to blundering predecessors who missed scuttling it only by fools' luck. But we are not in a position to jettison any part of it, except as we have substitute devices ready to hand that will serve the same essential purposes.

Vagaries of Reference

§ 26. VAGUENESS

In the preceding chapter we have imagined the progressive acquisition of terms and auxiliary particles by the child of our culture. Fullness of experimental detail was not an objective, but the genetic style of approach had conveniences: it helped us picture serially what devices there are to master and wherein their mastery consists, and it enabled us to study the referential claims of the devices in a cumulative order. Now in the present chapter we shall take the mastered language as a going concern and consider the indeterminacies and irregularities of reference that pervade it.

Such a study need not argue for language reform. We are accustomed daily to paraphrase our sentences under the stress or threat of failure of communication, and we can continue thus. Typical ways of doing just that are indeed all that this chapter will venture in a normative vein. The purpose of the study is to bring the referential business of our language more clearly into view.

Vagueness is a natural consequence of the basic mechanism of word learning (cf. § 18). The penumbral objects of a vague term are the objects whose similarity to ones for which the verbal response has been rewarded is relatively slight. Or, the learning process being an implicit induction on the subject's part regarding society's usage, the penumbral cases are the cases for which that induction is most inconclusive for want of evidence. The evidence is not there to be gathered, society's members having themselves had to accept similarly fuzzy edges when they were learning. Such is the inevitability of vagueness on the part of terms learned in the primitive way; and it tends to carry over to other terms defined on the basis of these.

Insofar as it is left unsettled how far down the spectrum toward yellow or up toward blue a thing can be and still count as green, 'green' is vague. Insofar as it is left unsettled where to withhold 'muddy water' in favor of 'wet mud', 'water' and 'mud' are vague. Insofar as it is left unsettled how far from the summit of Mount Rainier one can be and still count as on Mount Rainier, 'Mount Rainier' is vague. Thus vagueness affects not only general terms but singular terms as well. A singular term naming a physical object can be vague in point of the boundaries of that object in space-time, while a general term can be vague in point of the marginal hangers-on of its extension.

Commonly a general term true of physical objects will be vague in two ways: as to the several boundaries of all its objects and as to the inclusion or exclusion of marginal objects. Thus take the general term 'mountain': it is vague on the score of how much terrain to reckon into each of the indisputable mountains, and it is vague on the score of what lesser eminences to count as mountains at all. To a less degree 'organism' has both sorts of vagueness. Thus under the first heading there is the question at what stage of ingestion or digestion to count food a part of the organism; also whether to date the individual from conception or from severance of the cord or from some intermediate stage; also whether to count a slime mold as an organism or as a colony of organisms. Under the second heading there is the question whether to count filterable vira as organic at all.

The first of the two ways in which 'mountain' is vague causes an indeterminancy of count: it is not clear when to declare a saddle to be in the middle of one mountain and when between two mountains. The issue makes all the difference between one mountain and two. Correspondingly for 'organism': it is not clear in the case of pregnancy whether to say we have one organism or two, nor, in the case of slime mold, whether to say we have one or a thousand.

An extravagant degree of vagueness, if vagueness it be, is seen in 'big' and 'little'. Now part of the oddity of these words is that we speak of big butterflies and little elephants, meaning only that they are big for butterflies and little for elephants. This relativity to classes is not vagueness, but syncategorematic use (§ 27). But the words are used also apart from such allusions to classes, in ways that can be brought under control by retreat to the relative terms 'bigger' and 'smaller'. Similarly for 'hot' and 'cold', 'high' and 'low', 'smooth' and 'rough', 'heavy' and 'light'. Whether or not we call such relativization of polar words a resolution of vagueness, we can apply the same device to terms that are ordinarily called vague, such as 'green'. All worry over boundaries to the vague green part of the spectrum is resolved insofar as we can content ourselves with speaking of one thing as greener than another; sulphur is greener than blood, and the sky than violets.[1] Even this relative term 'greener' will indeed retain some vagueness, if it compares deviations from a central green norm which is itself not sharply specified, but it will retain no such wide-angled vagueness as that of the original vague 'green'. Much the same remedy is applicable, if less naturally, even to the vague singular term 'Mount Rainier': we can take to treating the mountain as a point, the summit, and then talk merely of relative distances down and out from that point. But this device does not afford an all-purpose resolution of vagueness; it can preclude or complicate the saying of some things in terms of 'green' and 'Mount Rainier' that we want to continue to be able to say. Alternative ways of resolving or diminishing vagueness, hereafter illustrated, serve some purposes better.

Good purposes are often served by not tampering with vagueness. Vagueness is not incompatible with precision. As Richards has remarked, a painter with a limited palette can achieve more precise representations by thinning and combining his colors than a mosaic worker can achieve with his limited variety of tiles, and the skillful superimposing of vaguenesses has similar advantages over the fitting together of precise technical terms.[2]

Also, vagueness is an aid in coping with the linearity of discourse. An expositor finds that an understanding of some matter A is necessary preparation for an understanding of B, and yet that A cannot itself be expounded in correct detail without, conversely, noting certain exceptions and distinctions which require prior understanding of B. Vagueness, then, to the rescue. The expositor states A vaguely, proceeds to B, and afterward touches up A, without ever having to call upon his reader to learn and unlearn any outright falsehood in the preliminary statement of A.

[1] But such ordering by frequency is perhaps not the most significant. See Land, pp. 89, 91.

[2] Richards, pp. 48 ff., 57 ff., 69.

Vagueness does not perturb the truth values of the usual sentences in which vague words occur. Typical truths about organisms are true by virtue of certain unmistakable organisms independently of any rulings on vira, embryos, slime mold, and cud. A sentence affirming the approximate height of Mount Rainier is independent of the vagueness of that singular term. Not so a sentence affirming the approximate area or population of Mount Rainier; but these are unusual aspects of a mountain to talk about. When sentences whose truth values hinge on the penumbra of a vague word do gain importance, they cause pressure for a new verbal convention or changed trend of usage that resolves the vagueness in its relevant portion. We may prudently let vagueness persist until such pressure arises, since meanwhile we are in an inferior position for judging which reforms might make for the most useful conceptual scheme.[3]

Sentences whose truth values hinge on vagueness usually command interest only in specialized studies, if at all, and the rulings adopted to resolve the obstructive vaguenesses are adopted only locally for the purposes in hand. One fertile field of illustration is law; another is that of almanac firsts.

Thus take the question of biggest fresh lake. Is Michigan-Huron admissible, or is it a pair of lakes? Here the briefest reflection on likely criteria will issue in a favorable verdict. Then take the question of longest river. Is the Mississippi-Missouri admissible, or is it a river and a half? The answer will depend on whether we decide to distinguish river from tributary by volume or by length.

Also, the length will depend on how we handle the sinuosities of the banks, for we might double the length by trebling our attention to minutiae. Here a possible definition is the length of the shortest wet curve from source to mouth. This aspect of the river problem recurs in the notion of length of seacoast, and can there be settled analogously by taking the shortest curve that is wet at high tide and dry at low.

And there is the question of the largest city, or of the number of cities of over a million, where 'city' is taken apolitically; for by gerrymandering you could count the whole human race into a region virtually as dense as can be. (One solution is to require convexity and some arbitrary density.) For that matter, our ambiguous term 'mountain' provides examples as good as any: how many mountains

[3] Cf. Waismann.

over 14,000 feet can be claimed by Colorado, or how many first
ascents by some doughty alpinist, will depend on how we settle
when a saddle forms the middle of one mountain and when it joins
two.

§ 27. AMBIGUITY OF TERMS

Ambiguity differs from vagueness. Vague terms are only dubi-
ously applicable to marginal objects, but an ambiguous term such
as 'light' may be at once clearly true of various objects (such as dark
feathers) and clearly false of them. Sometimes the ambiguity of a
word is resolved by the rest of the sentence that contains it; thus
'light' when followed by 'as a feather'. But sometimes the ambiguity
of a word infects the containing sentence; thus 'bore' in 'Our mothers
bore us'. Then either it is resolved by broader circumstances of
utterance, e.g. some contiguous remark on birth or boredom, or else
communication fails and a paraphrase is in order.

Lexicographers and grammarians have long permitted themselves
to treat words otherwise than as linguistic forms, by declaring of a
form that it functions sometimes as one word and sometimes as
another. Such are the so-called homonyms. And when shall we be
said to have two homonyms, rather than one ambiguous word?
An obvious sufficient condition is difference of etymology. But
words even of identical etymology are sometimes listed as two,
when from the typical speaker's point of view there remains no vivid
analogy between their uses. A man translating a foreign language
into his own may, moreover, even resort to the homonym split for no
better reason than that he needs two distinct correlates in his own
language to cover the ground of the foreign word.[1] In discriminat-
ing words thus beyond the dictates of form and etymology, lexicographers and grammarians suit their convenience. In particular
they find it trebly convenient to see the 'bore' of the above example
as a pair of homonyms, since there is divergence in etymology, in
intuitive sense, and in grammatical function. Grammarians will
maintain a neat exclusiveness of grammatical word classes at the
cost of multiplying homonyms. This is all very well as long as one
recognizes the problems of analysis thereby transferred into the

---

[1] Thus Malinowski; see above, § 13, note 1. But perhaps he would not, if
pressed, have insisted on distinguishing homonymy from ambiguity here. And
there is still a question of separating both of these from mere generality; but
I anticipate.

concept of word or lexical identity. For our own purposes, matters may most easily be kept straight by calling words identical that sound alike (or look alike, if writing is in question). Supplementary terminology can always be devised for supplementary distinctions.

Among the ambiguities that even those who talk of homonymy call ambiguities, there are the systematic ambiguities of verbal nouns. One pervasive type is the process-product ambiguity (Black), illustrated by 'assignment', which can refer to the act of assigning or to the thing assigned. Another is the action-custom ambiguity (Sigwart, Erdmann), illustrated by 'skater', which can refer to one who is skating and hence awake or merely to one who skates and is now perhaps asleep.

We deliberately create ambiguity when we name a child after someone. The name 'Paul', despite the thousands who bear it, is not a general term; it is a singular term with wide ambiguity. Each typical utterance of the word designates or purports to designate one specific man. We do not say, as we would with a general term, 'a Paul', 'the Paul', 'Pauls'—unless, facetiously, we use it in the sense of the genuinely general term 'man named 'Paul' '.

Such, in English, is the grammatical contrast between an ambiguous singular term and a general term. But now in the case of an admittedly general term how are we to say how much of the term's multiple applicability is ambiguity and how much is generality? Take 'hard' said of chairs and questions. As remarked, ambiguity may be manifested in that the term is at once true and false of the same things. This seemed to work for 'light', but it is useless for 'hard'. For can we claim that 'hard' as applied to chairs ever is denied of hard questions, or vice versa? If not, why not say that chairs and questions, however unlike, are hard in a single inclusive sense of the word? There is an air of syllepsis about 'The chair and questions were hard', but is it not due merely to the dissimilarity of chairs and questions? Are we not in effect calling 'hard' ambiguous, if at all, just because it is true of some very unlike things?

Relative to the initial phase of word learning we may quite reasonably call a word ambiguous (and not merely general) if it has been conditioned to two very unlike classes of stimulations, each a close-knit class of mutually similar stimulations. An instance of ambiguity at that level was cited in § 17: 'Mama' is reinforced as a response both to the looming of the mother and to the sound 'Mama'. There is a real difference genetically between conditioning a word to a continuous region of the child's evolving quality space and conditioning it to two widely disconnected regions. But 'hard' is not a case in point, because talk of hard questions is too abstract and sophisticated. It is acquired in middle childhood as a figurative extension of the primary use of 'hard'. Are we to treat this extension as a second sense of a thenceforward ambiguous term, or are we to treat it as an extended application of a thenceforward more general term?

Essentially this same question comes up in instances that are taken seriously. There are philosophers who stoutly maintain that 'true' said of logical or mathematical laws and 'true' said of weather predictions or suspects' confessions are two usages of an ambiguous term 'true'. There are philosophers who stoutly maintain that 'exists' said of numbers, classes, and the like and 'exists' said of material objects are two usages of an ambiguous term 'exists'. What mainly baffles me is the stoutness of their maintenance. What can they possibly count as evidence? Why not view 'true' as unambiguous but very general, and recognize the difference between true logical laws and true confessions as a difference merely between logical laws and confessions? And correspondingly for existence? [2]

The striking thing about the ambiguous terms 'light' and 'bore', or 'bore us', is that from utterance to utterance they can be clearly true or clearly false of one and the same thing, according as interpretative clues in the circumstances of utterance point one way or another. This trait, if not a necessary condition of ambiguity of a term, is at any rate the nearest we have come to a clear condition of it. We have taken account of ambiguity only insofar as it figures as a contributory cause of variation in the truth value of a sentence under variation of the circumstances of utterance.

Nor is even the variation in the truth value of a sentence from occasion to occasion necessarily to be laid to ambiguity. 'The door is open' changes its truth value with the movements of the door, such is the force of the present tense; and it varies in truth value simultaneously from door to door, such is the referential instability of the singular description. Yet to count any of its four words or

---

[2] For examples of what I am protesting see Ryle, *Concept of Mind*, p. 23, and Russell, *Problems of Philosophy*, Ch. IX. For a critical examination of the matter see White, *Toward Reunion in Philosophy*, Ch. IV. See further Wittgenstein, *Blue and Brown Books*, p. 58, and Richman, "Ambiguity and intuition."

their combinations as ambiguous on that account would not be typical use of 'ambiguous'. The shifting of the reference of 'the door' and of the truth value of 'The door is open' with circumstances of utterance are accounted normal to the meanings of the words concerned, whereas ambiguity is supposed to consist in indecisiveness between meanings. Our reflections in Chapter II encourage us little in distinctions of this kind; having no present technical need of the notion of ambiguity, however, I shall not try to improve the boundary, but will just go on using the word as a non-technical term where it seems appropriately suggestive.

Ambiguity can invest composite terms in special ways. One way it enters is through indeterminacy between the truly attributive and the syncategorematic (§ 21) use of certain adjectives. Thus consider the rich little word 'poor'. When it is ostensibly in attributive position it may either have truly attributive use, in which case it may either impute poverty or express pity, or it may be syncategorematic, suggesting 'badly'. If in 'poor violinist' we take the use of 'poor' as truly attributive, then poor violinists are poor (or perhaps pitiable) and they are violinists; if we take it in the syncategorematic way, then poor violinists need be neither poor nor pitiable nor even, by decent standards, violinists.

If in 'intellectual dwarf' we take the use of 'intellectual' as truly attributive, then anyone referred to will be both intellectual and a dwarf. If we take it in the syncategorematic way, then anyone referred to will be unintellectual and quite possibly gigantic.

The use of 'true' and 'false' in 'true artist' and 'false prophet' is syncategorematic; for a false prophet is no prophet, and a true artist, though truly an artist, is not an artist who is true. On the other hand true and false sentences are sentences that are true and false; here the use of the adjectives is truly attributive in sense. The term 'true love' is ambiguous on the point. Take the use of 'true' here as truly attributive in sense, and you construe 'true love' as referring to steadfast love, or perhaps to a steadfast or steadfastly loved one. Take the use of 'true' rather as syncategorematic, and you construe 'true love' as referring merely to that which is truly love, or perhaps to him or her who is truly loved.

A particularly prominent species of the syncategorematic use of adjectives is that in which an adjective that admits of comparison, e.g. 'big', is used with a substantive in the fashion 'F G' to express the sense 'G that is more F than the average G'; thus 'big butterfly'.

Jakobson has suggested to me that 'white wine', 'white man', and 'black bread' might best be construed under this head, with 'white' and 'black' as comparative adjectives. There is no threat of ambiguity between these senses and the categorematic or attributive ones, but only because, e.g., no wine is white stuff and no men are white things.

Where ambiguity turns on the syncategorematic use of an adjective, the ambiguous *term* is the compound and not the adjective; for an adjective in syncategorematic use is not used as a term. In any event one quite naturally speaks of ambiguity in wider application than was hinted for it at the beginning of this section. Thus one conveniently speaks of some indefinite singular terms as ambiguous, though they do not refer. An example is the ambiguity of 'a lion' as between 'some lion' and 'every lion'; compare 'A lion escaped' with 'A lion likes red meat'.

An indefinite singular term whose ambiguity has especially invited confusion, real and feigned, is 'nothing', or 'nobody'. As tired humor the device is quite familiar enough: Gershwin's "I got plenty o' nothin'," Lewis Carroll's " 'I passed nobody on the road.' 'Then nobody walks more slowly than you.' " Locke, if we go along with Hume's unsympathetic interpretation,[3] humorlessly succumbed to this same confusion in his defense of universal causality, arguing that if an event lacked a cause it would have nothing for a cause, and that nothing cannot be a cause. Heidegger, if we may read him straight,[4] was beguiled by the same confusion into his dictum *"Das Nichts nichtet."* And Plato evidently had his troubles with Parmenides over this little fallacy.

What is troublesome about the indefinite singular term 'nothing' is its tendency to masquerade as definite. The cause is evident. Sheer multiplicity serves as a reminder of indefiniteness when an indefinite singular term is built with 'some' or 'each', but that reminder is lacking when the particle is 'no'. Furthermore the idea of a zero quantity is fostered by consideration of limits, and, once embraced, is easily mistaken for a designation of 'nothing' *qua* definite singular term. The persistence of the confusion is attested daily, as in 'They fight over nothing'. Take 'nothing' strictly as indefinite singular term, and the sentence is consonant with peace

---

[3] Hume, p. 81.
[4] See Carnap's comments, "Ueberwindung," pp. 229 ff.

on earth; but in practice it is likely to mean that they fight without provocation.

§ 28.   SOME AMBIGUITIES OF SYNTAX

One extends the notion of ambiguity beyond terms to apply to particles—notably 'or', with its proverbial inclusive and exclusive senses—and even to syntax.   Thus attributive position might be said to be syntactically ambiguous as between the truly attributive use and the syncategorematic.   The same may be said of predicative position; for 'The violinist was poor' can mean that he was impoverished or that he played poorly.   (Curiously the third alternative, expression of pity, lapses in this position.)

There is scope for syntactical ambiguity in the versatility of plural subjects and objects of verbs.   Sometimes the plural form of a general term does the work merely of the singular form with 'every'; thus 'Lions like red meat', 'I dislike lions'.   Sometimes it does the work rather of a singular with 'an' or 'some', but with an added implication of plurality; thus 'Lions are roaring', 'I hear lions'. (Cf. § 24.)   Sometimes it does the work of an abstract singular term designating the *extension* of the general term (i.e., the class of all the things of which the general term is true); thus 'Lions are numerous', 'Lions are disappearing', 'Humble persons are rare' (§ 25).

Yet a further kind of work is done by the plural in such an example as 'Ernest is hunting lions', if what is meant is not that he is intent on a certain lion or lions but just that in his unfocused way he is out for lions.   Benighted persons can in this sense even hunt unicorns.   This use of 'hunt' and other verbs will be examined further in § 32.

Finally the plural form plays a special role as subject or object of a verb used *dispositionally*.   I may best illustrate this by dropping lions at last and switching to 'Tabby eats mice'.   The idea here is not just that there is, are, was, were, or will be a mouse or various mice that Tabby will have eaten; it is rather that Tabby is regularly disposed to eat mice given certain favorable and not exceptional conditions.

The syntactical ambiguities noted thus far, first in the categorematic and syncategorematic uses of adjectives and now in the various uses of plural substantives, are syntactical ambiguities only in that what are ambiguous are certain constructions. We turn now to syntactical ambiguities in a fuller sense: ambiguities of structure, ambiguities as to what is syntactically connected with what.

Notable among such syntactical ambiguities is that of pronominal reference. An example is quoted by Jourdain:

> And Satan trembles when he sees
> The weakest saint upon his knees.

Such ambiguity is partially prevented in familiar languages by the devices of gender, number, and person, but only hit and miss; thus for the prevention of the above case it would have sufficed that the weakest saint be female. But we can clear up this case by supplanting the troublesome pronoun by its grammatical antecedent, saying 'the weakest saint's knees'. What makes ambiguity of pronominal reference serious is that grammatical antecedents cannot always be thus repeated. We saw in § 23 that they cannot be repeated, unless with the wrong effect, when they are indefinite singular terms. The pronoun whose antecedent is indefinite is not dispensable as a mere abbreviation of the antecedent would be. An example of ambiguous cross-reference to indefinite antecedents is:

(1) Everything has a part smaller than it.

Another, adapted from an example with definite antecedents which Peirce quoted from Allen and Greenough,[1] is:

(2) A lawyer told a colleague that he thought a client of his more critical of himself than of any of his rivals.

One possible device for such cases is that of manifolding the pronominal 'it', or 'he', into 'former' and 'latter', or 'first', 'second', and 'third', etc. The device makes for very artificial English but reputedly for natural Chippeway.[2] The mathematicians, happily, have a more readable method. They use arbitrary letters instead of 'first', 'second', etc., introducing each letter in apposition with its intended grammatical antecedent, thus:

(3) Everything x has a part smaller than x.

---

[1] Peirce, vol. 2, paragraph 287. Against the popular misconception of pronouns as standing for nouns, see his footnote.

[2] Jespersen, *Philosophy of Grammar*, p. 220.

(4) A lawyer x told a colleague y that x [or y?] thought a client z of y [or x?] more critical of z [or y? or x?] than of any of z's [or y's? or x's?] rivals.

For unobvious though traceable reasons, arbitrary letters used for cross-reference as in (3) and (4) are called *variables*.

We remarked that the supplanting of a pronoun by its grammatical antecedent is an obvious solution of ambiguity of pronominal reference when the antecedent is a definite singular term, but that it is not permissible when the antecedent is an indefinite singular term. Note now that it is likewise not permissible, leading indeed simply to nonsense, in another case: where the antecedent is a relative pronoun, 'who' or 'which'. An example of ambiguous cross-reference to mixed antecedents, comprising one relative pronoun and two indefinite singular terms, is provided by this relative clause:

(5) who told a colleague that he thought a client of his more critical of himself than of any of his rivals.

Whereas (2) was a sentence, the relative clause (5) is a general term (cf. § 23); but in their ambiguity they are alike. Now in the case of a relative clause an obviously sensible preliminary step is expansion of the relative pronoun into 'such that' and an ordinary pronoun (cf. § 23); for this step segregates the referential function of the relative pronoun. Often also, in examples other than (5), it helpfully rectifies word order. Another good move is to recover and incorporate the term to which the relative clause was to have been attributively attached; for relative clauses occur only attributively. In the case of (5) the term was, we may suppose, 'lawyer'. We get:

(6) lawyer such that he told a colleague that he thought a client of his more critical of himself than of any of his rivals.

Now we are ready to introduce variables just as in (4):

(7) lawyer x such that x told a colleague y that [etc. as in (4)].

Note that though (5) may have been preceded in context by 'the lawyer' or 'a lawyer', it is still just to the general term 'lawyer' that (5) is attributive (cf. § 23). Accordingly (6) and (7), like (5), are framed as general terms, to which a 'the' or 'an' may or may not be superadded to derive a singular term. The example (7) contrasts instructively with (4) in exhibiting 'x' in apposition not to an indefinite singular term but to a general term.

In the context of a logical or semantical discussion the phrase 'cross-reference' is unfortunate in a way in which its French equivalent *renvoi* is not. For, a pronoun or other singular term may also be said to refer, permanently or in passing, to some person or other object. Reference in the latter sense is genuinely the relation of sign to object, whereas cross-reference is only a relation of sign to coordinate sign, a harking back of pronoun to grammatical antecedent. Logicians happily have another terminology for talking of cross-reference, where variables are concerned: they speak of *binding*. The introductory or appositive occurrence of 'x' is said to *bind* the various recurrences of 'x', insofar as they hark back to that apposition and not to some independent use of the letter.

If a sentence or relative clause contains an appositive or binding occurrence of 'x' and sundry recurrences of 'x', then ordinarily it will include a component sentence that contains some of the occurrences of 'x' but, within itself, none to bind them. Such a component sentence, considered by itself, is called an *open* sentence, and its unbound occurrences of variables are said to be *free* in it. Examples:

x has a part smaller than x.

x thought a client z of y more critical of z than of any of z's rivals.

Open sentences are sentences in form but, because of the free variables, neither true nor false.

Another structural species of syntactical ambiguity is ambiguity of grouping. We can make sense of 'pretty little girls' camp' in any of five groupings: '(pretty (little girls')) camp', '(pretty little) (girls' camp)', and so on. We cope with such ambiguity by variously stressing and pausing, by inserting particles for coordination or ballast, or by rephrasing altogether (thus 'rather little camp for girls').[3] A graphic means of marking grouping in mathematics is parentheses, as above.

[3] See further my *Elementary Logic*, §§ 11–13, whence the present example, or *Methods of Logic*, § 4.

§ 29. AMBIGUITY OF SCOPE

More subtle problems of grouping are presented by what is called *scope*. Thus take 'big European butterfly': is it to be true of just the European butterflies that are big for butterflies, or is it to be true of all the European butterflies that are big for European butterflies? The question may be phrased as a question whether the scope of the syncategorematic adjective 'big' is 'butterfly' or 'European butterfly'; and what is subtle about it is that it cannot be settled by a simple choice between two positions for parentheses. Perhaps the version allowing the wider scope could be rendered 'big (European butterfly)' and the other could be rendered with a comma: 'big, European butterfly'. Or, of course, we can paraphrase.[1]

No such problem of scope arises when adjectives are used categorematically, in the truly attributive way. Between 'round black box' as true of black boxes that are round, and 'round black box' as true of boxes that are black and round, no distinction is required.

I shall not find further occasion to pursue the syncategorematic use of adjectives. But there is also another connection in which ambiguity of scope obtrudes, and one that is peculiarly central to our language; viz., in connection with indefinite singular terms. Thus consider:

(1) If any member contributes, he gets a poppy.
(2) If every member contributes, I'll be surprised.

Sentence (1) makes of every member this assertion: if he contributes, he gets a poppy. Sentence (2) does not correspondingly make of every member the assertion: if he contributes, I'll be surprised. For that would mean that I expected no contributions, whereas all (2) says is that I expect less than unanimous contributions. It is rather the component clause 'every member contributes', in (2), that makes an assertion (however false) of every member; and then (2) as a whole is compounded of that closed-off clause and 'I'll be surprised'. The contrast between (1) and (2) brings out the idea of the scope of an indefinite singular term. The scope of 'any member' in (1) is (1) in its entirety, whereas the scope of 'every member' in (2) is just 'every member contributes'.

[1] This paragraph issued from a discussion with Jakobson.

The example 'I believe he saw a letter of mine', unlike (1) and (2), threatens ambiguity of scope. If the scope of the indefinite singular term 'a letter of mine' is taken to be just 'he saw a letter of mine', then the whole sentence 'I believe he saw a letter of mine' applies 'I believe' to the self-contained sentence 'he saw a letter of mine'. Under this interpretation the whole sentence amounts to saying merely that I believe he did not miss all my letters. If on the other hand the scope of 'a letter of mine' is taken to be the whole sentence including 'I believe', then the whole sentence amounts rather to saying that there are one or more letters of mine which, specifically, I believe he saw.

If in 'Each thing that glisters is not gold' [2] we take the scope of the indefinite singular term 'each thing' as the whole sentence, we have a falsehood: a sweeping denial of goldhood with respect to glistering things. If we take the scope rather as 'each thing that glisters is gold', and so reckon 'not' as an outside operator governing the whole, we have the truth that Shakespeare intended.

Sentences (1) and (2) were unambiguous for three instructive reasons. One is that (1') has 'he' in its second clause, with 'any member' as grammatical antecedent; we cannot take the scope of 'any member' as just the first clause of (1), on pain of leaving 'he' high and dry. A second reason is that 'every', by a simple and irreducible trait of English usage, always calls for the shortest possible scope. A third reason is that 'any', by a simple and irreducible trait of English usage, always calls for the longer of two possible scopes. This third reason is supernumerary for (1), on account of the 'he'; but it asserts itself in:

(3) If any member contributes, I'll be surprised.

This, in contrast to (2), asserts of every member that if he contributes I'll be surprised. Whereas the scope of 'every member' in (2) is just 'every member contributes', the scope of 'any member' in (3) is (3) as a whole. Here we see the reason for joint survival of the apparent synonyms 'any' and 'every': distinctive scope connotations. The same point is illustrated by the pair:

(4) I do not know any poem,
(5) I do not know every poem.

---

[2] I have changed Shakespeare's 'All' in order not to invite the proposal, irrelevant to present purposes, that 'all that glisters' be treated as a definite singular term designating the whole glistering content of space-time.

Since 'any' takes wide scope, (4) means that, given each poem in turn, I do not know it. Since on the other hand 'every' takes narrow scope, (5) merely denies that, given each poem in turn, I know it. The scope of 'any poem' in (4) is (4); the scope of 'every poem' in (5) is 'I know every poem', which (5) negates.

The remarkable divergence between (5) and:

(6) I am ignorant of every poem

can be accounted for by the affinity of 'every' for minimum scope. Sentence (6), unlike (5), contains no subsidiary sentence, since the negative 'i-' of (6), unlike the 'not' of (5), is inseparable. Thus whereas the scope of 'every' in (5) is not the whole of (5), the scope of 'every' in (6) is necessarily the whole of (6); and thus (6) is equivalent not to (5) but to (4).

A graphic means of exhibiting scope lies ready to hand in the 'such that' construction. Representing the indefinite singular term as 'b' and its scope as '$\ldots b \ldots$', we may sum the method up in this maxim: rewrite the scope '$\ldots b \ldots$' as 'b is such that $\ldots$ it $\ldots$'. Thus (1)–(5) become:

(7) Each member is such that if he contributes he gets a poppy.
(8) If each member (is such that he) contributes, I'll be surprised.
(9) Each member is such that if he contributes I'll be surprised.
(10) Each poem is such that I do not know it.
(11) Not each poem is such that I know it.

I have here rendered 'any' and 'every' indifferently as 'each', since the distinctions of scope so subtly indicated by one's choice between 'any' and 'every' are self-evident under 'such that'.

The two interpretations of 'I believe he saw a letter of mine' become:

(12) I believe that some letter of mine is such that he saw it,
(13) Some letter of mine is such that I believe that he saw it.

But there will be more to say of (13) in § 31.

This way of showing scope is essentially a matter of getting the indefinite singular term into the position of grammatical subject of a predication which is its scope, and so reducing the question of scope to the question of spotting a subject's predicate. The point of 'such that' is just that it enables us to convert anything '... *b* ...' that we might want to say, about anything *b*, into a single complex predicate 'such that ... it ...', attributable to *b*.

The special thing about (8) is that 'each member' is already the subject of its scope 'each member contributes', so that the 'such that' manoeuvre is superfluous. Sentence (8) is the ideally simple case. At the other extreme, the 'such that' clause may become so complex that we have to resort to variables to keep pronominal references straight. But this we are prepared for by recent pages; 'is such that ... it ...' merely gives way to 'is an object *x* such that ... *x* ...'. The intrusion of 'object' here, which substantivizes the adjectival 'such that' clause, is merely for the grammatical purpose of giving '*x*' something to stand in apposition with. Commonly also, in complex cases, one welcomes the opportunity to mark the limits of a scope by parenthesizing the 'such that' clause. Much of the value of the 'such that' manoeuvre in settling scope is that it makes scope more explicitly a matter of grouping, amenable to parentheses.

'Which' clauses are adjectives which, like 'mere', occur only in attributive and not predicative position. And reasonably enough, one might say; for predication of a 'which' clause would accomplish nothing that is not accomplished more simply by the clause alone, with 'which' supplanted by the subject of the predication. Much the same might have been said of 'such that' clauses: predication of a 'such that' clause accomplishes nothing that is not accomplished by the part after 'such that' alone, with its pronoun supplanted by the subject of the predication. Yet 'such that' clauses do occur, unlike 'which' clauses, in predicative position. And we now see that such use of them is not idle after all; for it is precisely the means of making scopes explicit, as in (7)–(13).

§ 30. REFERENTIAL OPACITY

Definite singular terms may shift in reference with occasions of use, either through ambiguity or through the peculiar functions of 'the', 'this', and 'that' (§ 27). Under some circumstances the term may simply fail of reference, through there being no object of the required sort. And there is a further kind of variation: in sentences there are positions where the term is used as a means simply of specifying its object, or purporting to, for the rest of the sentence to say something about, and there are positions where it is not. An example of the latter sort is the position of 'Tully' in:

(1) 'Tully was a Roman' is trochaic.

When a singular term is used in a sentence purely to specify its object, and the sentence is true of the object, then certainly the sentence will stay true when any other singular term is substituted that designates the same object. Here we have a criterion for what may be called *purely referential position:* the position must be subject to the *substitutivity of identity.*[1] That the position of 'Tully' in (1) is not purely referential is reflected in the falsity of what we get by supplanting 'Tully' in (1) by 'Cicero'.

If we understand the sentence:

(2) The commissioner is looking for the chairman of the hospital board

in such a way as to be prepared to affirm it and yet to deny:

(3) The commissioner is looking for the dean

even though, by recent appointment and unknown to the commissioner,

(4) The dean = the chairman of the hospital board,

then we are treating the position to the right of 'looking for' as not purely referential. On the other hand if, aware of the commissioner's persistent avoidance of the dean, we are still constrained by (2) and (4) to treat (3) as true, then we are indeed treating the position as purely referential.

Example (2), even if taken in the not purely referential way, differs from (1) in that it still seems to have far more bearing on the chairman of the hospital board, dean though he be, than (1) has on Tully. Hence my cautious phrase 'not purely referential', designed to apply to all such cases and to affirm no distinction among them. If I omit the adverb, the motive will be brevity.

An illustration of purely referential position is the position of singular terms under predication. For, the predication is true so long merely as the predicated general term is true of the object

---

[1] The concept and its criterion are due essentially to Frege, "On sense and reference." But there is much in his associated theory that I do not adopt; see end of § 31.

named by the singular term (§ 20); hence the substitution of a new singular term that names the same object leaves the predication true. In particular the question whether to take the main singular-term positions in (2) as purely referential is the question whether to treat (2) as a predication of a relative term 'looking for'.

The positions that we have been classifying into purely referential and other are positions of singular terms relative to sentences that contain them. Now it is convenient to extend the concept to apply also to positions of singular terms relative to singular terms that contain them. Thus, take quotation marks: applied to any sort of expression, what they produce is a singular term (naming, as it happens, the expression inside). It is convenient to be able to speak of the personal name in (1) as having non-referential position not only in the sentence (1), but equally in the singular term, of quotational form, that is the grammatical subject of (1). Indeed, it is rather the quotation than (1) as a whole that is primarily in point here; the personal name has non-referential position in (1) simply because of the quotation.

As a criterion of referential position, substitutivity of identity works as well for positions within singular terms as for positions within sentences. For positions in sentences, what it says is that the containing sentence keeps its truth value when the contained singular term is supplanted by any other having the same reference. For positions in singular terms, what it says is that the containing singular term keeps its reference when the contained singular term is so supplanted. Thus what shows the position of the personal name in the quotation:

(5)   'Tully was a Roman'

to be non-referential is that, though Tully = Cicero, yet

   'Tully was a Roman' ≠ 'Cicero was a Roman'.

Quotation, we see, gives rise to non-referential positions. Now this is not true of an alternative device to the same purpose as quotation, viz. *spelling*. Instead of (5) we can as well say:

   tee⌢yu⌢ell⌢ell⌢wye⌢space⌢doubleyu⌢ay⌢ess⌢space⌢ay⌢space⌢ar ⌢oh⌢em⌢ay⌢en,

thus using explicit names of the letters and an arch (following Tarski) to indicate concatenation. The shift from quotation to spelling has an independent advantage (cf. § 39), but incidentally it is instructive as stressing that any non-referential occurrences caused by quotation are surface appearances, dispelled by an easy change in notation.

Also apart from quotation there are frequent cases where a not purely referential occurrence of a singular term can be banished by paraphrase. But there is no compulsion upon us to banish all non-referential occurrences of singular terms, nor to reduce them to quotation. We are not unaccustomed to passing over occurrences that somehow "do not count"—'mary' in 'summary', 'can' in 'canary'; and we can allow similarly for all non-referential occurrences of terms, once we know what to look out for.

One and the same occurrence of a term may have purely referential position with respect to its immediate surroundings and not with respect to a broader context. For example, the personal name has purely referential position in the sentence:

(6) Tully was a Roman

and yet in neither of the more extended expressions (1) and (5). Quotation, which thus interrupts the referential force of a term, may be said to fail of referential *transparency*.[2]

Referential transparency has to do with constructions (§ 11); modes of containment, more specifically, of singular terms or sentences in singular terms or sentences. I call a mode of containment Φ referentially transparent if, whenever an occurrence of a singular term t is purely referential in a term or sentence $\psi(t)$, it is purely referential also in the containing term or sentence $\Phi(\psi(t))$. Take $\Phi(\psi(t))$ as (5), $\psi(t)$ as (6), and t as the personal name, and you have the referential opacity of quotation.

Alternation, in contrast, is referentially transparent. That is, if a sentence is compounded of component sentences by means of 'or', all purely referential positions in the component sentences qualify still as purely referential positions in the compound. Clearly any truth function (§ 13) is referentially transparent.

General terms predicatively used may be looked on as constructions: modes of containment of the subject singular terms in sentences. As constructions they are referentially transparent; for this is

[2] The term is from Whitehead and Russell, 2d ed., vol. 1, p. 665.

simply to say, what was remarked above, that the subject position in a predication is purely referential.

Again the construction 'looking for' counts as transparent if adjacent term positions are treated as referential, and not otherwise. In the one case 'look for' is a genuine relative term; in the other not. What it is in the other case will become clearer in § 32.

A construction that may be transparent or opaque is the belief construction, 'a believes that p'. Thus suppose that though

(7) Tom believes that Cicero denounced Catiline,

he is ill-informed enough to think that the Cicero of the orations and the Tully of *De Senectute* were two. Faced with his unequivocal denial of 'Tully denounced Catiline', we are perhaps prepared both to affirm (7) and to deny that Tom believes that Tully denounced Catiline. If so, the position of 'Cicero' in (7) is not purely referential. But the position of 'Cicero' in the part 'Cicero denounced Catiline', considered apart, is purely referential. So 'believes that' (so conceived) is opaque.

At the same time there is an alternative way of construing belief that is referentially transparent.[3] The difference is as follows. In the opaque sense of belief considered above, Tom's earnest 'Tully never denounced Catiline' counts as showing that he does not believe that Tully denounced Catiline, even while he believes that Cicero did. In the transparent sense of belief, on the other hand, Tom's earnest 'Cicero denounced Catiline' counts as showing that he does believe that Tully denounced Catiline, despite his own misguided verbal disclaimer.

'Cicero' has purely referential occurrence in (7) or not according as 'believes' is taken transparently or not. If belief is taken transparently, then (7) expresses an outright relation between the men Tom and Cicero, viz. the relation of deeming denouncer of Catiline; if belief is taken opaquely, then (7) expressly relates Tom to no man.

There will be more to say of the distinction between transparent and opaque belief. But note meanwhile that the distinction is unrelated to the familiar quirk of English usage whereby 'x does not believe that p' is equated to 'x believes that not p' rather than to 'It

[3] This is apparent from an example of Goodman cited by Scheffler, "On synonymy and indirect discourse," p. 42.

is not the case that x believes that p'. I have been avoiding the concatenation 'does not believe', lest this incidental idiomatic complication seem to figure in the reasoning.

It would be wrong to suppose that an occurrence of a term within an opaque construction is barred from referential position in every broader context. Examples to the contrary are provided by the occurrences of the personal name in:

(8) 'Tully was a Roman' is true,
(9) 'Tully' refers to a Roman.

Despite the opacity of quotation, these occurrences of the personal name are clearly subject to substitutivity of identity *salva veritate*, thanks to the peculiarities of the main verbs involved. On this account 'non-transparent' would be more suggestive than 'opaque'; but the term would be cumbersome, and it is rather a fine point.

§ 31.   OPACITY AND INDEFINITE TERMS

Since indefinite singular terms do not designate objects (§ 23), we have had only definite singular terms in mind in our considerations of referential position. The terms that we replace by others of like designation, in testing for substitutivity of identity, are definite singular terms. Still, what we are testing are positions, and indefinite singular terms can be put into them. Let us see with what effect.

We saw that the position after 'The commissioner is looking for' might or might not be taken as purely referential, with unlike effects. But if we put an indefinite singular term in it, say 'someone', we cease to be free to choose between two interpretations. To make proper sense of 'The commissioner is looking for someone' we have to think of the position as purely referential. For, who is this person the commissioner is looking for? The chairman of the hospital board, i.e., the dean. In the sense of 'looking for' in which the commissioner can be said to be looking for someone, (3) of § 30 has to be reckoned true along with (2). The treatment that would count (2) as true and (3) as false makes the truth value of such statements depend on what epithet is used in designating the sought person; and such a distinction is inapplicable in 'The commissioner is looking for someone', where the sought person is not designated at all.

To put the point paradoxically, indefinite singular terms need referential position because they do not refer.

The same consideration would seem to suggest that for purposes of 'Tom believes that someone denounced Catiline' we must take 'believes' transparently; i.e., take the position of 'someone' as referential. But this case is complicated by a second, intersecting ambiguity: a question of the scope of the indefinite singular term. According as that scope is taken as narrow or wide, the sentence is explained by one or the other of:

(1) Tom believes that someone (is such that he) denounced Catiline,

(2) Someone is such that Tom believes that he denounced Catiline.

Surely (1) is likelier than (2) to do justice to 'Tom believes that someone denounced Catiline'; the words 'is such that he' in (1) are indeed immediately felt as superfluous. But in (1), unlike 'The commissioner is looking for someone', we remain quite free to take the position of 'someone' as referential or not as we please. This is because 'someone' obviously and unequivocally occupies referential position in the subsidiary sentence 'someone denounced Catiline' considered alone. And just because the subsidiary sentence makes sense in any event, (1) does too. In short, therefore, the denouncing position in (1) can freely be taken as referential or non-referential in (1) as a whole. In other words, belief can be construed transparently or opaquely; (1) makes sense either way.

Not so (2), which may be put more idiomatically as 'There is (or was) someone whom Tom believes to have denounced Catiline'. Here it is that those reflections apply that applied to 'The commissioner is looking for someone'. For, who is this person whom Tom believes to have denounced Catiline? Cicero, i.e., Tully. In the sense of 'believes' in which there can be said to be someone whom Tom believes to have denounced Catiline, 'Tom believes that Tully denounced Catiline' has to be reckoned true along with 'Tom believes that Cicero denounced Catiline'. In short, belief must be taken transparently to make proper sense of (2), though it can be taken either way for (1).

The two interpretations of 'I believe he saw a letter of mine' (§ 29) are on this score quite like (1) and (2). Where transparency matters in relation to indefinite singular terms is that there must not be a pronominal cross-reference from inside an opaque construction to an indefinite singular term outside the construction. Such is the lesson of (2). Parallel considerations show also that there must not be a pronominal cross-reference from inside an opaque construction to a 'such that' outside the construction. Adapted to variables (§ 28) the maxim is this: an indefinite singular term outside an opaque construction does not bind a variable inside the construction.

The need of cross-reference from inside a belief construction to an indefinite singular term outside is not to be doubted. Thus see what urgent information the sentence 'There is someone whom I believe to be a spy' imparts, in contrast to 'I believe that someone is a spy' (in the weak sense of 'I believe there are spies'). The one corresponds to (2), the other to (1). Surely, therefore, the transparent sense of belief is not to be lightly dismissed. Yet let its urgency not blind us to its oddity. "Tully," Tom insists, "did not denounce Catiline. Cicero did." Surely Tom must be acknowledged to believe, in every sense, that Tully did not denounce Catiline and that Cicero did. But still he must be said also to believe, in the referentially transparent sense, that Tully *did* denounce Catiline. The oddity of the transparent sense of belief is that it has Tom believing that Tully did and that he did not denounce Catiline. This is not yet a self-contradiction on our part or even on Tom's, for a distinction can be reserved between (*a*) Tom's believing that Tully did and that Tully did not denounce Catiline, and (*b*) Tom's believing that Tully did and did not denounce Catiline. But the oddity is there, and we have to accept it as the price of saying such things as (2) or that there is someone whom one believes to be a spy.

Certainly we are not to blame the oddity on Tom's mere misunderstanding of a proper name, for there are parallel examples without names. Thus instead of having Tom say, "Tully did not denounce Catiline; Cicero did," have him say, "The dean is not married, but the chairman of the hospital board is," not appreciating that they are one.

Now if this much oddity on the part of the transparent sense of belief is tolerable, more remains that is not. Where 'p' represents a sentence, let us write 'δp' (following Kronecker) as short for the description:

the number x such that $((x = 1)$ and $p)$ or $((x = 0)$ and not $p)$.

We may suppose that poor Tom, whatever his limitations regarding Latin literature and local philanthropies, is enough of a logician to believe a sentence of the form '$\delta p = 1$' when and only when he believes the sentence represented by 'p'. But then we can argue from the transparency of belief that he believes everything. For, by the hypotheses already before us,

(3) Tom believes that δ(Cicero denounced Catiline) = 1.

But, whenever 'p' represents a true sentence,

$\delta p = \delta$(Cicero denounced Catiline).

But then, by (3) and the transparency of belief,

Tom believes that $\delta p = 1$,

from which it follows, by the hypothesis about Tom's logical acumen, that

(4) Tom believes that p.

But 'p' represented any true sentence. Repeating the argument using the falsehood 'Tully did not denounce Catiline' instead of the truth 'Cicero denounced Catiline', we establish (4) also where 'p' represents any falsehood. Tom ends up believing everything.[1]

Thus in declaring belief invariably transparent for the sake of (2) and 'There is someone whom I believe to be a spy', we would let in too much. It can sometimes best suit us to affirm 'Tom believes that Cicero denounced Catiline' and still deny 'Tom believes that Tully denounced Catiline', at the cost—on *that* occasion—of (2). In general what is wanted is not a doctrine of transparency or opacity of belief, but a way of indicating, selectively and changeably, just what positions in the contained sentence are to shine through as referential on any particular occasion.

A way of doing that is to agree to localize the failure of transparency regularly in the 'that' of 'believes that' and the 'to' of 'believes to', and not in the 'believes'. Thus we may continue to write 'Tom believes that Cicero denounced Catiline' when we are content to leave the occurrences of 'Cicero' and 'Catiline' non-referential, but write rather:

(5) Tom believes Cicero to have denounced Catiline

[1] See Church's review of Carnap for a related argument in another connection.

if we want to bring 'Cicero' into referential position.[2] Similarly we can get 'Catiline' into referential position thus:

> (6) Tom believes Catiline to have been denounced by Cicero.

If we want to get both into referential position, we are driven to something like:

> (7) Tom believes Cicero and Catiline to be related as denouncer and denounced.

On this convention 'believes that' is unequivocally opaque and (2) therefore simply goes by the board as a bad formulation involving cross-reference from inside an opaque construction to an indefinite singular term outside. What was offered before as an idiomatic equivalent of (2) remains legitimate, however: 'There is (or was) someone whom Tom believes to have denounced Catiline'. Similarly (13) of § 29 goes by the board, but the originally intended sense of it survives in the legitimate version 'There is (or was) a letter of mine which I believe to have been seen by him'.

Here as usual we can revise the relative clauses at will into 'such that' clauses (§ 23); thus '...whom Tom believes to...' and '...which I believe to...' become '...such that Tom believes him to...' and '...such that I believe it to...', without ever disturbing the insides of the opaque 'to' construction. Note that the 'that' of 'such that' is referentially transparent; it is only the 'that' of 'believes that', and the 'to' of 'believes to', that our convention counts opaque.

The constructions 'believes that', 'says that', 'wishes that', 'endeavors that', 'urges that', 'fears that', 'is surprised that', etc., are what Russell calls expressions of *propositional attitude*.[3] What has been observed of the first of them in recent pages applies equally to the lot. The contortions of (5)–(7) strain ordinary language in varying degrees when applied to the rest of the verbs of propositional attitude. 'Wishes', 'urges', and 'fears' fit (5)–(7) as naturally as 'believes' (except that 'urges' is inappropriate to our particular example on account of the past tense). 'Says' falls into

---

[2] Davidson points out to me that the rearrangement 'By Tom, Cicero is believed to have denounced Catiline' has, along with the drawback of unnaturalness, the virtue of being more graphic than (5) in two respects: it unifies the opaque 'believe to', and it displays the referential positions before mentioning belief. Similar rearrangements work for (6) and (7).

[3] *Inquiry into Meaning and Truth*, p. 210. See also Reichenbach, pp. 277 ff.

place with no great violence. 'Endeavors' and 'is surprised' have to be reworded in some such fashion as 'endeavors-to-cause' and 'is surprised-to-learn' when fitted to those positions.

An opaque construction is one in which you cannot in general supplant a singular term by a *codesignative* term (one referring to the same object) without disturbing the truth value of the containing sentence. In an opaque construction you also cannot in general supplant a general term by a *coextensive* term (one true of the same objects), nor a component sentence by a sentence of the same truth value, without disturbing the truth value of the containing sentence. All three failures are called failures of *extensionality*. A reason for stressing the first is that one rightly expects substitutivity of identity in discourse about the identical object, whereas no such presumption is evident for full extensionality. A related reason is that the first failure is what disallows cross-reference from inside opaque constructions. Frege was bound to stress all three failures, for he treated general terms and sentences as naming classes and truth values; all failures of extensionality became failures of substitutivity of identity.[4] Failures of substitutivity of identity, moreover, were in Frege's view unallowable; so he nominally rectified them by decreeing that when a sentence or term occurs within a construction of propositional attitude or the like it ceases to name a truth value, class, or individual and comes to name a proposition, attribute, or "individual concept." (In some ways this account better fits Church, who has sharpened and elaborated the doctrine.[5]) I make none of these moves. I do not disallow failure of substitutivity, but only take it as evidence of non-referential position; nor do I envisage shifts of reference under opaque constructions.

§ 32. OPACITY IN CERTAIN VERBS

We have hit upon a convenient trick of so phrasing our statements of propositional attitude as to keep selected positions referen-

---

[4] Even apart from this special doctrine, the following connection between referential transparency and extensionality can be established: if a construction is transparent and allows substitutivity of concretion (§ 48), it is extensional. The argument is obvious, but see Church's review of "On Frege's way out" for exposure of a fallacy in my adaptation of it to Whitehead and Russell's theory.

[5] Church, "A formulation of the logic of sense and denotation."

tial and others not. The device does not yet apply to our earlier example:

(1) The commissioner is looking for the chairman of the hospital board,

since this example contains no expression of propositional attitude. But it can be made to do so by expanding 'look for' into 'endeavor to find':

(2) The commissioner is endeavoring that the commissioner finds the chairman of the hospital board.

The point of the bad English is to stress the parallel of 'Tom believes that Cicero denounced Catiline'. Now if we carry over the convention of two pages back, the term 'the chairman of the hospital board' has non-referential position in (2). Sentence (2) expands (1) in a way that counts 'looking for . . .' opaque. To get an expansion of (1) in a transparent sense, we must operate on (2) to bring 'the chairman of the hospital board' out from under the opaque 'endeavoring that'. The desired operation on (2) is precisely the operation which, applied to 'Tom believes that Cicero denounced Catiline', gave 'Tom believes Cicero to have denounced Catiline'. Applied to (2), the operation delivers:

(3) The commissioner is endeavoring (-to-cause) the chairman of the hospital board to be found by the commissioner.

Note that the opaque 'to' of (3) is the one after 'board' and not the one in parentheses; the parenthetical expression is for our purposes merely part of the inflection of 'endeavor'. (See end of § 31.)

So (2) construes (1) with opaque 'looking for . . .', and (3) construes (1) with transparent 'looking for . . .'. Thus (2) construes (1) in such a way that substituting 'someone' for 'the chairman of the hospital board' produces nonsense; (3) construes (1) in such a way that substituting 'someone' makes sense. Again (2) construes (1) in such a way that substitution of 'the dean' produces falsity; (3) construes (1) in such a way that substitution of 'the dean' preserves truth.

In both (2) and (3), the first occurrence of 'the commissioner' has referential position and the second has not. Thus (1), no matter whether we take its 'looking for . . .' in the opaque manner of (2) or in the transparent manner of (3), is a sentence whose single grammatical subject implicitly plays two roles, a referential one and a non-referential one. An example in which this same phenomenon of two-role subject comes out more vividly is:

(4) Giorgione was so-called because of his size,

which anyone is ready enough to paraphrase into:

Giorgione was called 'Giorgione' because of his size.

Taking (4) as it stands, we have of course to reckon the position of the subject as not (purely) referential, because of the non-referential character of one of its two implicit roles. And the same conclusion emerges by the direct substitutivity criterion: substitution in (4) according to the identity 'Giorgione = Barbarelli' yields a falsehood.

'The commissioner' in (1) is likewise found to resist substitutivity, if (1) is construed as (2) or (3). Thus suppose the commissioner, for all his self-importance, is the least competent of the county officials. Substitution in (1) according to this identity would give 'The least competent official is endeavoring that the least competent official finds etc.', if we construe (1) as (2); and this, with opaque 'endeavoring that', is doubtless to be adjudged false. The case is similar when we construe (1) as (3).

Now the account of (4) was unexceptionable, but this parallel account of (1) is certainly a distortion.[1] Surely, on a fair account, 'the commissioner' should have referential position in (1), and be replaceable by 'the least competent official' *salva veritate*.

The non-referential status of the subject position in (4) excludes 'someone' from that position, and rightly; 'Someone was so-called because of his size' is nonsense. But the non-referential status of the subject position in (1) would likewise exclude 'someone' from that position; whereas we must surely insist on saying 'Someone is looking for the chairman of the hospital board'.

The upshot of these reflections is that (1) is wrongly construed in both (2) and (3). We must bring the second occurrence of 'the commissioner' into referential position by an additional twist, analogous to the one used on 'Cicero' in (5) or (7) of § 31. The proper account of (1) with opaque 'looking for...' is not (2) above, but rather this analogue of (5) of § 31:

---

[1] I am indebted here to a remark of Davidson's.

(5) The commissioner is endeavoring (-to-cause) himself to find the chairman of the hospital board.

The proper account of (1) with transparent 'looking for...' is not (3) above, but rather this analogue of (7) of § 31:

(6) The commissioner is endeavoring (-to-cause) himself and the chairman of the hospital board to be related as finder and found.

Sentences (2) and (3) remain all right in themselves, but not as versions of (1).

If (1) were construed as (2) or (3), which would be indefensible, and again if (1) is construed as (5), which is one of two admissible interpretations, the verb 'is looking for' does not count as a relative term; not as a term at all, but an opaque verb whose function is explained by the overall paraphrase. If (1) is construed as (6), on the other hand, 'is looking for' qualifies as a relative term. Subject and object in (1) have referential position when (1) is construed as (6). This does not make (6) preferable to (5). Sentence (5) explains (1) with 'looking for' taken as opaque and hence not as a term, and (6) explains (1) with 'looking for' taken as transparent and hence as a term; and both uses of 'looking for' have their place.

The contrast between the two uses of 'looking for' is the same as the contrast between hunting lions in the abstract and hunting or stalking known ones (§ 28). For, observe how lion-hunting turns out. Just as looking for is endeavoring to find, so hunting is endeavoring to shoot or capture. The difference between the two cases of 'Ernest is hunting lions' is *prima facie* a difference in scope:

(7) Ernest is endeavoring that some lion is such that Ernest shoots it,
(8) Some lion is such that Ernest is endeavoring that Ernest shoots it

(cf. (12) and (13) of § 29, also (1) and (2) of § 31). This symmetrical pair of formulations brings the contrast of scopes instructively to the fore, but we shall not want to leave them thus. Sentence (7), to begin with, can as well be put more concisely:

(9) Ernest is endeavoring that Ernest shoots a lion.

And (8) is simply wrong under the convention of § 31, for that convention counts 'is endeavoring that' unequivocally as opaque. Sentence (8) is like (2) of § 31 in involving a cross-reference from inside an opaque construction to an indefinite singular term outside. Correcting (8) as we did (2) of § 31, we have:

> There is a lion which Ernest is endeavoring (-to-cause) to be shot by Ernest,

or, if we feel we can keep the intended scope of the indefinite singular term in mind with less extravagant aids,

> (10) Ernest is endeavoring (-to-cause) a (certain) lion to be shot by Ernest.

Now note that (9) and (10) have the same forms as (2) and (3) of the present section, except that they use an indefinite singular term instead of a definite one. Consequently the objection to (2) and (3) as versions of (1) applies equally to (9) and (10) as versions of 'Ernest is hunting lions': they fail to give 'Ernest' purely referential position at its second occurrences. Rather, just as we dropped (2) and (3) (as versions of (1)) in favor of (5) and (6), so we must drop (9) and (10) (as versions of 'Ernest is hunting lions') in favor of:

> (11) Ernest is endeavoring (-to-cause) himself to shoot a lion,
> (12) Ernest is endeavoring (-to-cause) himself and a (certain) lion to be related as shooter and shot.

When 'Ernest is hunting lions' is construed as (12), 'hunt' qualifies as a straightforward relative term. 'Hunt' is so used in 'man-hunting', as applied to the police; not as applied to man-hunting lions. 'Hunt' in the latter use, and in 'unicorn-hunting' and in the commonest use of 'lion-hunting', is not a term; it is an opaque verb whose use is clarified by the paraphrase (11).

What we have been remarking of 'hunt' or 'look for' and 'endeavor' applies *mutatis mutandis* to 'want' and 'wish'; for to want is to wish to have. 'I want a sloop' in the opaque sense is parallel to (11): 'I wish myself to have a sloop (to be a sloop owner)'; 'I want a sloop' in the transparent sense, 'There is a sloop I want', comes out parallel to (12). Only in the latter sense is 'want' a relative term, relating people to sloops. In the other or opaque sense it is not a relative term relating people to anything at all, concrete or abstract, real or ideal. It is a shortcut verb whose use is set forth by 'I wish myself to have a sloop', wherein 'have' and 'sloop' continue to rate as general terms as usual but merely happen to have an opaque construction 'wish to' overlying them. This point needs to be noticed by philosophers worried over the nature of objects of desire.

Whenever sentences capable of containing 'want' or 'hunt' or 'look for' in an opaque sense are up for consideration in an at all analytic vein, it behooves us forthwith to paraphrase them into the more explicit idiom of propositional attitude. The question of transparency thereupon stands forth and can be settled, now as in (5) and (11) and now as in (6) and (12), in clear view of the alternative commitments and consequences. In general it is a good rule thus to try by paraphrase to account for non-referential positions by explicitly opaque constructions. And in the present instances there is also another benefit from the paraphrase: it exposes a structure startlingly unlike what one usually associates with the grammatical form of 'Ernest is hunting lions' and 'I want a sloop' (cf. 'I hear lions').

When 'hunt lions' and the like are meant rather in the transparent way, there is seldom call to paraphrase them into the idiom of propositional attitudes; for here the verb is a well-behaved relative term as it stands. Usually we are well enough off with 'There is a lion that Ernest is hunting', 'There is a sloop I want'; nothing is gained by expanding it in the grotesque manner of (12), except for purposes of comparisons of the sort in which we have just now been engaged. Our paraphrases, aimed at bringing out the distinction between referential and non-referential positions, have been cumbersome at best; but the most cumbersome ones are the ones least needed.

CHAPTER FIVE

Regimentation

§ 33. AIMS AND CLAIMS OF REGIMENTATION

Practical temporary departures from ordinary language have recommended themselves at various points in the foregoing chapter. Most of these were fairly representative of the departures that one actually adopts in various pursuits short of symbolic logic, and none was drastic. There were the provisional refinements of vague terms for special limited purposes of law or of almanacs. There was the still more transitory paraphrasing of ambiguous terms, simple or composite, for getting over a sudden block in communication; but generally these moves keep within ordinary usage. There was the resort to variables and parentheses to clear up structural ambiguities; and if these devices have come to dominate mathematical writing, it is largely because mathematical work is so liable to ambiguities of cross-reference and grouping that the easiest plan is to leave the devices hooked up for the duration. There was the 'such that' expedient for ambiguities of scope; this again is seldom called for except in connection with intricate communication, which takes place mostly in mathematics. Finally there was the resort to infinitive phrases to distinguish between those positions that are meant as referential and those that are not. Something of this sort can be needed once in a while to resolve doubts e.g. as to the locus of Tom's historical error or as to what is exercising the commissioner; still its main utility is rather for analytical studies of reference, belief, desire, than for the first-intension use of language in talking of other things.

Opportunistic departure from ordinary language in a narrow

sense is part of ordinary linguistic behavior. Some departures, if the need that prompts them persists, may be adhered to, thus becoming ordinary language in the narrow sense; and herein lies one factor in the evolution of language. Others are reserved for use as needed.

In relation to the concerns of this book, those departures have interested us less as general aids to communication than as present aids to understanding the referential work of language and clarifying our conceptual scheme. Now certain such departures have yet a further purpose that is decidedly worth noting: simplification of theory. A striking case is the use of parentheses. To say of parentheses that they resolve ambiguities of grouping gives little notion of their far-reaching importance. They enable us to iterate a few selfsame constructions as much as we please instead of having continually to vary our idioms in order to keep the grouping straight. They enable us thus to minimize our stock of basic functions, or constructions, and the techniques needed in handling them. They enable us to subject long expressions and short ones to a uniform algorithm, and to argue by substitutions of long expressions for short ones, and vice versa, without readjustments of context. But for parentheses or some alternative convention [1] yielding the foregoing benefits, mathematics would not have come far.

Simplification of theory is a central motive likewise of the sweeping artificialities of notation in modern logic. Clearly it would be folly to burden a logical theory with quirks of usage that we can straighten. It is the part of strategy to keep theory simple where we can, and then, when we want to apply the theory to particular sentences of ordinary language, to transform those sentences into a "canonical form" adapted to the theory. If we were to devise a logic of ordinary language for direct use on sentences as they come, we would have to complicate our rules of inference in sundry unilluminating ways. For example, we would have to make express provision for the contrasting scope connotations of 'any' and 'every' (§ 29). Again we would have to incorporate rules on agreement of tense, so as to disallow inference e.g. of

---

[1] Łukasiewicz has pointed out that the benefits of parentheses can be gained without their aid by adopting a prepositive symbol for each basic construction (in the sense of § 11) and fixing, for each such construction, the number of terms or sentences that it is to admit as immediate components. See Tarski, p. 39.

'George married a widow' from 'George married Mary and Mary is a widow'. By developing our logical theory strictly for sentences in a convenient canonical form we achieve the best division of labor: on the one hand there is theoretical deduction and on the other hand there is the work of paraphrasing ordinary language into the theory. The latter job is the less tidy of the two, but still it will usually present little difficulty to one familiar with the canonical notation. For normally he himself is the one who has uttered, as part of some present job, the sentence of ordinary language concerned; and he can then judge outright whether his ends are served by the paraphrase.

The artificial notation of logic is itself explained, of course, in ordinary language. The explanations amount to the implicit specification of simple mechanical operations whereby any sentence in logical notation can be directly expanded, if not into quite ordinary language, at least into semi-ordinary language. Parentheses and variables may survive such expansion, for they do not always go over into ordinary language by easy routine. Commonly also the result of such mechanical expansion will display an extraordinary cumbersomeness of phrasing and an extraordinary monotony of reiterated elements; but all the vocabulary and constituent grammatical constructions will be ordinary. Hence to paraphrase a sentence of ordinary language into logical symbols is virtually to paraphrase it into a special part still of ordinary or semi-ordinary language; for the shapes of the individual characters are unimportant. So we see that paraphrasing into logical symbols is after all not unlike what we all do every day in paraphrasing sentences to avoid ambiguity. The main difference apart from quantity of change is that the motive in the one case is communication while in the other it is application of logical theory.

In neither case is synonymy to be claimed for the paraphrase. Synonymy, for sentences generally, is not a notion that we can readily make adequate sense of (cf. §§ 12, 14); and even if it were, it would be out of place in these cases. If we paraphrase a sentence to resolve ambiguity, what we seek is not a synonymous sentence, but one that is more informative by dint of resisting some alternative interpretations. Typically, indeed, the paraphrasing of a sentence S of ordinary language into logical symbols will issue in substantial divergences. Often the result S' will be less ambiguous than S, often it will have truth values under circumstances under which S has none (cf. §§ 37 f.), and often it will even provide explicit references where S uses indicator words (cf. § 47). S' might indeed naturally enough be spoken of as synonymous with the sentence S" of semi-ordinary language into which S' mechanically expands according to the general explanations of logical symbols; but there is no call to think of S' as synonymous with S. Its relation to S is just that the particular business that the speaker was on that occasion trying to get on with, with help of S among other things, can be managed well enough to suit him by using S' instead of S. We can even let him modify his purposes under the shift, if he pleases.

Hence the importance of taking as the paradigmatic situation that in which the original speaker does his own paraphrasing, as laymen do in their routine dodging of ambiguities. The speaker can be advised in his paraphrasing, and on occasion he can even be enjoined to accept a proposed paraphrase or substitute another or hold his peace; but his choice is the only one that binds him. A foggy appreciation of this point is expressed in saying that there is no dictating another's meaning; but the notion of there being a fixed, explicable, and as yet unexplained meaning in the speaker's mind is gratuitous. The real point is simply that the speaker is the one to judge whether the substitution of S' for S in the present context will forward his present or evolving program of activity to his satisfaction.

On the whole the canonical systems of logical notation are best seen not as complete notations for discourse on special subjects, but as partial notations for discourse on all subjects. There are regimented notations for constructions and for certain of the component terms, but no inventory of allowable terms, nor even a distinction between terms to regard as simple and terms whose structure is to be exhibited in canonical constructions. Embedded in canonical notation in the role of logically simple components there may be terms of ordinary language without limit of verbal complexity. A *maxim of shallow analysis* prevails: *expose no more logical structure than seems useful* for the deduction or other inquiry at hand. In the immortal words of Adolf Meyer, where it doesn't itch don't scratch.

On occasion the useful degree of analysis may, conversely, be such as to cut into a simple word of ordinary language, requiring its paraphrase into a composite term in which other terms are compounded with the help of canonical notation. When this happens, the line of analysis adopted will itself commonly depend on what is sought in the inquiry at hand; again there need be no question of the uniquely right analysis, nor of synonymy.

Among the useful steps of paraphrase there are some, of course, that prove pretty regularly to work out all right, whatever plausible purposes the inquiry at hand may have. In them, one may in a non-technical spirit speak fairly enough of synonymy, if the claim is recognized as a vague one and a matter of degree. But in the pattest of paraphrasing one courts confusion and obscurity by imagining some absolute synonymy as goal.

To implement an efficient algorithm of deduction is no more our concern, in these pages, than was the implementation of communication. But the simplification and clarification of logical theory to which a canonical logical notation contributes is not only algorithmic; it is also conceptual. Each reduction that we make in the variety of constituent constructions needed in building the sentences of science is a simplification in the structure of the inclusive conceptual scheme of science. Each elimination of obscure constructions or notions that we manage to achieve, by paraphrase into more lucid elements, is a clarification of the conceptual scheme of science. The same motives that impel scientists to seek ever simpler and clearer theories adequate to the subject matter of their special sciences are motives for simplification and clarification of the broader framework shared by all the sciences. Here the objective is called philosophical, because of the breadth of the framework concerned; but the motivation is the same. The quest of a simplest, clearest overall pattern of canonical notation is not to be distinguished from a quest of ultimate categories, a limning of the most general traits of reality. Nor let it be retorted that such constructions are conventional affairs not dictated by reality; for may not the same be said of a physical theory? True, such is the nature of reality that one physical theory will get us around better than another; but similarly for canonical notations.

§ 34. QUANTIFIERS AND OTHER OPERATORS

Where the objective of a canonical notation is economy and clarity of elements, we need only to show how the notation *could* be made to do the work of all the idioms to which we claim it to be adequate; we do not have to use it. Notations of intermediate richness can be less laborious to use, and different forms have advantages for different purposes. So, reassured that we are in no way compromising our freedom, we can be uncompromising in our reductions.

One striking reduction is already suggested by what we saw in § 29: we can hold our indefinite singular terms to subject position. The idea in § 29 was that this be done just when ambiguity of scope threatens; but now we can as well insist on it as a regular condition of a narrowly canonical grammar. We can even standardize their manner of occurrence a bit further, insisting specifically that they occur always followed by a predicate of the form 'is an object x such that ... x ...'. For this is just the position that an indefinite singular term does end up in once we apply the 'such that' procedure of § 29 and then substantivize the 'such that' clause by prefixing 'object' in order to accommodate variables.

Also we can dispense with almost the entire category of indefinite singular terms. To begin with, the need for a distinction between 'any' and 'each' or 'every' is already removed by our recourse to 'such that' (cf. § 29). 'No', as of the indefinite singular terms 'no poem', 'nobody', 'nothing', can be paraphrased by means of 'each' and negation. The essential forms of indefinite singular terms reduce thus to 'every F' and 'some F' (in the sense of 'a certain F'), where 'F' stands for any general term in substantival form. But now for the striking economy: these two classes of indefinite singular terms are in turn dispensable in favor of just the two indefinite singular terms 'everything' and 'something'. For, as noted in the preceding paragraph, 'every F' and 'some F' are needed only in the positions 'Every F is an object x such that ... x ...' and 'Some F is an object x such that ... x ...'; and obviously we can paraphrase these in turn respectively as:

(1) Everything is an object x such that (if x is an F then ... x ...),

(2) Something is an object x such that (x is an F and ... x ...).

Thus all the indefinite singular terms are got down to 'everything' and 'something', and even these two come never to occur except followed by the words 'is an object x [or y, etc.] such that'. Hence we may conveniently subject 'everything' and those ensuing words to condensed symbolization; and correspondingly for 'something'. Usual notations for these respective purposes are '(x)' and '$(\exists x)$', conveniently read 'everything x is such that' and 'something x is such that'. These prefixes are known, for unobvious but traceable reasons, as *quantifiers*, universal and existential.

A small further economy is still possible: of our two surviving indefinite singular terms, 'everything' and 'something', one only is needed. In other words, existential quantifiers can be paraphrased with help of universal ones and vice versa, as is well known: '$(\exists x)(\ldots x \ldots)$' becomes 'not (x) not $(\ldots x \ldots)$' and conversely.

This last reduction is of little moment. The reduction of all indefinite singular terms to the two sorts of quantifiers is more significant, concentrating as it does the whole bewildering phenomenon of indefinite singular terms in two instances, 'everything' and 'something'. And much more significant still was the stage reached already in § 29: the clear isolation of the scopes of indefinite singular terms. I have explained the idea of quantification in stages, separating its several significant aspects; but Frege achieved the whole thing at once, right down to the final reduction to universal quantifiers, in his *Begriffsschrift* (1879), a thin book that may be said to mark the start of mathematical logic.

The indefinite singular terms were built upon general terms. They have now disappeared into quantification. But there remain definite singular terms that are likewise built upon general terms: notably singular descriptions and demonstrative singular terms (§ 21). Now we can assimilate the demonstrative singular terms to singular descriptions, treating 'this (that) apple' as 'the apple here (there)', *'der hiesige (dortige) Apfel'*. This use of the indicator words 'here' and 'there' as general terms attributively adjoined to 'apple' depends on pointing just as did the use of 'this' and 'that': no less and no more. In the case of 'this (that) apple' the question of spatiotemporal extent, left open by the pointing gesture, was conveniently settled by the general term 'apple' (cf. § 21); but the same happens in the general term 'apple here (there)', for it is true only of things of which both components are true.

A further sort of definite singular term which, like the singular description, is built on a general term, is the class-name. In it the general term in its substantival form is followed by '-kind', or pluralized and preceded by 'the class of the'. Another is the attribute-name (cf. § 25), in which the general term in its adjectival form is followed perhaps by '-ness', or '-ity', or in its verbal form is inflected infinitively or gerundively: 'to be a dog', '(the attribute of) being a dog', 'to be human', 'to err', 'to bake pies'. Another is the relation-name, similarly formed: 'nextness', 'superiority', 'giving'.

We can gain some simplicity of structure and also expedite subsequent developments by regimenting these definite singular terms as follows. Consider the singular description, 'the F'. The general term in the role of 'F' here may be simple or composite; in particular it may have the form 'object x such that ... x ...'. Now we may arbitrarily insist on its having the latter form invariably, since 'F' itself can be expanded at will to 'object x such that Fx'. The canonical form for singular description thus becomes:

(3) the object x such that ... x ... .

Similarly the canonical forms for class abstraction (as it is called) and attribute abstraction become:

(4) the class of the objects x such that ... x ... ,
(5) to be an object x such that ... x ... .

Relations can be forced somewhat into line thus:

(6) to be objects x and y such that ... x ... y ... .

It must be conceded that (6), with its tandem variables 'x' and 'y', strains the 'such that' idiom beyond what we hitherto reckoned on. Moreover (3)–(6) all seem gratuitous inflations of what there had been. But the gain is this: we can now take the further step of treating the whole complex prefixes of (3)–(6) as unitary operators, absorbing the 'such that'. This is just what we did with the complex prefixes of (1) and (2) when we rendered them as simple quantifiers '(x)' and '$(\exists x)$'.

The prefixes 'the object x such that' and 'the class of the objects x such that' have figured prominently among the basic operators of mathematical logic from Frege and Peano onward, commonly in the condensed notations '$(\imath x)$' and '$\hat{x}$'. For the prefixes in (5) and (6) let us use just the unmodified variables themselves, and then enclose the governed sentence distinctively in brackets. Thus (3)–(6) become:

(7) $(\imath x)(\ldots x \ldots)$, $\hat{x}(\ldots x \ldots)$, $x[\ldots x \ldots]$, $xy[\ldots x \ldots y \ldots]$.

In the last two we have abstraction notations for *intensions*: monadic intensions, or attributes, and dyadic intensions, or relations. In the same spirit we might adopt simply the brackets without prefix to express abstraction of medadic (0-adic) intensions, or propositions; thus '[Socrates is mortal]' would amount to the words 'that Socrates is mortal', or 'Socrates's being mortal', when these are taken as referring to a proposition. It will be noted that in conformity with modern philosophical practice I am using the term 'proposition' not for a sentence, but for an abstract object which is thought of as designated by a 'that'-clause. Such an object, e.g. that Socrates is mortal, is thought of as related to a sentence, 'Socrates is mortal', in the way that an attribute, e.g. to be a dog or to bake pies, is related to a general term, 'dog', 'bakes pies'. I would be among the last to discourage the question what manner of objects these might be, but it belongs to a critical phase proper to the next chapter.

The four prefixes in (7) are, like the quantifiers, *variable-binding* operators (§ 28). There is the difference only that whereas quantifiers attach to sentences to produce sentences, these four new operators all attach to sentences to produce singular terms. The sentence to which an operator is attached is called the *scope* of the operator. The scope of a quantifier is not quite the scope, in the sense of § 29, of the indefinite singular term 'everything' or 'something' which the quantifier has absorbed; for the scope of an indefinite singular term included the term itself. The scope of a quantifier or other variable-binding operator is rather the clause governed by the 'such that' which the operator has absorbed.

Actually our operators here are somewhat excessive. That of class abstraction is, as already hinted by the initial 'the' of its verbalization in (4), reducible to that of singular description; for we can paraphrase '$\hat{x}(\ldots x \ldots)$' as:

(8) $(\imath y)(x)(x \in y$ if and only if $\ldots x \ldots)$ [1]

where '$\in$' is short for the relative term 'is a member of'. If we keep '$\hat{x}$' nevertheless, we do so in the spirit in which we keep '$(\exists x)$' despite its reducibility to universal quantification; viz., as a convenient abbreviation.

This method of eliminating class abstraction fails, by the way, for intensional abstraction. We cannot, on the analogy of (8), paraphrase '$x[\ldots x \ldots]$' as:

(9) $(\imath y)(x)(x$ has y if and only if $\ldots x \ldots)$.

[1] This formula needs modification for some forms of class theory. See my *Mathematical Logic*, pp. 131 ff., 155–166, and "On Frege's way out," pp. 153 ff.

That (8) succeeds where (9) fails is due to a difference in identity conditions for classes and attributes. Since classes with the same members are identical, the condition following '$(\imath y)$' in (8) fixes y uniquely. Since on the other hand attributes are not in general supposed to be identical just because the same things have them, the condition following '$(\imath y)$' in (9) cannot in general be depended on to single out any one attribute y.

§ 35. VARIABLES AND REFERENTIAL OPACITY

Variables now having been brought into increased prominence, it will be worth while to consider more expressly their connection with referential opacity. Each of our variable-binding operators came as a condensation of 'such that' and trimmings; and the variable that the operator binds is the variable bound by the absorbed 'such that'. The bearing of opacity on variables is consequently implicit already in what was said in § 31: that there can be no cross-reference from inside an opaque construction to a 'such that' outside. Rephrased for quantification and other variable-binding operations, this says that *no variable inside an opaque construction is bound by an operator outside.* You cannot quantify into an opaque construction.

When 'x' stands inside an opaque construction and '(x)' or '$(\exists x)$' stands outside, the attitude to take is simply that that occurrence of 'x' is then not bound by that occurrence of the quantifier. An example is the last occurrence of 'x' in:

(1) $(\exists x)(x$ is writing '$9 > x$').

This sentence is true when and only when someone is writing '$9 > x$'. Change 'x' to 'y' in its first two occurrences in (1), and the result is still true when and only when someone is writing '$9 > x$'. Change the last 'x' to 'y', and the case is otherwise. The final 'x' of (1) does not refer back to '$(\exists x)$', is not bound by '$(\exists x)$', but does quite other work: it contributes to the quotational name of a three-character open sentence containing specifically the twenty-fourth letter of the alphabet.

The case of:

(2) $(\exists x)$(Tom believes that x denounced Catiline)

is similar in that 'x' is inside and '$(\exists x)$' outside an opaque construction (if we keep to the convention of § 31). So here again we may say that the '(∃x)' fails to bind that occurrence of 'x'. But (2) differs from (1) in that (1) still makes sense while (2) does not.

Of course these make sense:

(3) (∃x)(Tom believes x to have denounced Catiline),
(4) Tom believes that (∃x)(x denounced Catiline).

But in each of these the 'x' is bound by '(∃x)'. In (3), 'x' and '(∃x)' are both outside the opaque construction; in (4) they are both inside.

Referential position is primarily thought of, naturally enough, as a position for a singular term that names; and the criterion of such position, viz. substitutivity of identity, was accordingly stated in relation to such terms. Derivatively we have been able to speak of variables in referential position, though they do not name; for the positions remain the same however filled. Section 31 opened on a parallel remark. But now it is time to notice also that the substitutivity criterion can be trained upon the variables directly, without prior talk of constants. For, the substitutivity of identity can be stated with variables as a quantified conditional:

(5) $(x)(y)($ if $x = y$ and $\ldots x \ldots$ then $\ldots y \ldots)$

where '$\ldots x \ldots$' stands for the sentence in which 'x' is said to have purely referential position. Special importance attaches to our being able thus to explain referential position without talking of singular terms other than variables, because in § 38 singular terms other than variables will be eliminated. The notion of referential position will remain.

In (5) the substitutivity of identity takes on a somewhat different air from what it has in:

(6) If Tully = Cicero and $\ldots$ Tully $\ldots$ then $\ldots$ Cicero $\ldots$.

We easily produce quite natural sentences for the role of '$\ldots$ Tully $\ldots$' that violate (6), and hence we see (6) not as a law of identity but merely as a condition of referentiality of the position of 'Tully' in '$\ldots$ Tully $\ldots$'. On the other hand (5) does have the air of a law; one feels that any interpretation of '$\ldots x \ldots$' violating (5) would be simply a distortion of the manifest intent of the blanks. Anyway I hope one feels this, for there is good reason to. Since there is no quantifying into an opaque construction, the positions of 'x' and 'y' in '$\ldots x \ldots$' and '$\ldots y \ldots$' must be referential if 'x' and 'y' in those positions are to be bound by the initial '(x)' and '(y)' of (5) at all. Since the notation of (5) manifestly intends the quantifiers to bind 'x' and 'y' in all four shown places, any interpretation of '$\dots x \dots$' violating (5) would be a distortion.

Evidently then a more fundamental characterization of referential position than (5), from the point of view of variables, is the point about binding: occurrences of variables have to be referential relative to the scope of the quantifier that binds them. But if in trying to settle whether a position is referential we feel uncertain of our intuitions about quantifiers and what they bind, we can always fall back on (5) or even on substitutivity of identity for constant terms.

Variable-binding operators, as well as variables, were brought into increased prominence in § 34. We have now got a better perspective on referential position, from the point of view of variables. It turns out that we can also add a certain vividness to the treatment of propositional attitudes (§§ 31, 32) by exploiting certain of the operators. For, the verbs of propositional attitude may be viewed as relative terms predicable of objects some of which are propositions, attributes, or relations. Thus 'Tom believes that Cicero denounced Catiline', 'Tom believes Cicero to have denounced Catiline', and 'Tom believes Cicero and Catiline to have been related as denouncer and denounced' (§ 31) become respectively:

(7) Tom believes [Cicero denounced Catiline],
(8) Tom believes Cicero $x[x$ denounced Catiline],
(9) Tom believes Cicero and Catiline $xy[x$ denounced $y]$.

We may for greater clarity rearrange (8) and (9) thus:

(8) Tom believes $x[x$ denounced Catiline] of Cicero,
(9) Tom believes $xy[x$ denounced $y]$ of Cicero and Catiline.

This move is not an adoption of the Frege-Church theory (§ 31). In sentences of propositional attitude I am taking only each whole opaquely enclosed portion as naming an intension. I do not take its component terms and sentences as naming intensions, nor impute shifts of reference. Why I prefer to touch intensional objects so lightly will appear in Chapter VI, when I undertake to get rid of them altogether.

Sentences (7)–(9) have the respective forms 'Fab', '$Fabc$', '$Fabcd$'. In (7) 'believes' figures as a dyadic relative term, predicated of a man and a proposition. In (8) 'believes' figures as a part of a triadic relative term 'believes of', predicated of a man, an attribute, and a man. In (9) 'believes' figures as a part of a tetradic relative term 'believes of and', predicated of a man, a relation, and two men. Each of the positions represented by 'a', 'b', 'c', and 'd' here is, as always, purely referential. The opaque constructions, marked in the verbal formulations by the 'that' and 'to' associated with 'believes', are marked uniformly in (7)–(9) by the brackets of intensional abstraction.

This opacity of intensional abstraction is no mere consequence of our reading these constructions into the idioms of propositional attitude. For presumably identity of propositions and of attributes is to be construed in such a way that

[the number of the major planets $> 4] \neq [9 > 4]$ and

x[the number of the major planets $> x] \neq x[9 > x]$

even though the number of the major planets = 9. This failure of substitutivity of identity shows that the position of '9' is not referential in '$[9 > 4]$' or '$x[9 > x]$'. But it is referential in '$9 > 4$' and '$9 > x$'. So abstraction of propositions and attributes is opaque. That of relations fares similarly.

Or again let 'p' and 'q' represent any two true sentences such that $[p] \neq [q]$. Presumably then

$[\delta p = 1] \neq [\delta q = 1]$

(cf. § 31), even though $\delta p = \delta q$; so once more propositional abstraction proves opaque. For a parallel argument regarding attribute abstraction, let A and B be coextensive but distinct attributes. (If there were no such, we could forget attributes and talk instead always of classes.) Presumably then

$x[x \in \hat{y}(y \text{ has } A)] \neq x[x \in \hat{y}(y \text{ has } B)]$

even though $\hat{y}(y \text{ has } A) = \hat{y}(y \text{ has } B)$.

Note that in the abstraction of attributes the opaque construction takes in the initial 'x' along with the brackets. Otherwise the initial 'x' would be an operator outside, and thus powerless to bind an inside variable.

The topic of opacity will be resumed in § 41.

§ 36. TIME.
CONFINEMENT OF GENERAL TERMS

Our ordinary language shows a tiresome bias in its treatment of time. Relations of date are exalted grammatically as relations of position, weight, and color are not. This bias is of itself an inelegance, or breach of theoretical simplicity. Moreover, the form that it takes—that of requiring that every verb form show a tense—is peculiarly productive of needless complications, since it demands lip service to time even when time is farthest from our thoughts. Hence in fashioning canonical notations it is usual to drop tense distinctions.

We may conveniently hold to the grammatical present as a form, but treat it as temporally neutral. One does this in mathematics and other highly theoretical branches of science without deliberate convention. Thus from 'Seven of them remained and seven is an odd number' one unhesitatingly infers 'An odd number of them remained', despite the palpable fallacy of the analogous inference from 'George married Mary and Mary is a widow'. One feels the 'is' after 'seven' as timeless, unlike the 'is' after 'Mary', even apart from any artifice of canonical notation.

Where the artifice comes is in taking the present tense as timeless always, and dropping other tenses. This artifice frees us to omit temporal information or, when we please, handle it like spatial information. 'I will not do it again' becomes 'I do not do it after now', where 'do' is taken tenselessly and the future force of 'will' is translated into a phrase 'after now', comparable to 'west of here'. 'I telephoned him but he was sleeping' becomes 'I telephone him then but he is sleeping then', where 'then' refers to some time implicit in the circumstances of the utterance.

This adjustment lays inferences such as the above ones about seven and George conveniently open to logical inspection. The valid one about seven becomes, with present tenses read timelessly, 'Seven of them then remain and seven is an odd number; therefore an odd number of them then remain.' In this form the inference no longer has an invalid analogue about George and Mary, but only a valid one: 'George marries before now Mary and Mary is a widow now; therefore George marries before now (one who is) a widow now.' (Whether to write 'marries before now' as here, or 'then marries' in parallel to the example about seven, is merely a question whether to suppose that the sentences came on the heels of some reference to a specific past occasion. I have supposed so in the one example and not in the other.)

Such rephrasing of tense distorts English, though scarcely in an unfamiliar way; for the treating of time on a par with space is no novelty to natural science. Of the perplexities that are thus lessened, instances outside the domain of logical deduction are not far to seek. One is the problem of Heraclitus (§ 24). Once we put the temporal extent of the river on a par with the spatial extent, we see no more difficulty in stepping into the same river at two times than at two places. Furthermore the river's change of substance, at a given place from time to time, comes to be seen as quite on a par with the river's difference in substance at a given time from place to place; sameness of river is controverted no more on the one count than on the other.

The problem of Heraclitus was already under control in § 24, without help of the alignment of time with space; but intuitively the alignment helps. Similarly for perplexities of personal identity: the space-time view helps one appreciate that there is no reason why my first and fifth decades should not, like my head and feet, count as parts of the same man, however dissimilar. There need be no unchanging kernel to constitute me the same man in both decades, any more than there need be some peculiarly Quinian textural quality common to the protoplasm of my head and feet; though both are possible.[1]

Physical objects, conceived thus four-dimensionally in space-time, are not to be distinguished from events or, in the concrete sense of the term, processes.[2] Each comprises simply the content, however heterogeneous, of some portion of space-time, however disconnected and gerrymandered. What then distinguishes material substances from other physical objects is a detail: if an object is a substance, there are relatively few atoms that lie partly in it (temporally) and partly outside.

---

[1] Cf. Goodman, *Structure of Appearance*, p. 94.

[2] They are what Strawson (*Individuals*, pp. 56 f.) has dismissed as *process-things*, "not to be identified either with the processes which things undergo *or* with the things which undergo them. . . . I was concerned to investigate . . . the categories we actually possess; and the category of process-things is one we neither have nor need." He supports his distinctions with examples of usage. Given his concern with usage conservation, I expect he is in the right. But our present concern is with canonical deviations.

Zeno's paradoxes, if they can be made initially puzzling, become less so when time is looked upon as spacelike. Typical ones consist essentially in dividing a finite distance into infinitely many parts and arguing that infinite time must be consumed in traversing them all. Seeing time in the image of space helps us appreciate that infinitely many periods of time can just as well add up to a finite period as can a finite distance be divided into infinitely many component distances.

Discussion of Zeno's paradoxes, as of much else, is aided by graphing time against distance. Note then that such graphs are quite literally a treatment of time as spacelike.

Just as forward and backward are distinguishable only relative to an orientation, so, according to Einstein's relativity principle, space and time are distinguishable only relative to a velocity. This discovery leaves no reasonable alternative to treating time as spacelike. But the benefits surveyed above are independent of Einstein's principle.[3]

Tense, then, is to give way to such temporal qualifiers as 'now', 'then', 'before t', 'at t', 'after t', and to these only as needed. These qualifiers may be systematized along economical lines, as follows.

Each specific time or epoch, of say an hour's duration, may be taken as an hour-thick slice of the four-dimensional material world, exhaustive spatially and perpendicular to the time axis. (Whether something is an epoch in this sense will depend on point of view, according to relativity theory, but its existence as an object will not.) We are to think of t as an epoch of any desired duration and any desired position along the time axis.[4] Then, where x is a spatiotemporal object, we can construe 'x at t' as naming the common part of x and t. Thus 'at' is taken as tantamount to the juxtapositive notation illustrated in the singular term 'red wine' (§ 21). Red wine is red at wine.

---

[3] Einstein's discovery and Minkowski's interpretation of it provided an essential impetus, certainly, to spatiotemporal thinking, which came afterward to dominate philosophical constructions in Whitehead and others. But the idea of paraphrasing tensed sentences into terms of eternal relations of things to times was clear enough before Einstein. See e.g. Russell, *Principles of Mathematics* (1903), p. 471. For further discussion of tense elimination see my *Elementary Logic*, pp. 6 f., 111–115, 155 ff.; Goodman, *Structure of Appearance*, pp. 296 ff.; Reichenbach, pp. 284–298; Taylor; Williams.

[4] The question of an instant, or epoch of no duration, is best set aside now and subsumed under § 52.

We easily extend 'at' to classes. Where z is mankind, z at t may be explained as the class $\hat{y}(\exists x)(y = (x$ at $t)$ and $x \in z)$ of appropriate man stages.

We can treat the indicator words 'now' and 'then' on a par with 'I' and 'you', as singular terms. Just as the temporary and shifting objects of reference of 'I' and 'you' are people, those of 'now' and 'then' are times or epochs. 'I now' and 'I then' mean 'I at now', 'I at then'; the custom just happens to be to omit the 'at' here, as in 'red wine'.[5]

'Before' can be construed as a relative term predicable of times. Such constructions as 'x is eating y before t' and 'x is eating y after t' then come through thus:

$$(\exists u)(u \text{ is before } t \text{ and } x \text{ at } u \text{ is eating } y),$$

$$(\exists u)(t \text{ is before } u \text{ and } x \text{ at } u \text{ is eating } y).$$

In this example I have used the progressive aspect 'is eating', in preference to 'eats', because what is concerned is the state and not the disposition; contrast 'Tabby eats mice' (§ 28). Temporal qualifications apply to the latter as well, for there may have been a time when Tabby had no taste for mice, and a time may come when she will lose it. Thus we may say 'Tabby now eats mice', 'Tabby at t eats mice', as well as 'Tabby at t is eating mice', but in the one case we report a phase in her evolving pattern of behavior while in the other we report an incident in her behavior.

In the devices of canonical notation thus far before us there is no suggestion for analyzing the terms 'is eating' and 'eats mice', or even 'eats mice' and 'eats fish', into any common elements. Nor will later pages help us much in the matter. For I know of no general analysis of such terms that improves the situation, however unsatisfactory, in which ordinary language leaves them. For

---

[5] In *Individuals*, p. 216, Strawson argues against viewing 'now' as a singular term. His argument is that 'now' sets no temporal boundaries. One possible answer might be to defend vagueness; another would be to construe the temporal boundaries as those of the shortest utterance of sentential form containing the utterance of 'now' in question. The latter answer is in our present spirit of artificial regimentation, and we must note that the Strawson passage has a different context. I even share, in a way, an ulterior doctrine that he is there engaged in supporting, for I think it is of a piece with my reflections on the primacy of unanalyzed occasion sentences in the theory of radical translation and of infant learning.

special purposes one may well paraphrase a dispositional sentence like 'Tabby eats mice' into a more elaborate sentence built of canonical notations, the progressive form of the verb, and other materials; but the paraphrase may be expected to include details that suit only the case and purposes at hand and afford no general paradigm. For that matter, our analysis in § 35 left us with no suggestion for analyzing the relative terms 'believes', 'believes of', 'believes of and', etc. into any common elements either.

Where canonical notation is cut off, leaving unanalyzed components, will usually vary with one's purposes (§ 33). But what typically remains unanalyzed has the form of a term; indeed a general term, for we shall see how to eliminate singular terms (§ 38). Moreover, this residual general term regularly ends up in predicative position. We have already been witnessing the trend of general terms to predicative position under regimentation of notation. Thus 'I now have a dog' and 'Every dog barks' show the general term 'dog' as part of an indefinite singular term; their paraphrases:

$(\exists x)(x$ is a dog and I now have $x)$,

$(x)(\text{if } x$ is a dog then x barks$)$

give it predicative position. In 'Turtles are reptiles', 'Paul and Elmer are sons of colleagues', 'Buffaloes have dwindled', and 'I now hear lions', six general terms appear in the plural; in the paraphrases:

$(x)(\text{if } x$ is a turtle then x is a reptile$)$,

$(\exists x)(\exists y)(\text{Paul is son of } x$ and Elmer is son of y and x is colleague of $y)$,

$(\exists t)(t$ is before now and $\hat{x}(x$ is a buffalo) now is smaller than $\hat{x}(x$ is a buffalo) at $t)$,[6]

$(\exists x)(x$ is a lion and I now hear x and $(\exists y)(y \neq x$ and y is a lion and I now hear $y))$ (cf. § 24)

all six have predicative position. Occurrences of general terms in singular terms, in the fashion 'the F' and 'to be F', likewise resolve into predicative position: $(\imath x)Fx$, $x[Fx]$.

---

[6] See the account, two pages back, of a class at t.

Ways in which one general term can occur in another general term were noted in §§ 21 and 22. One was where a (relative) general term was applied to a singular term to obtain a general term of the form 'F of b'. One was where one general term was adjoined attributively to another; thus 'F G', 'red ball'. Now in both cases the composite general term can, in predicative position, be dissolved: '(F G)x' reduces to 'Fx and Gx', and '(F of b)x' to 'Fxb'. The components end up in predicative position. Similarly for other algebraic modes of composition: thus 'F and G' and 'F or G'. The predication '(F or G)x' dissolves to 'Fx or Gx', and the predication '(F and G)x' dissolves to 'Fx and Gx'.

Such algebraic constructions are in effect cases of the 'such that' form: 'F of b' is 'object x such that Fxb', 'F G' is 'object x such that Fx and Gx', and so on. The observed dissolution of such constructions in predicative position is thus in effect merely the dissolution of 'such that' in predicative position (§ 29). It is notable that the 'such that' construction—or, what comes to the same thing, the relative clause—has no place in the canonical notation. The construction had been crucial, but in § 34 it was absorbed, in its useful functions, into other more special variable-binding operators.

There do remain unreduced ways in which one general term can occur in another. There is the application of an adverb or syncategorematic adjective to a general term, yielding a more complex general term (§§ 21, 22, 27, 28). There is the juxtaposing of substantival general terms, in the often haphazard senses that such juxtaposition may bear (§ 21). For that matter, there are dispositional combinations like 'eats mice'. I do not say the component general terms in such cases reduce to predicative position; the whole residual general term at which our paraphrasing leaves off is what gets predicative position, not its parts. The internal structure of these recalcitrant compounds is, relative to canonical notation, just not structure. Or, if for special purposes such a term is paraphrased with help of the canonical notation in *ad hoc* ways, then its component terms likewise settle into predicative position. In brief the point is that the only canonical position of a general term is predicative position, whatever the term's uncanonical substructure.

This is still not to say that general terms end up without canonical substructure. But the fact is that they do, except when a certain variant line is adopted that will be considered in § 44. Even that line accords general terms no general terms as immediate components, but it does accord some of them sentences as immediate components.

§ 37. NAMES REPARSED

A constant singular term, simple or complex, will seldom be used in purely referential position unless the speaker believes or makes believe that there is something, and just one, that the term designates. For us who know there is no such thing as Pegasus, the sentence 'Pegasus flies' counts perhaps as neither true nor false. (Cf. § 23.)

There are sentences containing 'Pegasus' that we do count true or false. One example is 'Homer believed in Pegasus', to which we shall recur; but here the position may be held not to be referential. Another example is 'Pegasus exists', or 'There is (such a thing as) Pegasus'; and let us consider whether the position of 'Pegasus' there is purely referential. Certainly, if a sentence of the form '. . . exists' is true, and its subject is supplanted by another term that designates the same thing as it does, the result will be true; so by that standard the position is indeed purely referential. Yet oddly so; for there is little evident sense in '$(x)(x$ exists)' or '$(\exists x)(x$ exists)'.

A look at '$(\exists x)(x$ exists)' suggests that our embarrassment may be one of riches: that 'exists' has perhaps no independent business in our vocabulary when '$(\exists x)$' is at our disposal. May we not better spell 'Pegasus exists' itself out as '$(\exists y)(y = \text{Pegasus})$'? On this plan '$(x)(x$ exists)' and '$(\exists x)(x$ exists)' become '$(x)(\exists y)(y = x)$' and '$(\exists x)(\exists y)(y = x)$' and thus trivially true. What we have done here is to construe 'exists' as an ordinary general term, or predicate, but a trivial one: we have taken 'x exists' as '$(\exists y)(y = x)$', which, like '$x = x$', is true of everything. Still this course leaves anomalies. It seems odd, if '$(x)(x$ exists)' is true and 'Pegasus' has purely referential position in 'Pegasus exists', for 'Pegasus exists' to be false. This anomaly withstands the proposed expansion of 'exists': it still seems odd, if '$(x)(\exists y)(y = x)$' is true and 'Pegasus' has purely referential position in '$(\exists y)(y = \text{Pegasus})$', for '$(\exists y)(y = \text{Pegasus})$' to be false. Also there is a certain anomaly in that despite the general tendency mentioned at the beginning of this section we want to single out 'Pegasus exists' or '$(\exists y)(y = \text{Pegasus})$' as false, rather than neither true nor false. Finally, independently of all such technicalities, there is just something wrong about admitting that 'Pegasus' can ever have purely referential position in truths or falsehoods; for the intuitive idea behind "purely referential position" was supposed to be that the term is used purely to specify its object, for the rest of the sentence to say something about (§ 30).

Singular terms which, like 'Pegasus', lack their objects thus raise problems; and not only in connection with the concept of purely referential position. The mere occurrence of truth-value gaps, as we may call them—cases where, in Strawson's phrase, the question of truth value does not arise—would add irksome complications to deductive theory if allowed for. We have indeed never been worried that open sentences lack truth values (§ 28), but open sentences are notationally recognizable. A special awkwardness of the truth-value gaps here under consideration is that they cannot be systematically spotted by notational form. Whether 'Pegasus flies' has a truth value is made to depend on whether there is such a thing as Pegasus. Whether a sentence containing 'the author of *Waverley*' has a truth value is made to depend on whether *Waverley* was written by one man or two. Even such truth-value gaps can be admitted and coped with, perhaps best by something like a logic of three truth values. But they remain an irksome complication, as complications are that promise no gain in understanding.

Let it not be supposed that these various perplexities and complications issue merely from a pedantic distinction between what is false and what is neither true nor false. Nothing would be gained by pooling those two categories under the head of the false; for they are distinguished, under whatever names, in that the one category contains the negations of all its members while the other contains the negations of none of its members.

Such, then, are characteristic troubles over singular terms that fail to designate. The original sin is recorded, after a fashion, in § 22. It was the forming of composite singular terms, and the example was 'this apple'. The following impractical sort of reform may therefore suggest itself. We might insist that a singular term (variables aside) never be permitted the form of a single word unless it was learned in that form, like 'mama' and 'water', through the primitive kind of conditioning that antedated the learning of compound singular terms. We might insist that all other singular terms (variables aside) be rendered as compounds, in ways reflecting how they were learned. Then we might devise techniques for meeting possible failures of designation on the part of these visibly structured singular terms, secure meanwhile in the existence of the designata of the simple ones. This sort of approach recalls, if only in caricature, Russell's early philosophy of proper names and descriptions. Anyway it is hopeless, in that everybody has his peculiar history of term-learning and nobody keeps track of it. Moreover there is no evident reason to depend, for improvements of our conceptual apparatus, upon emended re-enactments of genesis. Continued evolution, sped and guided by creative imagination, has served science better.

The following observation will helpfully narrow our problem. Think of 'a' as a singular term, and '$\ldots a \ldots$' as any sentence containing 'a' in purely referential position. By the substitutivity of identity, since the position is purely referential,

(1) (x)(if $x = a$ and $\ldots x \ldots$ then $\ldots a \ldots$).

I shall suppose 'x' foreign to the sentence represented by '$\ldots a \ldots$'. (Otherwise take another letter.) But then (1) is equivalent, by the elementary logic of quantification, to:

(2) If $(\exists x)(x = a$ and $\ldots x \ldots)$ then $\ldots a \ldots$.

Conversely, moreover,

(3) If $\ldots a \ldots$ then $(\exists x)(x = a$ and $\ldots x \ldots)$;

for, if $\ldots a \ldots$ then $a = a$ and $\ldots a \ldots$. Now (2) and (3) combine to show that '$\ldots a \ldots$' is equivalent to '$(\exists x)(x = a$ and $\ldots x \ldots)$', which contains 'a' only in the position '$= a$'.[1]

This shows that the purely referential occurrences of singular terms other than variables can be got down to the type '$= a$'. It does not show the same for variables, for see the manifold occurrences of 'x' needed in '$(\exists x)(x = a$ and $\ldots x \ldots)$' itself; but no matter, since the singular terms that raised problems were not the variables.

Now an interesting thing about our being able to manoeuvre those singular terms into a standard position '$= a$' is that '$= a$' taken as a whole is in effect a predicate, or general term; and general terms raise none of the problems that singular terms raise. What suggests itself is that '$=$ Pegasus', '$=$ mama', '$=$ Socrates', etc. be

---

[1] I may mention in passing, what is familiar to logic students, that this transformation is not unique. Often there is a choice between fixing upon longer or shorter segments of text for the role of '$\ldots a \ldots$'.

parsed anew as indissoluble general terms, no separate recognition of singular terms 'Pegasus', 'mama', 'Socrates', etc. being needed for other positions.

The equation '$x = a$' is reparsed in effect as a predication '$x = a$' where '$= a$' is the verb, the 'F' of 'Fx'. Or look at it as follows. What was in words 'x is Socrates' and in symbols '$x =$ Socrates' is now in words still 'x is Socrates', but the 'is' ceases to be treated as a separate relative term '$=$'. The 'is' is now treated as a copula which, as in 'is mortal' and 'is a man', serves merely to give a general term the form of a verb and so suit it to predicative position. 'Socrates' becomes a general term that is true of just one object, but general in being treated henceforward as grammatically admissible in predicative position and not in positions suitable for variables. It comes to play the role of the 'F' of 'Fa' and ceases to play that of the 'a'.

This reparsing depended on a theorem of confinability of singular terms to the position '$= a$'. But the theorem applied only to purely referential uses of the terms. What of their use, so hard to classify and so beset with anomalies, before 'exists'? It turns out to perfection. Our ill-starred previous suggestion of '$(\exists x)(x = \text{Pegasus})$', as a paraphrase of 'Pegasus exists', comes into its own when '$x = \text{Pegasus}$' is reparsed as 'x is Pegasus' with 'Pegasus' as general term. 'Pegasus exists' becomes '$(\exists x)(x$ is Pegasus$)$', and straightforwardly false; 'Socrates exists' becomes '$(\exists x)(x$ is Socrates$)$', with 'Socrates' as general term, and probably true (with timeless 'is', of course). 'Socrates' is now a general term, though true of, as it happens, just one object; 'Pegasus' is now a general term which, like 'centaur', is true of no objects. The position of 'Pegasus' and 'Socrates' in '$(\exists x)(x$ is Pegasus$)$' and '$(\exists x)(x$ is Socrates$)$' is now certainly inaccessible to variables and certainly no purely referential position, but only because it is simply no position for a singular term; 'x is Pegasus' and 'x is Socrates' now have the form of 'x is round'.

There remain unaccommodated those not purely referential uses of singular terms that had other forms than 'a exists'; thus perhaps 'Homer believed in Pegasus'. This example may be expanded to show a sentence within a sentence, thus 'Homer believed that Pegasus exists' or 'Homer believed [Pegasus exists]', the contained sentence being of a form already dealt with. There are other examples that cannot so obviously be accommodated under the propositional attitudes; thus 'Tom is thinking of Pegasus', 'is imagining Pegasus', 'is describing Pegasus', 'is drawing Pegasus'.[2]   But perhaps they can with some torturing.   Perhaps 'Tom is drawing Pegasus' can be managed somewhat in the fashion 'Tom is making a sketch which he imagines to resemble Pegasus', i.e.:

($\exists y$)(Tom now is making y and Tom now is imagining $x[x$ resembles Pegasus] of y).[3]

Perhaps 'Tom is imagining Pegasus' can be managed as 'Tom is imagining himself to see Pegasus', i.e.:

Tom now is imagining $x[x$ is seeing Pegasus] of Tom.

The point of such efforts would be to give the singular term referential position with respect to its immediately containing sentence, and so render it amenable to reparsing within that immediate context, opaque though the wider context be.[4]

The proposed reparsing of singular terms as general terms should, on pain of introducing new problems of analysis of general terms, be limited to those singular terms that have no internal structure we care to perpetuate.   Which terms these are is a question not of how the terms were first learned, nor of whether they are single English words, but of the particular needs of the argument or investigation that we may imagine ourselves engaged in.   The singular terms, other than variables, that are treated as simple in this sense might suggestively be called *names*—namehood then being purely relative to varying projects in hand.[5]   The proposed reparsing is then a reparsing of names as general terms.

[2] Cf. Chisholm, "Sentences about believing."

[3] Cf. (8) of § 35.   To my treatment of the present example, one is tempted to object that the imagined resemblance on the part of y is not as of now, while y is still in the making; but the answer is that there is no 'now' on the last 'y'.

[4] If the opaque wider context is a quotation, any reparsing within it would indeed be unallowable.   But we can suppose quotation antecedently dissolved into spelling; cf. § 30.

[5] But note that this use of 'name' is akin to the use in grammar of 'proper name'.   In some writings I have used 'name' rather in the sense of 'that which names'—an extragrammatical sense implying existence of a named object. Hochberg, "The ontological operator," pp. 253 f., wrongly assumes that I equate the latter or referential sense of namehood with the grammatical one.

§ 38. CONCILIATORY REMARKS.
ELIMINATION OF SINGULAR TERMS

We can encourage a feeling for the reparsing by letting the epithet 'name' accompany 'Socrates' and the like into their new estate, thus saying that the category of names is not dissipated but only reconstrued as subordinate to that of general terms instead of to that of singular terms.   In thus construing names as general terms, what we deviate from is only in part usage, and largely attitude toward usage: the policy of parsing names on a par with singular pronouns and indefinite singular terms.   That attitude was even somewhat artificial, for it meant construing the natural 'is' sometimes as copula and sometimes as '='.   Nor was it the invariable attitude of logicians in past centuries; they commonly treated a name such as 'Socrates' rather on a par logically with 'mortal' and 'man', and as differing from these latter just in being true of fewer objects, viz. one.   Again Leśniewski (1930) is best construed as assimilating names to general terms, though he does not so phrase the matter.[1]   Ryle took a step in the same direction in 1933, when, talking specifically of the context 'x exists', he urged that "the term 'x' which from the grammar seems to be designating a subject of attributes, is really signifying an attribute."[2]   In § 20, we in turn felt that one might naturally wonder if the distinction between general and singular terms were not overrated.   Our assimilation of names into the category of general terms is a partial restoration of that in some ways more natural point of view.

Any question of a distinction between singular and general terms is irrelevant to stimulus synonymy (cf. § 12).   Furthermore it is irrelevant to the infantile phase at which such terms as 'mama' are learned (§ 19).   Some arbitrariness persists when we apply the distinction to mass terms (cf. § 20).   And then there is the arbitrariness of deciding when to treat 'is' as '=' and when as copula. All in all, who shall say whether English is more radically modified by a canonical notation in which names consort with the singular pronouns and indefinite singular terms or by one in which they consort with the general terms?

[1] See Leśniewski or Lejewski.

[2] Ryle, "Imaginary objects."   In writing "The analysis, which seems to me to be the correct one, is this," he goes farther than I, suggesting that there is but one right analysis.

A conspicuous way in which our reparsing of names as general terms deviates from ordinary usage, as distinct from ordinary categorizations of usage, is in its closing of truth-value gaps. But this was a purpose of the reparsing. It would have been wrong if paraphrase carried a synonymy claim; but it does not (§ 33). A paraphrase into a canonical notation is good insofar as it tends to meet needs for which the original might be wanted. If the form of paraphrase happens incidentally to produce sense where the original suffered a truth-value gap and so was wanted for no purpose, we may just let the added cases turn out as they will. (Example: 'Pegasus flies', originally neither true nor false, now gets paraphrased as '$(\exists x)(x$ is Pegasus and x flies)' and hence becomes false.) Such waste cases, what the computing-machine engineers call don't-cares, are a frequent feature of good paraphrases, as we shall have further occasion to note.

There is a feeling that in reparsing the names as general terms we forfeit part of their meaning, viz. the purport of uniqueness.[3] The notion is that 'Socrates' as general term would be true of one and only one thing just as a matter of contingent fact, whereas the uniqueness of designation of 'Socrates' as singular term is claimed in the very character of the word. This intuitive appeal to meaning may even be conceded to be somewhat intelligible (cf. §§ 12, 14), whatever its cogency. But remember that general terms frequently obey laws that seem accountable to the meanings of the terms and not to contingent fact; witness the law of symmetry of the relative term 'cousin', or of transitivity of 'part'. One might equally well recognize uniqueness—anyway in the weak sense "one at most"—as similarly implicit in the very meaning of certain general terms, viz. ones like 'Socrates'. Such general terms might on that very account be denominated, more particularly, names.

Terms like 'Socrates' do ordinarily purport uniqueness of reference not only in the weak sense but in the sense of 'one exactly'. They purport it on pain of truth-value gaps; but we are well rid of that sanction. Any existence claim that is felt to inhere in the meanings of singular terms is well eliminated.

If we liked we could, alternatively, eliminate 'Socrates' as singular term by reconstruing the name as a general term true of many objects; viz., Socrates's spatiotemporal parts (cf. p. 52). For the old

[3] Thus perhaps Hochberg, "On pegasizing."

force of 'x = Socrates' can then still be recovered in paraphrase, this time as:

$(y)(y$ is a socrates if and only if y is part of $x)$.

A possible interest of this alternative is that the uniqueness of such an object x then follows from the logic of the part-whole relation, independently of any special trait of 'socrates' beyond its being true of one or more objects of the sort that can be parts.

Let us now turn our attention from names to singular descriptions. In ordinary discourse the idiom of singular description is normally used only where the intended object is believed to be singled out uniquely by the matter appended to the singular 'the' together perhaps with supplementary information to be gleaned from the context or circumstances of utterance. When we turn to canonical notation, we have to imagine that supplementary information made explicit as part of the perhaps complex sentence represented by the '$\ldots x \ldots$' of '$(\imath x)(\ldots x \ldots)$'. This eking out bears witness to what was said in § 33: that no synonymy claim is involved, and that paraphrasing depends on what we are trying to prove or find out. Eking out descriptions is pragmatic, like settling ambiguities, tenses, and indicator words. Seldom in practice do these things have to be done in full, even when we propose to reason within the outward structure of our canonical notation. We settle points that are crucial to the particular formal manoeuvres envisaged, and just imagine the rest filled in anyhow. But the logical theory which the canonical framework makes possible treats the ambiguous terms and the indicator words as having fixed references, supposed intended, even where we do not need to say which; and it treats the '$\ldots x \ldots$' of '$(\imath x)(\ldots x \ldots)$' as if it were eked out in supposedly intended ways, even when we do not need to say how. If someone is persuaded that the sentence represented by '$\ldots x \ldots$', even including all plausibly intended supplementations, is fulfilled by more than one object x or by none, then for him the question of truth or falsity of sentences containing referential occurrences of '$(\imath x)(\ldots x \ldots)$' tends, as noted at the beginning of § 37, to lapse. He will normally abstain from the discussion proper, in favor of a discussion of its propriety.

Compare now the identity '$y = (\imath x)(\ldots x \ldots)$' with the quantification:

(1) $(x)(\ldots x \ldots$ if and only if $x = y)$,

which may be briefly read '... y ... and y only'. Presumably, if either '$y = (\imath x)(\ldots x \ldots)$' or '... y ... and y only' is true of an object y, both are. Still the two formulas may diverge in their falsity conditions, on account of truth-value gaps; for these gaps may be viewed as rendering '$y = (\imath x)(\ldots x \ldots)$' innocent of truth value for each object y if not true of one, whereas '... y ... and y only' is simply false for each object y if not true of one. Hence our opposition to truth-value gaps is readily acted on: we can simply equate '$y = (\imath x)(\ldots x \ldots)$' with '... y ... and y only', thus filling the truth-value gaps of '$y = (\imath x)(\ldots x \ldots)$' with falsity. Now this move enables us to sweep singular descriptions away altogether. For, we saw earlier (§ 37) how to limit the occurrences of any singular terms other than variables to occurrences as right members of equations and as subjects of 'exists'. Where the term is '$(\imath x)(\ldots x \ldots)$', we have thereafter only to paraphrase the equations and the existence sentence away by paraphrasing '$y = (\imath x)(\ldots x \ldots)$' as '... y ... and y only', or (1), and '$(\imath x)(\ldots x \ldots)$ exists' as '$(\exists y)(\ldots y \ldots$ and y only)'. Such is Russell's elimination of the singular description.[4]

Singular terms other than variables have been reparsed where simple, and dissolved where of the form of descriptions. What now of that further important class of singular terms, the *algebraic* type '$\sqrt{x}$', '$x + y$', '$x + 5$', '$x + y^z$', etc.? These are the singular terms that have as their immediate constituents not sentences, as descriptions do, but further singular terms. An example not concerned with number is afforded by concatenation, § 30: '$x \frown y$'. Another is the treatment of 'at' suggested in § 36: 'x at t'. But we can reduce this whole algebraic category to the category of descriptions, by adopting an appropriate relative term in lieu of each of the algebraic operators. For example, to get rid of '$+$' we adopt a triadic relative term 'Σ' and reckon 'Σwxy' as true when and only when $w = x + y$; thenceforward we can render anything of the form '$a + b$', however complex the terms represented by 'a' and 'b', as '$(\imath w)\Sigma wab$'. What this reduction amounts to is a reparsing of the '$=$' and '$+$' of '$w = x + y$' as a simple triadic relative term; the 'Σ' is only for vividness.

Thus '$x + y^z$' goes first into '$(\imath w)\Sigma wxy^z$'. But 'y^z' in turn goes

---

[4] Russell, "On denoting"; also Whitehead and Russell. By retracing the relevant reasoning of § 37 in addition to the above, the reader can see that the manner of eliminating descriptions here is really the same as Russell's despite differences in approach.

into '$(\imath u)Puyz$', where '$Puyz$' is taken as amounting to '$u = y^z$'. So '$x + y^z$' becomes '$(\imath w) \Sigma w x (\imath u)Puyz$'. Again '$x + y + z$' can be explained as '$x + (y + z)$' and hence ultimately as '$(\imath w) \Sigma w x (\imath u)\Sigma uyz$'. Similarly '$x \frown y$' can be handled as '$(\imath w)Cwxy$', '$x \frown y \frown z$' as '$(\imath w) C w x (\imath u)Cuyz$', and so on.

There are still some forms of complex singular terms to consider which, like descriptions, contain sentences. Class abstraction is one that need not detain us, for we saw in (8) of § 34 how it reduces to description. As for intensional abstraction, it can be got down to description by substantially the same reparsing trick that we just now used on '$w = x + y$'. Thus, consider the brackets of propositional abstraction. Instead of viewing them as an operator that applies to a sentence to form a singular term, and then viewing '$=$' in '$a = [p]$' as a relative term that applies to the two singular terms to form a sentence, we can reparse '$= [\quad]$' as an irreducible operator that applies outright to 'a' and 'p' to form a sentence '$a = [p]$'. Thus suppose we rewrite that newly indivisible operator for vividness as 'O', so that '$a = [p]$' becomes 'aOp'; then the old '$[p]$' comes out as '$(\imath w)(wOp)$'. Attribute abstraction can be treated analogously, by reparsing '$a = x[\ldots x \ldots]$' as formed by an irreducible two-place variable-binding operator in the fashion '$aO_x(\ldots x \ldots)$'; then the old '$x[\ldots x \ldots]$' comes out as '$(\imath w)(wO_x(\ldots x \ldots))$'. Similarly for the abstraction of relations. Thus evidently nothing stands in the way of our making a clean sweep of singular terms altogether, with the sole exception of the variables themselves.[5]

[5] Strawson, "Singular terms, ontology, and identity," pp. 446 f., 453, has supposed that demonstrative singular terms somehow defy such a program. That this is a mistake is evident from the paraphrasing of such terms into descriptions in § 34. The indicator words 'here' and 'there', with which § 34 left us, stay on as general terms; the indicator words 'now' and 'then', treated as singular terms in § 36, become reparsed as general terms. There is no evident reason to infer survival of singular terms from survival of indicator words. Cf. Russell, "Mr. Strawson on referring." Strawson's notion is doubtless causally connected somehow with an unsuccessful effort to read between my lines; he writes (p. 443), "Quine does not explicitly claim . . . elimination [of indicator words] as a merit of the recommended procedure [of eliminating singular terms]; but I think it certain that he would regard it as one." I do not. — Incidentally, let me take this opportunity to deny also the motivation hinted on p. 444, where Strawson writes, "And though I do not think he has explicitly done so, Quine might well claim [eliminations of failure of substitutivity of identity] as a further simplification to be gained by the elimination of singular terms." On the contrary, see § 35 above, especially (5), and also

That variables alone remain as singular terms may be seen as testifying to the primacy of the pronoun. One is reminded of Peirce's mot about "the noun, which may be defined as a part of speech put in place of a pronoun." [6]

Thus winnowed, what does canonical notation retain? Those of its sentences that contain no sentences as parts are composed each of a general term, without recognized internal structure (§ 36), standing in predicative position complemented by one or more variables. That is, the atomic sentences have the forms 'Fx', 'Fxy', etc. The rest of the sentences are built from the atomic ones by truth functions, quantifiers, and perhaps other devices. Three such further devices of sentence composition are the operators 'O' and 'O_x' just now noted and their analogue 'O_{xy}' for relations; but they will be reconsidered in § 44.

§ 39. DEFINITION AND THE DOUBLE LIFE

The elimination of singular terms depended on fusing '=' with some further bit of text. This does not mean that in the end we are rid of '=', along with the singular terms. For though singular terms (other than variables) are gone, '=' continues to occur flanked by variables. Like all general terms, it stays on in predicative position with variables and thus only. Indeed the very forms '... y ... and y only' and '$(\exists y)(\ldots y \ldots$ and y only)', which served in § 38 to supplant the immediate contexts of descriptions, contain '$x = y$' (when spelled out according to (1) of § 38). Again the uniqueness sentences which may be expected to come into prominence with the reparsing of names require '=' flanked by variables; that one and only one thing is Socrates, e.g., runs '$(\exists y)(y$ is Socrates and y only)', or:

(1) $(\exists y)(x)(x$ is Socrates if and only if $x = y)$.

The elimination of singular terms other than variables was attended with a considerable simplification of logical theory in the closing of truth-value gaps. But now it may be feared that a comparable loss

From a Logical Point of View, pp. 144 ff., 152. These passages serve also in answer to Pap, "Belief and propositions," p. 124 n. In another paper, Strawson showed cognizance of such passages; see "A logician's landscape," pp. 234 ff., where his misgivings take other lines.

[6] Peirce, vol. 5, paragraph 153.

of simplicity is suffered on other counts. The logical laws governing '=' are applicable automatically to 'x is Socrates' *qua* 'x = Socrates', but *prima facie* irrelevant to 'x is Socrates' *qua* 'Fx'; irrelevant again to '$z = x + y$' *qua* 'Σzxy'. Moreover, inference by substitution of singular terms other than variables for variables of universal quantifications is obstructed. What would have been:

(2) If $(z)(\ldots z \ldots)$ then $\ldots$ Socrates $\ldots$,
(3) If $(z)(\ldots z \ldots)$ then $\ldots x + y \ldots$

are now:

(4) If $(z)(\ldots z \ldots)$ then $(\exists z)(z$ is Socrates and $\ldots z \ldots)$,
(5) If $(z)(\ldots z \ldots)$ then $(\exists z)(\Sigma zxy$ and $\ldots z \ldots)$.

And these, besides being cumbersome, are not even valid except on the supplementary existence premisses '$(\exists z)(z$ is Socrates)' and '$(\exists z)\Sigma zxy$'.

What seems here a complication is, however, in a way a boon. As long as singular terms other than variables are accepted at face value, the logic of quantification must somehow allow for (2) and (3); but then how exclude their 'Pegasus' analogue? What had been a tacit premiss of existence comes out into the open when, eliminating singular terms other than variables, we switch from (2) and (3) to (4) and (5).

Directness aside, no losses are sustained. It can be shown that everything that used to be demonstrable or deducible from given premisses when 'Socrates' was manipulated unquestioningly as a singular term is still demonstrable or deducible from those same premisses with the added help of the uniqueness premiss '$(\exists y)(y$ is Socrates and y only)', or (1), when 'Socrates' is reparsed as a general term. Likewise everything that could be done with '+' can still be done, in translation, in terms of 'Σ', given this uniqueness premiss for 'Σ':

(6) $(x)(y)($if x is a number and y is a number then $(\exists z)(\Sigma zxy$ and z only$))$.

More generally, everything that could be done with '$(\imath x)(\ldots x \ldots)$' can still be done, in translation, on the premiss '$(\exists y)(\ldots y \ldots$ and y only)'. These supporting premisses are less to be deplored as uneconomical than prized as an unfolding of tacit assumptions, an articulation of the inarticulate.

But there is no blinking the added complications. Certainly (4) and (5) are more cumbersome than (2) and (3). Certainly '$(\exists x)(x$ is Socrates and x is Greek)', of the form '$(\exists x)(Fx$ and $Gx)$', is more cumbersome than 'Socrates is Greek' conceived as of the form 'Ga'. It is convenient to be able to bandy names as singular terms, and descriptions likewise, substituting them for variables and predicatively applying general terms to them. When we come to the shift exemplified by that from '$+$' to 'Σ', indeed, the loss in facility is staggering; we sacrifice precisely the moves that typify mathematics at its fleetest. Not to allow the nesting of singular terms within singular terms within singular terms without limit, in polynomial fashion, and not to allow the facile substitution of complexes for variables and equals, would diminish the power of mathematics catastrophically, even though only practically and not in principle. Happily, though, this looming dilemma can be solved.

For an endearing trait of canonical notations is that they do not bind; we can vacillate between two, opportunistically enjoying their incompatible advantages. What modern logicians call *definitions* are largely instructions for doing just that. Thus we can cleave theoretically to a canonical notation in which there are no singular terms but variables, but at the same time we can define, relative to that notation, a shorthand use of the other singular terms after all. Through the medium of such definitions we can even resuscitate (2) and (3) and the like as working rules, by showing that what they yield is, under the definitions, mere shorthand for what could be got longhand from premisses such as (1) and (6). Yet when our problems are of a kind that respond better to economy in the roots of the theory than to brevity of paraphrase and swiftness of deduction, we are still free to play the narrower canonical notation straight.

The purpose of the definitions is to enable us to lapse back into the eliminated notation, or a convenient approximation, while maintaining a key to how the strict canonical transcription would run. Substantially the appropriate definitions are therefore before us, in the very transformations already cited to show the dispensability of singular terms other than variables. Such definitions have the virtue, incidentally, of restoring singular terms in all their flexibility without reviving the nuisance of the truth-value gaps. The definition for singular description becomes simply this: write '$y = (\imath x)(\ldots x \ldots)$' and '$(\imath x)(\ldots x \ldots)$ exists' as notational variants of '$\ldots y \ldots$ and y only' and '$(\exists y)(\ldots y \ldots$ and y only)', and, harking back now to the reasoning in § 37, write '---$(\imath x)(\ldots x \ldots)$---' as an abbreviation of:

(7) $(\exists y)(y = (\imath x)(\ldots x \ldots)$ and ---y---).

(In this exposition we understand '---y---' as an arbitrary open sentence, and '---$(\imath x)(\ldots x \ldots)$---' as the same with the singular description in place of 'y'.)

The three parts of the above definition suffice, when applied successively and in iteration, to restore '$(\imath x)(\ldots x \ldots)$' to every position of occurrence of which a free variable is capable. Actually the definition needs some tightening, in known ways.[1] But enough; logic students know this logic of descriptions, essentially Russell's, and my purpose has been rather a philosophical clarification of its business.

Along with the practical resuscitation thus of descriptions, the various other singular terms that were reduced to descriptions in § 38 are resuscitated too—notably the terms of algebraic type. This is a convenient channel also for reintroducing names as singular terms: 'Socrates' as singular term can be defined as '$(\imath x)(x$ is Socrates)' on the basis of 'Socrates' as general term. In practice the defined singular term 'Socrates' and the defining general term 'Socrates' would doubtless be rendered distinctively, say by lowering one initial 'S' to 's' or even by leaving the singular term as '$(\imath x)(x$ is Socrates)'. Technically we could keep 'Socrates' for both, since in a well-formed notation the positions open to general and singular terms will be mutually exclusive and so avert any ultimate ambiguity. But what is particularly to be noted is that it would be pointless to defend either the singular term or the general term as *the* regular counterpart of the name 'Socrates' of ordinary language. In paraphrasing some sentences for some purposes the singular term will come in handy; on other occasions the general term works better. We are reminded once again that paraphrase makes no synonymy claim. As for the epithet 'name', it applies first and foremost to the 'Socrates' of ordinary language and derivatively to either of its formalizations; when our intention is more specific we can say so, as e.g. in the provisional convention at the end of § 37.

The virtues of definition as a method of eating one's cake and having it are strikingly illustrated by quotation and concatenation. Quotation, which produces names of linguistic forms by picture-writing, has the overwhelming practical convenience of visible reference. But it has the drawback, for some purposes of systematic

---

[1] Thus see § 37, note 1.

theory, that the names which it produces are, regardless of length, logically unstructured. Hence the main virtue of spelling, which comes properly apart. Spelling, however protracted, analyzes into iteration of the one little two-term algebraic operation of concatenation plus a small stock of names of letters. Spelling also has the virtue of shattering the non-referential occurrences of terms which quotation engenders (cf. § 30); but this is an incidental surface effect. Then, finally, there is the elimination in turn of concatenation in favor of the triadic relative term 'C'. The advantage here is theoretical simplicity, through the elimination of complex singular terms; and the disadvantage is cumbersomeness, the sacrifice of algebraic facility. Now thanks to the device of definition we can enjoy each of these benefits without foreswearing the others. We theorize within the 'C' theory secure in the knowledge that the luxuries of spelling and even of quotation can be restored, by definition, at will. It is one of the consolations of philosophy that the benefit of showing how to dispense with a concept does not hinge on dispensing with it.

Flight from Intension

§ 40. PROPOSITIONS AND ETERNAL SENTENCES

In the preceding chapter a certain air of innovation prevailed, but only the blandest. Ways were shown of paraphrasing sentences to gain clarity of structure and economy of constructions at little or no cost except of brevity and familiarity of expression. The paraphrases were such as to meet most or all the likely purposes for which the originals might be used, except insofar as such needs include brevity or familiarity. There was little or no banning of locutions without benefit of passable paraphrase. The nearest we came to that was perhaps the banning of quantification into opaque constructions, but even there no clear loss was sustained, no loss that would be felt as such from any very plausible point of view; useful cases of apparent quantification into opaque contexts were generally salvaged by paraphrase. There was no banning of abstract objects on scruples of nominalism; no banning of intensional objects on scruples of extensionalism; nor any banning of indicator words on scruples of absolutism. In this chapter such issues will begin to come to the fore.

A sentence is not an event of utterance, but a universal: a repeatable sound pattern, or repeatedly approximable norm. Truth cannot on the whole be viewed as a trait, even a passing trait, of a sentence merely; it is a passing trait of a sentence for a man. 'The door is open' is true for a man when a door is so situated that he would take it as the natural momentary reference of 'the door' and it is (whether he knows it or not) open. The individual event of utterance can still be described as true absolutely, since a time and

191

a man are specific to it; but talk of sentences as true for men at times covers more ground, for it includes cases where the sentence is not uttered by the man in question at the time in question.

Relativity to times and persons can be awkward on account of the supplementary specifications in which it keeps involving us. This is no doubt one reason why philosophers have liked to posit supplementary abstract entities—*propositions*—as surrogate truth vehicles. This done, they speak of the sentence as expressing now one proposition and now another for this man and that, while allowing each such proposition itself to remain steadfastly true or false without respect to persons.

This posit is not altogether the philosopher's doing. Ordinary language has its 'that' clauses, and such clauses (with 'that' as conjunction, not as relative or demonstrative pronoun) function grammatically as singular terms (except when preceded by 'such'), thus evidently purporting to designate something. Their purported objects are what the philosopher takes up and calls, subject to certain refinements, propositions. It is because of the place in ordinary language of the 'that' clauses in question that it suited the half uncritical mood of the preceding chapter to make a place in canonical notation for what we called propositional abstraction and provisionally to recognize objects, called propositions, for the singular terms thus formed to designate. Since a prominent use of the 'that' clauses is as grammatical objects of the so-called verbs of propositional attitude, we found ourselves taking propositions in particular as the things that people believe, affirm, wish, etc. Russell's term 'propositional attitude' is a reminder that we were not first in so doing.

It is irrelevant that the notation of propositional abstraction, along with singular terms generally other than variables, dropped out in § 38. None of the eliminations of singular terms in §§ 37 and 38 eliminated objects. By the very nature of the elimination technique, propositions stayed on as denizens of the universe alluded to in the 'everything' and 'something' of '(x)' and '$(\exists x)$'; as values, in short, of the variables.[1] The object x concerned in the notation

[1] Mistaken critical remarks keep one reminded that there are those who fancy the mathematical phrase 'values of the variables' to mean 'singular terms substitutable for the variables'. It is rather the object designated by such a term that counts as a value of the variable; and the objects stay on as values of the variables though the singular terms be swept away.

'xOp' that supplanted 'x = [p]' is still the proposition [p], nameless though it be forevermore. Anyway I have no intention of adhering to a canonical notation without singular terms other than variables; it is enough that we have seen how we can switch to it. (Cf. § 39.)

The newly remarked purpose of propositions as surrogate truth vehicles demands that propositions resist variation in truth value, but this demand was already implicit also in their use as objects of propositional attitudes. If the sentence:

(1) Tom believes [the door is open]

as affirmed on some occasion is to be viewed as holding however momentarily of the objects Tom and [the door is open], then certainly the two objects must themselves be quite specific objects once and for all, however inadequately singled out by the words of (1). Tom must be the specific human filler of a couple of serpentine stere-years somewhere-when in past and future space-time, though we must depend heavily on our own knowledge of the circumstances of utterance of (1) in deciding among various possible ones of that name; and [the door is open] must be a proposition specific as to door and time concerned, though again we must depend on our knowledge of the circumstances of utterance of (1) in deciding which. Vagueness, ambiguity, fugacity of reference, are traits of verbal forms and do not extend to the objects referred to.

If we want to identify Tom by explicit elaboration of (1), rather than leaving the matter to circumstances of utterance, we may supply surname and address or other details. If we want to identify [the door is open] by explicit elaboration of (1), rather than leaving the matter to circumstances of utterance, we may specify where the door is and what time is intended. In general, to specify a proposition without dependence on circumstances of utterance, we put for the 'p' of '[p]' an *eternal* sentence: a sentence whose truth value stays fixed through time and from speaker to speaker.

Eternal sentences are standing sentences (§ 9) of an extreme kind; many standing sentences, e.g. 'The *Times* has come', are not eternal. Theoretical sentences in mathematics and other sciences tend to be eternal, but they have no exclusive claim to the distinction. Reports and predictions of specific single events are eternal too, when times, places, or persons concerned are objectively indicated rather than left to vary with the references of first names, incomplete descriptions, and indicator words. Nor need eternal sentences be empty of stimulus meaning; a speaker may quite well be prompted by one stimulation to assent to an eternal sentence and by another to dissent from it. But when this happens he says he has been wrong and has changed his mind in the light of new evidence, rather than that the sentence has changed in truth value as 'The *Times* has come' is wont to do.

An eternal sentence may be expected to be free of indicator words, but there is no bar to its containing names, however parsed (§ 37), or other ostensively learned terms. Terms present may well have been learned with help of indicator words.

Already in § 36 we supposed tense banished from the canonical language. But the advantages of that move did not include conversion to eternal sentences. The effect on (1) of banishment of tense is merely to insert 'now' twice and rate the two verbs as tenseless. To finish the job of eternalizing the sentence in the brackets we have to supplant the 'now' by a date and clock reading or the like, and put something more into the description 'the door'. We can go on to eternalize the outer parts too if we like, by supplanting its 'now' similarly and enlarging on Tom. (But see § 45 for an obstacle to thus eternalizing statements of propositional attitude in the general case.)

I find no good reason not to regard every proposition as nameable by applying brackets to one or another eternal sentence. An alternative plan would be to allow for inexpressible propositions, but no evident purpose would be served.[2] A more humdrum reason for supposing that the propositions outrun the eternal sentences could be that for many propositions the appropriate eternal sentences, though utterable enough, just happen never to get uttered (or written). This point is mistaken but worth examining, for the answer to it is important also apart from the present connection.

Prima facie the answer is that a sentence is not an event of utterance but a linguistic form that may be uttered often, once, or never; and that its existence is not compromised by failure of utterance. But we must not accept this answer without considering more precisely what these linguistic forms are. If a sentence were taken as the class of its utterances, then all unuttered sentences would reduce to one, viz., the null class; they might as well not exist so far as prop-

2 For a consideration of this point see Pap, "Belief and propositions," p. 134.

ositions are concerned, for all distinction lapses among them. Nor should I like to take a sentence as an attribute of utterances; for in § 43 I shall argue for dropping attributes. But there is another way of taking sentences and other linguistic forms that leaves their existence and distinctness uncompromised by failure of utterance. We can take each linguistic form as the *sequence*, in a mathematical sense, of its successive characters or phonemes. A sequence $a_1, a_2, \ldots, a_n$ can be explained as the class of the n pairs $\langle a_1, 1\rangle$, $\langle a_2, 2\rangle$, $\ldots$, $\langle a_n, n\rangle$. (On pairs see § 53.) We can still take each component character a_i as a class of utterance events, there being here no risk of nonutterance.

§ 41. MODALITY

There are some obscure idioms that seem much like those of the propositional attitudes except that they lack the personal reference; viz., the so-called logical modalities 'Necessarily . . .', Possibly . . .'.

In ordinary non-philosophical usage 'possibly' usually serves merely as a modestly impersonal rewording of what is really a personal idiom of propositional attitude after all: 'I am not sure but what'. Ordinarily the construction 'necessarily' does not, curiously enough, carry the corresponding sense 'I am sure that'. Often it connotes rather a propositional attitude of purpose or resolve. Sometimes, also, 'necessarily' and 'possibly' provide a condensed way of saying that a sentence follows from or is compatible with some fixed premiss understood as background. And sometimes they provide little more than a variant style for 'all' and 'some'.

But what is called logical modality is none of these things. Used as a logical modality, 'necessarily' imputes necessity unconditionally and impersonally, as an absolute mode of truth; and 'possibly' denies necessity, in that sense, of the negation.

Modal logic as we now know it was started by Lewis in 1918.[1] His interpretation of necessity, sharpened in formulation by Carnap,[2] is that a sentence beginning with 'necessarily' is true if and only if the rest of it is analytic. What with our reservations over analyticity (§ 14), this account leaves something to be desired; but let us go along with it for a while. If for the sake of argument we accept the term 'analytic' as predicable of sentences (hence as at-

---

[1] *Survey of Symbolic Logic*, Ch. 5. See also Lewis and Langford, pp. 78–89, 120–166.

[2] *Meaning and Necessity*, § 39.

tachable predicatively to quotations or other singular terms designating sentences), then 'necessarily' amounts to 'is analytic' plus
an antecedent pair of quotation marks. For example, the sentence:

(1) Necessarily 9 > 4

is explained thus:

(2) '9 > 4' is analytic.

It is doubtful that Lewis would ever have started this if Whitehead and Russell, who followed Frege in defending Philo of
Megara's version of 'If p then q' as 'Not (p and not q)', had not
made the mistake of calling the Philonian construction "material
implication" instead of the material conditional. Lewis protested
that a material implication so defined would have to be not merely
true but analytic in order to qualify as implication properly so-
called. Such was his account of "strict implication."

'Implies' and 'is analytic' are best viewed as general terms, to be
predicated of sentences by predicative attachment to names (e.g.
quotations) of sentences. In this they contrast with 'not', 'and',
and 'if-then', which are not terms but operators attachable to the
sentences themselves. Whitehead and Russell, careless of the
distinction between use and mention of expressions, wrote 'p implies
q' (in the material sense) interchangeably with 'If p then q' (in the
material sense). Lewis followed suit, thus writing 'p strictly implies q' and explaining it as 'Necessarily not (p and not q)'. Hence
his development of a modal logic of 'necessarily' as an operator on
sentences. The contrast between that operator and the term 'is
analytic', drawn by the quotation marks in (2), did not concern
Lewis. But it emerges when, as in Carnap's writings, the distinction between use and mention is carefully maintained; indeed it
emerges as the very distinction between modal logic and ordinary
talk of analyticity.[3]

Proponents of modal logic need not all be concerned with
necessity in this extreme sense. The necessity concerned might be
construed rather as some sort of physical necessity, without modify-
ing the form of the system. Or it might be construed as conditional

[3] See further my "Three grades of modal involvement."

necessity, relative to some unspecified set of premisses as parameter.[4] My remarks on modal logic will be predicated on the original or extreme interpretation. How far they apply to other possible uses of the same formal system is a family of separate questions that I shall leave aside.

So suppose (1) explained as in (2). Why, one may ask, should we preserve the operatorial form as of (1), and therewith modal logic, instead of just leaving matters as in (2)? An apparent advantage is the possibility of quantifying into modal positions; for we know we cannot quantify into quotation, and (2) uses quotation. Lewis surely intended modal positions to be quantified into, but he did not develop a quantified modal logic. Miss Barcan has subsequently done so.

But is it more legitimate to quantify into modal positions than into quotation? For consider (1) even without regard to (2); surely, on any plausible interpretation, (1) is true and this is false:

(3) Necessarily the number of major planets > 4.

Since 9 = the number of major planets, we can conclude that the position of '9' in (1) is not purely referential and hence that the necessity operator is opaque.[5]

Such illustrations of opacity depend on the existence of appropriately stubborn objects. The stubbornness of 9 consists in its being specifiable in ways that fail of necessary equivalence (e.g. as numbering the major planets and as succeeding 8), so that various traits (such as greaterness than 4) are entailed with necessity under one specification of 9 and not under another. Now if we narrow the universe of objects available as values of variables of quantification so as to exclude such stubborn objects, there ceases to be any such objection to quantifying into modal position.[6] Thus we can legitimize quantification into modal position by postulating that whenever each of two open sentences uniquely determines one and the same object x, the sentences are equivalent by necessity. Schematically we can put the postulate as follows, using 'Fx' and

[4] On these alternatives see Reichenbach, §§ 65 f. For a reinterpretation in terms of time see Prior, pp. 32 f.

[5] Hintikka offers a novel account of what makes for the opacity of modal contexts.

[6] Cf. Church's review of my "Notes on existence and necessity."

'Gx' (now) for arbitrary open sentences and using 'Fx and x only' as short for '$(w)(Fw$ if and only if $w = x)$': [7]

(4) If Fx and x only and Gx and x only then (necessarily (w) (Fw if and only if Gw)).

But this postulate annihilates modal distinctions; for we can deduce from it that 'Necessarily p' holds no matter what true sentence we put for 'p'. The argument is as follows. Let 'p' stand for any true sentence, let y be any object, and let $x = y$. Obviously then

(5) (p and $x = y$) and x only   and
(6) $x = y$ and x only.

By (4), next, with its 'Fx' taken as 'p and $x = y$' and its 'Gx' as '$x = y$', we can conclude from (5) and (6) that

(7) Necessarily $(w)((p$ and $w = y)$ if and only if $w = y)$.

But the quantification in (7) implies in particular '(p and $y = y$) if and only if $y = y$', which in turn implies 'p'; so from (7) we conclude that necessarily p.

Modal logic as systematized by Miss Barcan and by Fitch allows unrestricted quantification into modal contexts. How to interpret such a theory, without making the disastrous assumption (4), is by no means clear. It would seem, failing (4), that we must somehow distinguish between necessary and contingent ways of uniquely specifying one and the same object.[8]

Church's system is different.[9] He indirectly limits quantification, by reinterpreting variables and other symbols in modal positions. For him as for Frege, a sentence under a modal operator comes to designate a proposition. The operator is a predicate applied to it.

Let us then see what happens if we stop trying to quantify systematically into modal positions, and handle modalities rather as we

---

[7] Cf. (1) of § 38; also § 20, note 1.

[8] Carnap's system of modal logic in *Meaning and Necessity*, § § 10 and 40, is essentially one in which all objects are intensional. In presenting his system he propounds a curious double interpretation of variables; but, in a criticism which he generously included in that book, § 44, I have argued that this manoeuvre only obscures the intensional character of his objects and makes no difference to the essential theory. This being the case, I should expect his theory to fulfill (4), by interpretation at least, and so to be vitiated by the above deduction.

[9] Church, "A formulation of the logic of sense and denotation."

have handled propositional attitudes. Thus to begin with we might depict (1) as:

(8) [9 > 4] is necessary

and so pin the opacity on intensional abstraction. What are necessary and possible would thus be taken to be propositions. Then, following the model of § 35 further, we might try rendering modality selectively transparent on demand by switching selectively from propositions to attributes. We get:

(9) $x[x > 4]$ is necessary of 9,

which contrasts with (8) in giving '9' purely referential position, susceptible to quantification and to substitution of 'the number of major planets'. Now the manoeuvre seemed rewarding enough in the case of the propositional attitudes, when we wanted to be able to say e.g. that there is someone whom I believe to be a spy (§ 31). But in connection with the modalities it yields something baffling—more so even than the modalities themselves; viz., talk of a difference between necessary and contingent attributes of an object.

Perhaps I can evoke the appropriate sense of bewilderment as follows. Mathematicians may conceivably be said to be necessarily rational and not necessarily two-legged; and cyclists necessarily two-legged and not necessarily rational. But what of an individual who counts among his eccentricities both mathematics and cycling? Is this concrete individual necessarily rational and contingently two-legged or vice versa? Just insofar as we are talking referentially of the object, with no special bias toward a background grouping of mathematicians as against cyclists or vice versa, there is no semblance of sense in rating some of his attributes as necessary and others as contingent. Some of his attributes count as important and others as unimportant, yes; some as enduring and others as fleeting; but none as necessary or contingent.

Curiously, a philosophical tradition does exist for just such a distinction between necessary and contingent attributes. It lives on in the terms 'essence' and 'accident', 'internal relation' and 'external relation'. It is a distinction that one attributes to Aristotle (subject to contradiction by scholars, such being the penalty for attributions to Aristotle). But, however venerable the distinction, it is surely indefensible; and surely then the construction (9) which so smoothly implements it must go by the board.

We cannot in conscience blame these varied sorrows of modality on the notion of analyticity. The latter can be had without the former. Necessity as quantified into, and necessity as just now predicated of intensional objects, are burdens that are not forced upon one by merely explaining (1) and the like as (2) and the like; such a definition would not of itself yield all that. However, as long as propositional abstraction is admitted, there is a definition alternative to the plan of (1) and (2) that also commits us to at least a bit of something like modal logic: we can define 'P is necessary' as '$P = [(x)(x = x)]$'. Whether this makes (8) true, whether it conforms to the equating of (1) with (2) at all, will depend on how narrowly we construe propositions in point of their identity. Actually the answer is negative if propositions are construed narrowly enough to suit the propositional attitudes (cf. § 42). But the fact remains that this definition of necessity, however Pickwickian, yields something isomorphic to unquantified modal logic. We may then well ask whether a parallel definition of 'A is necessary of a', say as '$A = x[x$ has A or $x = a]$', has power to renew the horrors of (9). I shall leave the reader to ponder that one, meanwhile contenting myself with the prospect, in § 43, of renouncing intensional objects altogether.

§ 42.   PROPOSITIONS AS MEANINGS

A large part of learning 'apple' or 'river' was learning what counts as the same apple or river re-exposed and what counts as another. Similarly for 'proposition': little sense has been made of the term until we have before us some standard of when to speak of propositions as identical and when as distinct. Not being physical, a proposition cannot, like an apple or river, be exposed and re-exposed; but it admits of something analogous. The question of identity of propositions is the question how two eternal sentences should be related in order that, where 'p' and 'q' stand for them, we be entitled to say that $[q]$ is the same proposition as $[p]$ rather than another.

A usual answer is that the sentences are to be synonymous. One who gives this answer can as well go on to say that the proposition is the meaning of the sentence; and this again is a well-known line.

Not that meanings of declarative sentences are all to count as propositions; a likelier position is that 'The door is open' stays unchanged in meaning while the associated proposition differs from occasion to occasion of utterance. But propositions would be said to be the meanings of eternal sentences.

One must remember that an expression's meaning (if we are to admit such things as meanings) is not to be confused with the object, if any, that the expression designates. Sentences do not designate at all (variant conventions such as Frege's apart), though words in them may; sentences are simply not singular terms. But sentences still have meanings (if we admit such things as meanings); and the meaning of an eternal sentence is the object designated by the singular term formed by bracketing the sentence. That singular term will have a meaning in turn (if we are prodigal enough with meanings), but it will presumably be something further.[1] Under this approach the meaning (if such there be) of the non-eternal sentence 'The door is open' is not a proposition, and so is not named by '[the door is open]'; what '[the door is open]' names on the occasion concerned is a proposition which is the meaning not of 'The door is open' but of some other sentence, some eternal one that is an appropriate elaboration of 'The door is open' for the occasion concerned.

If we are content to define identity of propositions by synonymy of sentences, there is no evident objection to calling propositions meanings of eternal sentences. Misgivings as to what sort of object such a meaning might be could be allayed, if one pleases, by identifying it with the very class of all those mutually synonymous sentences that are said to have it.[2] The worry that remains is the worry over a suitable notion of synonymy of eternal sentences.

If propositions are to serve as objects of the propositional attitudes, then the broad sort of sentence synonymy talked of in § 14 would be unsatisfactory as a standard of identity of propositions even if adequately formulated. It would be too broad. For it would reckon all analytic sentences as meaning an identical proposition; yet surely one would not want to regard all analytic sentences as

[1] Cf. Frege, "On sense and reference," and my From a Logical Point of View, pp. 9, 21 f., 47, 62, 163.
[2] Thus Ayer, p. 88. Bergmann, if I rightly interpret his "Intentionality," p. 179, takes propositions rather as certain attributes of events of awareness and the like.

interchangeable in contexts of belief or indirect quotation, especially if all mathematical truths are regarded an analytic. Hence Lewis and Carnap have resorted to narrowed derivative relations of synonymy, or *intensional isomorphism* in Carnap's phrase, as better suited to interchange in contexts of propositional attitude.[3] The manner of derivation was sketched early in § 14.

The broader synonymy remains the basic one for both authors. It is to it that they fit modal logic, and by it that they gauge the identity of propositions. In their terminology, therefore, the objects of the propositional attitudes are not propositions; they are more finely individuated objects, called by Lewis *analytic meanings*. On the other hand Church reserves the word 'proposition' for the latter purpose. I prefer to follow Church in this; for it is the propositional attitudes above all, it seems to me, and not modal logic, that clamor for positing propositions or the like. As for the purpose of truth vehicles, it is served by propositions in either sense.

Gauging the identity of propositions to suit the propositional attitudes does not disallow the modal use made of propositional abstraction in § 41. The effect of the tightened identity is merely that if the meaning of every analytic sentence continues to be rated as necessary, there will be many necessary propositions. The minimum interchangeability relation for modal logic—strict equivalence, Lewis calls it—merely ceases to imply identity, and 'P is necessary' ceases to be definable as '$P = [(x)(x = x)]$'. A reinterpretation of modal logic remains thus definable, but its necessity is narrower than analyticity (cf. § 41). In any event I feel that the best claim of modal logic upon our attention is rather as a by-product of positing propositions than as a purpose of positing them.

Mates, Church, and Scheffler have argued that Carnap's intensional isomorphism (and Lewis's earlier construction of similar character) is still too broad for interchange in contexts of propositional attitude. Putnam and Church have responded with proposals for further tightening the relation. Scheffler still finds loopholes,[4] but part of his criticism can be annulled by limiting the question

[3] Lewis, "Modes of meaning"; Carnap, *Meaning and Necessity*, §§ 14–16.

[4] Mates, "Synonymity," p. 215; Church, "Intensional isomorphism and identity of belief"; Scheffler, "On synonymy and indirect discourse"; Putnam, "Synonymity and the analysis of belief sentences." See also Pap, "Belief, synonymy, and analysis" and "Belief and propositions."

of interchange, in contexts of propositional attitude, to the interchange of eternal sentences. Each non-eternal sentence should be
filled out into an eternal one suitable to the circumstances of the
supposed affirmation of propositional attitude, before we put a
standard of propositional identity to the test. This plan is manda-
tory if we take the objects of the propositional attitudes as propositions and propositions as meanings of eternal sentences; and anyway it is a natural separation of problems, since eternalization is
often in order also apart from propositional attitudes.

Little would be gained here by examining the historical details
of intensional isomorphism and its variants, for the constructions
have depended on the notion of sentence synonymy in the broad
sense, or, what is an equivalent assumption, the notion of analyticity. Section 14 left us little expectation of making approximately
suitable sense of a general boundary between analytic sentences
and others, on the basis even of the totality of dispositions to speech
behavior.

We do have our analyticity intuition, but it grades off. It is a
question of how heavily communication is felt to depend on acceptance of the sentences concerned (§ 14). It is question of how
much facility would be gained by departing from homophonic
translation in dealing with a compatriot who denies such a sentence. Now there is no objection to a graded notion of synonymy
or of analyticity, supposing it made reasonably clear; but it is unlikely to contribute directly or indirectly to a standard of identity
of propositions. For propositions have to be the same or distinct
absolutely; identity, properly so-called, knows no gradations.

These reflections count only against hoping to base identity of
propositions on some sort of intensional isomorphism derived from
the broad sort of sentence synonymy which is interdefinable with
analyticity. We might still hope to construct some approximation
to intensional isomorphism suitable for identity of propositions, in
some other way than from the elusive broad notion of sentence
synonymy. For we saw in § 12 how to define stimulus synonymy
of general terms using stimulus analyticity, and in Chapter V how
to regiment the structure of sentences in terms of a few fixed constructions. At the height of the regimentation, sentences were
constructible only by adjoining general terms (including '=' and
'ϵ') predicatively to variables and applying quantification, truth
functions, and other operations on sentences (thus the 'O', 'O_x',

etc. of § 38). Here, then, is a definition of structural synonymy to consider: sentences in this canonical form of notation are synonymous if one can be transformed into the other by transformations of the logic of quantification and truth functions together with substitution of general terms for stimulus-synonymous general terms. May we not take eternal sentences in canonical notation to mean the same proposition when and only when they are synonymous in this sense? Let us survey the objections.

(1) The transformability of one sentence into another by the logic of quantification and truth functions can elude even the specialist in logic for indefinite periods; there is no general limit to the length of inquiry that may be required.[5] Evidently then to identify propositions on this basis would disqualify them as objects of belief.[6] We might meet this objection by counting only certain less far-reaching logical transformations into our synonymy definition, or even none.[7]

(2) Perhaps the stimulus synonymy of general terms, on which our definition depends, is too loose a synonymy to give the desired effect—particularly when the terms do not denote fairly observable objects. (Cf. § 12.)

(3) Whether a general term in a sentence of ordinary language survives in a canonical paraphrase of the sentence, or disappears in favor of a more minute analysis, depends only on one's momentary purposes in paraphrasing; and so does the nature of the more minute analysis, if any. (Cf. § 33.) Therefore our suggested notion of structural synonymy, with its emphasis on general terms, is mainly relevant to a wholly casual feature of our use of canonical notation. Nor should we care to meet this objection by specifying

[5] This is a way of stating an important discovery of Church. See my *Methods of Logic*, revised edition, § 32.

[6] This objection is similar in principle to objections leveled against Carnap's intensional isomorphism in the papers of Scheffler and Church last cited.

[7] Counting none of them in is Putnam's course and Church's in their last-cited papers. Note that making the synonymy relation thus excessively narrow is more defensible than leaving it excessively wide; for when we count two sentences not synonymous and hence not interchangeable in belief contexts we still leave people free to believe both. Because of this, the first of the two problematic cases that Scheffler notes, *op. cit.*, top of p. 42, may be taken lightly. All that is wanted to clear up his other case, by the way, is the technique of selective transparency in § 31.

or imagining some absolute vocabulary of simple general terms, as canonical all-purpose elements of paraphrase.[8] If the positing of propositions as objects is serious, any such arbitrarily assembled groundwork for propositional identity must be seen as gratuitous.

(4) The proposed concept of structural synonymy, limited as it is to canonical notation, covers too special a subclass of the eternal sentences. Now insofar as this objection is aimed e.g. at the absence of singular terms, it is minor. Mechanical transformations are at hand in § 39 for eliminating and restoring singular terms, and we can read these operations into our definition of structural synonymy, if we like, on a par with the logical transformations and the substitutions under stimulus synonymy. But as an objection to limiting oneself to the canonical notation in other respects, it is serious; for the conversions to canonical notation are in general no more mechanical than foreign translation. The objection can be put simply as the objection that we are explaining propositional identity relative only to one language. The objection applies in particular also to the dependence of our concept upon that of the stimulus synonymy of terms; for this latter, unlike stimulus synonymy of sentences, was tied to English from the start (§ 12). Now to say that we can always adhere to our own language, and to the canonical part of it, is no adequate defense. For if the posit of propositions is to be taken seriously, eternal sentences of other languages must be supposed to mean propositions too; and each of these must be identical with or distinct from each proposition meant by an eternal sentence of our own, even if we never care which. Surely it is philosophically unsatisfactory for such questions of identity to arise as recognized questions, however academic, without there being in principle some suggestion of how to construe them in terms of domestic and foreign dispositions to verbal behavior.

This last point has the germs of an argument not only against our specific plan of a structural-synonymy concept as a standard of propositional identity, but against the whole idea of positing propositions. For, insofar as we take such a posit seriously, we thereby concede meaning, however inscrutable, to a synonymy relation that can be defined in general for eternal sentences of distinct languages

[8] Cf. § 47. It is on this point that Carnap's use of his intensional isomorphism differs most radically. He imagines a fixed, closed vocabulary of simple terms.

as follows: sentences are synonymous that mean the same proposition. We would then have to suppose that among all the alternative systems of analytical hypotheses of translation (§§ 15, 16) which are compatible with the totality of dispositions to verbal behavior on the part of the speakers of two languages, some are "really" right and others wrong on behaviorally inscrutable grounds of propositional identity. Thus the conclusions reached in § 16 may of themselves be said implicitly to scout the whole notion of proposition, granted a generally scientific outlook. The difficulties cited earlier in the present section are merely by the way. The very question of conditions for identity of propositions presents not so much an unsolved problem as a mistaken ideal.

§ 43. TOWARD DISPENSING WITH INTENSIONAL OBJECTS

A need to posit propositions—or perhaps "statements," as Strawson uses this word—has been felt or imagined in a number of connections. Propositions or other sentence meanings have been wanted as translational constants: as things shared somehow by foreign sentences and their translations. They have been wanted likewise as constants of so-called philosophical analysis, or paraphrase: as things shared by analysanda and their analysantia. They have been wanted as truth vehicles and as objects of propositional attitudes. The want has been felt so strongly as to encourage philosophers to defend a notion of sentence synonymy such as the identity of propositions demands, and to defend it by flimsier arguments than they might have permitted themselves if no preconceptions had been at stake. One of those arguments involves the fallacy of subtraction: it is argued that if we can speak of a sentence as meaningful, or as having meaning, then there must be a meaning that it has, and this meaning will be identical with or distinct from the meaning that another sentence has.[1] This is

[1] Thus Grice and Strawson, p. 146: "We want only to point out that if we are to give up the notion of sentence-synonymy as senseless, we must give up the notion of sentence-significance (of a sentence having meaning) as senseless too." The same subtractive fallacy can perhaps be imputed to Rynin, p. 381, where he seems to regard his defense of the notion of "knowing the meaning" as a defense of the notion of "meaning"; and again to Gewirth, note 48. And see Xenakis, p. 20, where from my remark that we give the mean-

urged without any evident attempt to define synonymy in terms of meaningfulness, nor any notice of the fact that we could as well justify the hypostasis of sakes and unicorns on the basis of the idioms 'for the sake of' and 'is hunting unicorns'.[2] Also we find it argued that the standard of clarity that I demand for synonymy and analyticity is unreasonably high;[3] yet I ask no more, after all, than a rough characterization in terms of dispositions to verbal behavior.

Another defense cites our undeniable intuitions of synonymy and analyticity. These I recognize, but I have urged (§§ 14, 42) that they do not sustain a synonymy concept suited to identity of propositions, or meanings. It should be said also that the arguments deplored in the preceding paragraph were doubtless meant in part as defenses merely of the intuitions and not of a synonymy adequate to propositional identity, though the distinction never gets drawn. As defenses of the intuitions those arguments may be acknowledged as fair enough, always excepting the one involving the fallacy of subtraction. But so construed the arguments are no defense of propositions, however strongly motivated by a wish to defend them.

Whistling in the dark is not the method of true philosophy. Let us review the situations that prompted the positing of propositions, and consider what can be done without that expedient. Now to begin with it is a mistake to suppose that the notion of propositions as shared meanings clarifies the enterprise of translation. The totality of dispositions to speech behavior is compatible with alternative systems of sentence-to-sentence translation so unlike one another that translations of a standing sentence under two such systems can even differ in truth value (§ 16). Were it not for this situation, we could hope to define in behavioral terms a general relation of sentence synonymy suited to translational needs, and our objection to propositions themselves would thereby be dissipated. Conversely, since the situation does obtain, the positing of propo-

---

ing of x by giving a synonym of x he deduces that "the meaning of x is a synonym of x." (But he is encouraged here by the familiar use of 'means' as short for 'means the same as'.)

[2] Nor any notice of my own caveats over this point, in the very book that the argument is directed against: *From a Logical Point of View*, pp. 11 f., 22 n., 48 f.

[3] Grice and Strawson, pp. 145 f.; Kemeny, review; Martin, "On 'analytic' "; Mates, "Analytic sentences," pp. 528 ff.; Richman, "Neo-pragmatism," p. 36. See also Gewirth, p. 400.

sitions only obscures it. The notion of proposition seems to facilitate talk of translation precisely because it falsifies the nature of
the enterprise. It fosters the pernicious illusion of there being a
uniquely correct standard of translation of eternal sentences (cf.
§ 42).

It is no less a mistake to suppose that the notion of propositions
as shared meanings clarifies the paraphrastic enterprises of philosophical analysis. On the contrary, as stressed in Chapter V, synonymy claims would generally be out of place in such connections
even if the notion of synonymy as such were in the best of shape.

We come next to the appeal to propositions as truth vehicles.
But instead of appealing here to propositions, or meanings of eternal
sentences, there is no evident reason not to appeal simply to the
eternal sentences themselves as truth vehicles. If we undertake to
specify the proposition "expressed" by the utterance of some non-
eternal sentence, e.g. 'The door is open', on some particular occasion,
we do so by bracketing some eternal sentence that means the proposition; thus we have had to compose an appropriate eternal sentence anyway, and we could as well stop there.

To stop there opens the question how this eternal sentence is
related to the given utterance of the non-eternal one. If the
question how the proposition was related to the utterance seemed
less urgent, it was because of a false sense of security induced by
the facile word 'expressed' and the unexamined ontology of propositional "thought" that it connotes. If talking of eternal sentences
instead of propositions brings the question to consciousness, so much
the better. In vague terms the answer to it is much the same as
in the case of paraphrasing sentences into canonical notation (§ 33):
the eternal sentence will be one that the original speaker could
have uttered in place of his original utterance in those original
circumstances without detriment, so far as he could foresee, to the
project he was bent on. I need hardly say that there is scope here
for refinement, but let it not be supposed that acquiescence in talk
of expressed propositions provides it.

It may seem that in talking of eternal sentences instead of propositions, whether as truth vehicles or in other connections, we cut
ourselves off from cases where the proposition is referred to as a
function of some variable: [x is mortal], where 'x' is bound only
by some quantifier farther forward in the context. The argument
would be that reference to the sentence 'x is mortal' itself, in place

of the propositional reference, would violate the restriction against quantifying into quotation. Actually there is no loss on this score; for quantification into the brackets of propositional abstraction is ruled out to begin with. Cf. § 35.

So much for propositions as truth vehicles. We have still to consider the problem of dispensing with propositions as objects of the propositional attitudes; but meanwhile let us pause for a word on the intensional objects other than propositions.

The strictures against propositions apply with equal force to attributes and relations. Just as propositions purport to be meanings of eternal closed sentences, so attributes and relations might be looked upon as meanings of eternal open sentences: open sentences which, for each choice of values of their free variables, take on truth values independent of speaker and occasion. The objection to propositions on the score of identity applies unchanged to attributes and relations. We shall want to dispense with attributes and relations as objects of the propositional attitudes, if we can, along with propositions.

Attributes and relations, or something rather like them, are needed also for various purposes apart from the propositional attitudes. Some of those purposes can be met by talking simply of the corresponding eternal open sentences or general terms—just as the purpose of propositions as truth vehicles seems to be met by eternal closed sentences. Others of those purposes, and very important ones they are, have no analogues among the purposes for which propositions might seem to be wanted; nor can they be met by talking of open sentences or general terms. We shall see later (§§ 48, 53 ff.) what some of those purposes are. But we shall find that those further purposes of attributes are well served by classes, which, after all, are like attributes except for their identity condition. Classes raise no perplexities over identity, being identical if and only if their members are identical.

Not only is the use of classes instead of attributes, where possible, to be desired on account of the identity question. It is also important in that intensional abstraction is opaque whereas class abstraction is transparent. Much of the power of class abstraction is due to our freedom to quantify into it, as in Cantor's theorem:

$$(x)(\hat{y}(y \text{ is a subclass of } x) \text{ has more members than } x)$$

or again in the law of counting:

(x)(if x is a positive integer then $\hat{y}$(y is a positive integer $\leqq x$) has x members).

Such quantification into intensional abstraction, on the other hand, is obstructed by opacity.

What classes are to attributes (thus dogkind to caninity), classes of ordered pairs are to relations. Insofar as purposes of attributes are met by classes, the analogous purposes of relations are met by classes of ordered pairs. But here there is a terminological quirk to look out for: classes of ordered pairs are in modern logic and mathematics customarily called relations too. To avoid confusion one often speaks of relations in the former or intensional sense as relations-in-intension.

The words 'attribute' and 'relation' turn up so often in the best discourse on the best of subjects that one may be taken aback by talk of renouncing attributes and relations. We now perceive that the renunciation, whatever its difficulties, is not as drastic as it sounds, since so much of what is said by ostensible reference to attributes or relations can be construed to refer at worst to open sentences, general terms, classes, or relations in the sense of classes of ordered pairs. Often even, as in the case of colors and substances, scattered concrete objects will fill the bill (§ 20).

Not that I would undertake to limit my use of the words 'attribute' and 'relation' to contexts that are excused by the possibility of such paraphrase. For consider how I have persisted in my vernacular use of 'meaning', 'idea', and the like, long after casting doubt on their supposed objects. True, the use of a term can sometimes be reconciled with rejection of its objects (cf. §§ 48 ff.); but I go on using the terms without even sketching any such reconciliation. What is involved here is simply a grading of austerity. I can object to using a certain dubious term at crucial points in a theory, on the ground that to use it would deprive the theory of its desired explanatory force; but I can still use and condone the term in more casual or heuristic connections, where less profundity of theoretical explanation is professed. Such grading of austerity is a natural adjunct of the scientific enterprise, if we see that enterprise in Neurath's way. There will be more to say of it in §§ 45 ff.

But let us get back, meanwhile, to the question how to accomplish specific purposes of intensional objects by means of substitute devices; for our troubles in that quarter are not over. For one thing, we have still to see what can be done about attributes and relations-in-intension, as well as propositions, in their capacity of objects of propositional attitudes.

§ 44. OTHER OBJECTS FOR THE ATTITUDES

When we handle propositional attitudes with intensional abstraction as in § 35, their opacity becomes localized in that of intensional abstraction. It follows that the work of attributes as objects of propositional attitudes cannot be done by the corresponding classes; for class abstraction is transparent. Or, to argue from example, let $x[Fx]$ be an attribute for which it is false that

(1) Tom believes $x[Fx]$ of a.

Still, endowed as he is with some trace of logical sense,

(2) Tom believes $x[Fx$ or $x = a]$ of a.

Suppose further that, unbeknownst to Tom, Fa. Then $\hat{x}(Fx) = \hat{x}(Fx$ or $x = a)$; so the required independence between (1) and (2) would be lost under class abstraction.

What thus disqualifies classes as objects of propositional attitudes is laxity of the condition of class identity: for two open sentences to determine the same class they need only be coextensive, i.e., fulfilled by the same values of the variable. Disqualification even of intensional objects as objects of propositional attitudes was to be feared on the same count, under certain contemplated conditions of identity of such objects; cf. objection (1) of § 42. Anyway we saw strong reasons not to welcome the intensional objects. The idea next suggests itself of taking as objects of the propositional attitudes things whose identity conditions are even stronger than the propositional attitudes require.

Such a course disturbs only some rather special sentences. Examples are 'Paul and Elmer agree on just three things', 'Paul believes only one thing that Elmer does not'; the effect of excess strength in the identity conditions could be upward revision of the numbers three and one in those examples, even to infinity. But these examples seem queer to begin with. That they do is indeed indicative of how uncertain one feels about sufficient conditions for identity of objects of the propositional attitudes.

Besides these trivial examples, there is indirect quotation to consider; it is one idiom of propositional attitude that might seem vulnerable to excessively strong identity conditions. Thus imagine hereafter in place of 'p' and 'q' two eternal sentences that are more or less equivalent intuitively speaking, and suppose the former uttered by w at t. One is tempted to think that an identity condition so strong as to distinguish between the objects of 'w says at t that p' and 'w says at t that q' would make 'w says at t that q' false. One is tempted to think thus about indirect quotation and not about belief, since w can believe all manner of distinct things at t but can utter only one sentence. However, this reasoning is wrong. In uttering his one sentence, w can be regarded as "saying" (in the sense of indirect quotation) as many distinct "things" (in the sense of objects of the propositional attitude of indirect quotation) as we like. Strong identity conditions are compatible with any amount of liberality over indirect quotation; they constrain us only in the more negligible connections noted in the preceding paragraph.

Such being the case, we might try repeating for propositional attitudes the line already urged in § 43 for truth vehicles: we might try using, instead of the intensional objects, the sentences themselves.[1] Here the identity condition is extreme: notational identity. The rough idea would be to rephrase (7)–(9) of § 35 thus:

(3) Tom believes-true 'Cicero denounced Catiline',
(4) Tom believes-true 'y denounced Catiline' of Cicero,
(5) Tom believes-true 'y denounced z' of Cicero and Catiline.

I modify 'believes' as 'believes-true' to alleviate the sense of oddity.

The plan has its recommendations. Quotation will not fail us in the way that class abstraction did. Moreover, conspicuously opaque as it is, quotation is a vivid form to which to reduce other opaque constructions. And we can even dissolve it altogether, into spelling, when we please (§ 30).

Intensional abstraction is in a very different position from class abstraction. We could scarcely afford to switch from class abstraction to quotation and so dispense with classes. The difference is our freedom to quantify into class abstraction (cf. § 43). To drop class theory in favor of quotation, into which there is no quantifying, would mean giving up most of the power that a class theory confers (whereof more anon: § 55). Intensional abstraction, on the

---

[1] Thus Carnap, *Logical Syntax*, p. 248.

other hand, was pressed into duty in § 35 with full acceptance of opacity; so its absorption into quotation means no such loss.

The proposal of (3)–(5) applies equally to other propositional attitudes. 'Tom says that Cicero denounced Catiline', or 'Tom says [Cicero denounced Catiline]', would become:

(6) Tom says-true 'Cicero denounced Catiline'.

This new verb is not to be confused with the 'says' of direct quotation; (6) is meant to retain the freedom of indirect quotation.

In general, thus, the objects of propositional attitudes would be taken simply to be eternal sentences, open and closed. In limiting them to eternal sentences we do not prohibit other sentences in contexts of propositional attitude; the point is merely that it is not these, but only eternal paraphrases of them, that count as the objects of the attitudes. In this respect the situation remains somewhat as it was when we were still using intensional abstraction; cf. § 40. Part of what is bewildering in analyses of the propositional attitudes is cleared up by keeping in mind that only the switch to eternal sentences makes the objects of the attitudes explicit, whether in propositional abstraction or in quotation.

Taking the objects of propositional attitudes as sentences does not require the subject to speak the language of the object sentence, or any. A mouse's fear of a cat is counted as his fearing true a certain English sentence. Yet there remains, as Church has remarked,[2] a certain relativity to language that needs still to be made explicit. Quotations are names merely of the forms therein exhibited, regardless of what language they belong to. What then if by coincidence those same forms quoted in (3)–(6) make sense in another language, and sense other than we intend? The coincidence is not excluded; indeed for Church it is even inevitable, for he counts as languages all possible languages and not just those actually used. Evidently therefore we should amend (3) to read:

(7) Tom believes-true in English 'Cicero denounced Catiline';

and correspondingly for (4)–(6) and other cases.

But there is still, according to Church,[3] a fundamental difficulty in treating the objects of propositional attitudes thus as linguistic

---

[2] "On Carnap's analysis of statements of assertion and belief."

[3] *Op. cit.* He credits Langford with the point.

forms. A German translation of (7) might run, inelegance for inelegance, thus:

(8) Tom glaubt wahr auf Englisch „Cicero denounced Catiline."

Yet a German ignorant of English will not get from (8) the information about Tom that he would get from a full German translation of:

(9) Tom believes that Cicero denounced Catiline.

Since (8) reproduces the meaning of (7), then, (7) must miss that of (9).

This argument I find inconclusive because it turns on a notion of likeness of meaning. After all, it was misgivings over that notion that impelled us to drop propositions in the first place.[4] True, I cannot reject the argument on that score and then hold that (7) is like (9) in meaning. But likeness of meaning is not my aim; cf. § 33. One could still hold that (7) well enough serves any purposes of (9) that seem worth serving.

But I find (7) and its train unsatisfactory on another count: the dependence on the notion of *a* language. The underlying form of (7) is 'w believes-true s in l', relating a man, a linguistic form, and a language. What are languages, and when do they count as identical or distinct? Clearly such questions should be unconnected with the propositional attitudes. It would be better to refer here not to a language l but to a speaker z, thus: 'w believes-true s in z's sense'. We have then an irreducibly triadic relative term '. . . believes-true . . . in . . .'s sense', relating a man, a linguistic form, and a man. The corresponding adjustment applies to the higher cases (4) and (5) and to the other propositional attitudes, including indirect quotation. In practice of course the appropriate substitute for 'z' will regularly be the indicator word 'me', since 'that' clauses are always given in our own language.

Scheffler has an alternative suggestion.[5] Consider all those events of utterance (or inscription), in all languages, that may fairly be counted as cases of saying that Cicero denounced Catiline. Let us call each such event an utterance that Cicero denounced Catiline. In effect Scheffler's plan is to adopt as basic this operator 'utterance

---

[4] This point was made by Pap in "Belief, synonymity, and analysis."
[5] "An inscriptional approach to indirect quotation."

that', which applies to a sentence to form a composite general term true of utterance events. Then he explains 'w says that p' as 'w makes an utterance that p'. Since an actual utterance event normally belongs to a unique language even if the form uttered does not, no auxiliary specification is required of Scheffler on that score.

Let it not be objected just here that there is no evident way of telling how far an utterance may be allowed to differ from the sentence appearing in the position of 'p' and still be counted as an utterance that p. The objection is correct, and doubly so when we think of what is involved in translation from foreign languages (Ch. II); and Scheffler appreciates it. But it is out of order just now, for it concerns indirect quotation however analyzed, and has no special relevance to Scheffler's contribution.

When Scheffler extends his method to idioms of propositional attitude other than indirect quotation,[6] however, a peculiar difficulty does arise: how are we to say e.g. that Paul believes something that Elmer does not? It will not do to say that Paul believes-true some utterance that Elmer does not believe-true, for it may happen that no such utterance exists or ever will; believing does not, like saying, produce utterances. This defect may be counted as favoring sentences over utterance events as objects of propositional attitudes; for, under the construction at the end of § 40, sentences are undisturbed by failure of utterance.

Still, the defect is limited to quantifications. It does not touch the explicit idiom 'w believes that p', construed as 'w believes-true an utterance that p'; for, once 'w believes that p' is itself uttered, there has been created a sample utterance that p.[7] Perhaps, after all, the quantifications affected—'Paul believes something that Elmer does not', 'Eisenhower and Stevenson agree on something', and the like—are expendable; for such quantifications tend anyway to be pretty trivial in what they affirm, and useful only in heralding more tangible information. Already earlier we were prepared not to care how the truth values of such sentences as 'Paul and Elmer agree on just three things' might turn out; perhaps now we can find it in us to be indifferent toward these others too.

But if so, there is no need to recognize 'believes' and similar verbs as relative terms at all; no need to countenance their predicative use

---

[6] He does so in "Thoughts on teleology," pp. 280 f.

[7] Scheffler notes this, p. 280 n.

as in 'w believes x' (as against 'w believes that p'); no need, therefore, to see 'that p' as a term. Hence a final alternative that I find
as appealing as any is simply to dispense with the objects of the
propositional attitudes. We can continue to formulate the propositional attitudes with help of the notations of intensional abstraction
as in § 35 but just cease to view these notations as singular terms
referring to objects. This means viewing 'Tom believes [Cicero
denounced Catiline]' no longer as of the form 'Fab' with a = Tom
and b = [Cicero denounced Catiline], but rather as of the form
'Fa' with a = Tom and complex 'F'. The verb 'believes' here ceases
to be a term and becomes part of an operator 'believes that', or
'believes [ ]', which, applied to a sentence, produces a composite
absolute general term whereof the sentence is counted an immediate
constituent. Similarly the 'believes' in 'Tom believes y[y denounced
Catiline] of Cicero' becomes part of a variable-binding operator
which, applied directly to an open sentence 'y denounced Catiline'
and a variable 'y', produces a relative general term 'believes y[y
denounced Catiline] of'. Correspondingly for two and more variables; and correspondingly for other verbs of propositional attitude.
In a word, we take the notation of § 35 simply as a stylization of the
verbal treatment of § 31 rather than as a deeper analysis of it that
makes reference to intensional objects.

This course supersedes the 'O', 'O_x', etc. of § 38. They belonged
to the program of eliminating singular terms, as it applied to
intensional abstracts when intensional abstracts were singular terms.
In their new status of non-terms, the intensional abstracts stay
on irreducibly as portions of composite general terms. General
terms, for their part, cease to count always as simple from the point
of view of canonical notation, and come to admit closed sentences
or open sentences and variables as immediate constituents.

§ 45. THE DOUBLE STANDARD

Even this course, for all its sacrifices, leaves us with a very way-
ward set of idioms. To have cleared away the ontology of the
propositional attitudes is not to have made scientific sense of them.
Thus, take indirect quotation again: the question how far it may
allowably deviate from direct quotation remains alive as ever, repudiate the supposed objects of indirect quotation though we may.

The problem here has evident affinities with that of translation.

It even includes the latter, when the indirect quotation occurs between languages. And indeed that most primitive phase of translation, the translation of observation sentences by stimulus synonymy, serves indirect quotation well enough within the limits of observation sentences; thus 'He says there is a rabbit there' is plausibly interpreted as 'He says something that has for him the stimulus meaning that 'There is a rabbit there' has for us'.

We can do as much for belief, if we abstract for the moment from liars and dumb animals. 'He believes there is a rabbit there' is plausibly interpreted as 'He would, if asked, assent to some sentence that has for him the stimulus meaning that 'There's a rabbit' has for us'.[1] This in turn, by our definition of stimulus meaning, amounts to saying two things: that he has just had a stimulation belonging to the stimulus meaning of 'There's a rabbit' for us, and that he knows the use of a sentence whose stimulus meaning for him is the same. If in place of this latter requirement we will settle for some nonlinguistic discriminatory disposition toward rabbits, we may even make sense of 'The dog believes there is a rabbit there'.[2]

Observation sentences are not eternal. In examining them thus directly under propositional attitudes, instead of first paraphrasing them into eternal sentences, we therefore abandon the precept of § 42; but so we must if we are to make much use here of their stimulus meanings. Anyway the reason for the precept, insofar as it turned on propositions, has now lapsed.

We know from § 11 that stimulus synonymy can be used as a standard of translation not only for observation sentences but for occasion sentences generally, thanks to the devices of socialized intrasubjective synonymy and bilinguals. One may reasonably expect comparable success in construing indirect quotations and belief sentences whose contained sentences are occasion sentences, though some tinkering with times and indicator words can be called for. The efficacy of the approach even extends to cases where the contained sentences are standing sentences, but it grades off with the richness of their stimulus meanings. It is perhaps partly because so substantial a portion of propositional-attitude discourse is thus straightforwardly empirical that people proceed so confidently with the rest of it.

---

[1] Cf. Carnap, *Meaning and Necessity,* p. 55.

[2] In this paragraph and the preceding one I am indebted to Davidson.

For the case of sentences generally, however, or even the case of eternal sentences generally, surely there is nothing approaching a fixed standard of how far indirect quotation may deviate from the direct.[3] Commonly the degree of allowable deviation depends on why we are quoting. It is a question of what traits of the quoted speaker's remarks we want to make something of; those are the traits that must be kept straight if our indirect quotation is to count as true. Similar remarks apply to sentences of belief and other propositional attitudes. Thus even if we eternalize the contained sentence and also rid the containing sentence of such sources of truth-value variation as inadequate descriptions, indicator words, and the like, still the whole may in some cases remain capable of varying in truth value from occasion to occasion, counting as true on occasions where no capital is to be made of the contained sentence's divergences from direct quotation, and false otherwise. Evidently we must recognize in indirect quotation and other idioms of propositional attitude a source of truth-value variation comparable to the indicator words, though more restrained in its effects. It will often happen also that there is just no saying whether to count an affirmation of propositional attitude as true or false, even given full knowledge of its circumstances and purposes.

A reason for gravitating to indirect quotation as prime example of the propositional attitudes is that the quoted speaker's actual utterance exists as a standard with which to compare the variants, whereas in the case of believing, wishing, and the rest there is usually no such fixed point to work from. Not, of course, that this trait makes indirect quotation humanly dispensable. We tend, even if we hear a remark directly and not by hearsay, to forget its exact words and remember only enough to report by indirect quotation.[4] Hence the main utility of indirect quotation. And there is its utility also as a medium of translation. Indirect quotation is here to stay, and so, for similar and further reasons, are the other idioms of propositional attitude.

In general the underlying methodology of the idioms of propositional attitude contrasts strikingly with the spirit of objective science at its most representative. For consider again quotation,

---

[3] Thus I agree on the general point with Scheffler, "On synonymy and indirect discourse," despite the reservations in § 42.

[4] See Chisholm, *Perceiving*, p. 160.

direct and indirect. When we quote a man's utterance directly we report it almost [5] as we might a bird call. However significant the utterance, direct quotation merely reports the physical incident and leaves any implications to us. On the other hand in indirect quotation we project ourselves into what, from his remarks and other indications, we imagine the speaker's state of mind to have been, and then we say what, in our language, is natural and relevant for us in the state thus feigned. An indirect quotation we can usually expect to rate only as better or worse, more or less faithful, and we cannot even hope for a strict standard of more and less; what is involved is evaluation, relative to special purposes, of an essentially dramatic act. Correspondingly for the other propositional attitudes, for all of them can be thought of as involving something like quotation of one's own imagined verbal response to an imagined situation.

Casting our real selves thus in unreal roles, we do not generally know how much reality to hold constant. Quandaries arise. But despite them we find ourselves attributing beliefs, wishes, and strivings even to creatures lacking the power of speech, such is our dramatic virtuosity. We project ourselves even into what from his behavior we imagine a mouse's state of mind to have been, and dramatize it as a belief, wish, or striving, verbalized as seems relevant and natural to us in the state thus feigned.

In the strictest scientific spirit we can report all the behavior, verbal and otherwise, that may underlie our imputations of propositional attitudes, and we may go on to speculate as we please upon the causes and effects of this behavior; but, so long as we do not switch muses, the essentially dramatic idiom of propositional attitudes will find no place.

The Scholastic word 'intentional' was revived by Brentano in connection with the verbs of propositional attitude and related verbs of the sort studied in § 32—'hunt', 'want', etc. The division between such idioms and the normally tractable ones is notable. We saw how it divides referential from non-referential occurrences of terms. Moreover it is intimately related to the division between behaviorism and mentalism,[6] between efficient cause and final cause, and between literal theory and dramatic portrayal.

[5] This adverb allows for § 18.
[6] See Chisholm, "Sentences about believing"; Bergmann, "Intentionality," p. 211.

The analysis in § 32 was such as to spare us any temptation to posit peculiar "intentional objects" of hunting, wanting, and the like. But there remains a thesis of Brentano's, illuminatingly developed of late by Chisholm,[7] that is directly relevant to our emerging doubts over the propositional attitudes and other intentional locutions. It is roughly that there is no breaking out of the intentional vocabulary by explaining its members in other terms. Our present reflections are favorable to this thesis. Even indirect quotation, for all its tameness in comparison with other idioms of propositional attitude, and for all its concern with overt speech behavior, seems insusceptible to general reduction to behavioral terms; the best we can do with it is switch to direct quotation, and this adds information. And when we turn to belief sentences the difficulty is doubled. For, first there is trouble, e.g. over dumbness or mendacity, in explaining belief as disposition to assent to sentences at all; and second there remains, much as in the case of indirect quotation, the question what deviations to allow between the sentences actually assented to and the second-hand reports.

Chisholm counts the semantical terms 'meaning', 'denote', 'synonymous', and the like into the intentional vocabulary, and questions the extent to which such terms can be explained without the help of other semantical or intentional ones. Adapted to the example 'Gavagai' (Ch. II), the sort of difficulty he has in mind is this: we cannot equate 'Gavagai' and 'Rabbit' as outright responses to rabbits, for assent to these sentences is prompted not by the presence of rabbits but by their believed presence; and belief is intentional. Now we cleared this obstacle in § 8 by equating 'Gavagai' and 'Rabbit' on the basis of stimulations rather than rabbits. Stimulations, however deceptive, go by face value, and match up well enough from speaker to speaker to sustain the equation. There is the possibility that informants may lie to us, but one assumes that such deviations, where undetected as lies, are rare enough not to spoil a significant approximation of stimulus meanings.

But the predicament that Chisholm anticipates is still encountered when we turn from the stimulus synonymy of occasion sentences to the construing of terms. This is a step that requires analytical hypotheses, undetermined by verbal dispositions (§§ 12, 16); yet it is a step that the intentional vocabulary would represent as determinate. For, using the intentional words 'believe' and 'ascribe',

---

[7] See Chisholm, *Perceiving*, Ch. 11, and his references to Brentano.

one could say that a speaker's term is to be construed as 'rabbit' if and only if the speaker is disposed to ascribe it to all and only the objects that he believes to be rabbits. Evidently, then, the relativity to non-unique systems of analytical hypotheses invests not only translational synonymy but intentional notions generally. Brentano's thesis of the irreducibility of intentional idioms is of a piece with the thesis of indeterminacy of translation.

One may accept the Brentano thesis either as showing the indispensability of intentional idioms and the importance of an autonomous science of intention, or as showing the baselessness of intentional idioms and the emptiness of a science of intention. My attitude, unlike Brentano's, is the second. To accept intentional usage at face value is, we saw, to postulate translation relations as somehow objectively valid though indeterminate in principle relative to the totality of speech dispositions. Such postulation promises little gain in scientific insight if there is no better ground for it than that the supposed translation relations are presupposed by the vernacular of semantics and intention.

Not that I would forswear daily use of intentional idioms, or maintain that they are practically dispensable. But they call, I think, for bifurcation in canonical notation. Which turning to take depends on which of the various purposes of a canonical notation happens to be motivating us at the time. If we are limning the true and ultimate structure of reality, the canonical scheme for us is the austere scheme that knows no quotation but direct quotation and no propositional attitudes but only the physical constitution and behavior of organisms. (It would be pointless to exempt from this ban even those favored sentences of propositional attitude that can be explained in terms of stimulus synonymy; for when they can be thus paraphrased they are certainly dispensable.) If we are venturing to formulate the fundamental laws of a branch of science, however tentatively, this austere idiom is again likely to be the one that suits. But if our use of canonical notation is meant only to dissolve verbal perplexities or facilitate logical deductions, we are often well advised to tolerate the idioms of propositional attitude. Our purposes may then be well served by admitting the apparatus of propositional attitudes as of the end of § 44—hence minus the right to quantify over the attitudinal objects.[8]

---

[8] On the austere scheme, which Bergmann ("Intentionality") calls L_c, see further § 47. Its more liberal variant, accommodating intentional idioms,

§ 46. DISPOSITIONS AND CONDITIONALS

Let us turn now to a further idiom that is similar in a way to those of propositional attitude: the strong or subjunctive conditional. What sets this apart from the ordinary conditional is not falsity of its antecedent or 'if'-clause, but the fact that the conditional can be seriously entertained and affirmed or denied in full cognizance of the falsity of the antecedent. An ordinary conditional forfeits our interest and ceases to be affirmed or denied once we are satisfied of the truth value of its antecedent.[1]

The subjunctive conditional depends, like indirect quotation and more so, on a dramatic projection: we feign belief in the antecedent and see how convincing we then find the consequent. What traits of the real world to suppose preserved in the feigned world of the contrary-to-fact antecedent can be guessed only from a sympathetic sense of the fabulist's likely purpose in spinning his fable. Thus consider the pair (Goodman's, nearly enough):

If Caesar were in command, he would use the atom bomb;

If Caesar were in command, he would use catapults.

We are likelier to hear the former, but only because that one is likelier to fit a lesson that a speaker would try to dramatize.

We recall of indirect quotation that it has no general translation into quoted speech, though each specific true case has a quotable actual utterance behind it. Similarly the subjunctive conditional is an idiom for which we cannot hope to find a satisfactory general substitute in realistic terms, though ordinarily in a particular case we can see how to restate the relevant point straightforwardly enough.

The subjunctive conditional is seen at its most respectable in the disposition terms. To say that an object a is (water-) *soluble* at time t is to say that if a were in water at t, a would dissolve at t. To say that a is *fragile* at t is to say that if a were struck smartly at

answers in spirit though not in detail to Bergmann's *L*. In his kindliness toward the intentional, Bergmann is nearer Brentano than I; but it is a difference not easily assessed, for we are agreed both that the intentional does not reduce and that it is at least in a practical way indispensable.

[1] For a closer analysis of the distinction see Stanley.

t, a would break at *t*. The ordinary conditional would not suffice here, for it loses its point when the truth value of its antecedent is known. We want to speak of *a* as soluble or fragile at *t* though knowing that it is not immersed or struck at *t*. Clearly the subjunctive conditional is the one involved. Yet it retains here little of the erratic quality seen in the Caesar examples.

The difference is that here a stabilizing factor is intruded: a theory of subvisible structure. What we have seen dissolve in water had, according to the theory, a structure suited to dissolving; and when now we speak of some new dry sugar lump as soluble, we may be considered merely to be saying that it, whether destined for water or not, is similarly structured. Fragility is parallel.

True, men talked equally easily of solubility before those explanations were at hand; but only because they already believed there was a hidden trait of some sort, structural or otherwise, that inhered in the substance and accounted for its dissolving on immersion. It was enough to suppose that if an erstwhile object *a* had the hypothetical characteristic (as seen by its having dissolved), and if the stuff of *b* seemed just like that of *a*, then probably *b* had it too. Something of the kind is still afoot whenever we infer one trait from another on the ground of widespread observation of association of the traits but in ignorance of the connecting mechanism, as for instance in psychiatric prognoses based on syndromes: an appropriate mechanism is believed present in the structure of the behaving organism, though all unknown.

Dispositions are, we see, a better-behaved lot than the general run of subjunctive conditionals; and the reason is that they are conceived as built-in, enduring structural traits. Their saving grace extends, moreover, to many subjunctive conditionals that do not happen to have acquired one-word tags like 'soluble' and 'fragile'. An example was the 'would prompt assent' of § 8. For there again a disposition was concerned, albeit unnamed: some subtle neural condition, induced by language-learning, that disposes the subject to assent to or dissent from a certain sentence in response to certain supporting stimulations.

Disposition terms such as 'soluble' and 'fragile' show their dispositionality in their suffixes, and the nature of the disposition in their verb stems. It is only on this etymological count, if at all, that such a term as 'red' might not be said to be dispositional as well. An object is red if it is disposed, given a chance, to reflect a certain range of low frequencies selectively. Redness of things is like solubility in that the pattern of subvisible structure concerned now happens to be fairly well understood and was once, without hindrance to the use of the term, known only by its fruits. Apart from etymology, therefore, the notion of disposition term proves to be a pretty idle one unless taken in a relativized sense: 'soluble' is dispositional relative to 'dissolve', 'red' relative to 'reflect low visible frequencies selectively'. Doubts connected with the subjunctive conditional concern not the several terms but rather the disposition operator '-ble', conceived as generally applicable to terms in order to generate new terms that are dispositional relative to them. Any specific terms got by that operator may still be accepted on their merits as simple terms. There is no reason to hesitate over admitting the general terms 'soluble' and 'fragile' to one's theoretical vocabulary, any more than 'red'. Each is a term that we attribute to physical objects on the strength often of direct observation, by way of simply conditioned response, and often of theory.

The special problem of disposition terms is therefore this: must we treat the etymologically dispositional words 'soluble', 'fragile', etc. as simple and irreducible general terms on a par with 'red', or can the sentences that contain them be systematically paraphrased so as to drop those disposition terms in favor of their root verbs? Of course they can if we allow subjunctive conditionals; but the problem is to manage also without that aid—or, what is equivalent, to paraphrase subjunctive conditionals themselves insofar as they can be fairly viewed as expressing dispositions.

The objective would not be synonymy, but just approximate fulfillment of likely purposes of the original sentences; cf. § 33. The objective is wholly vague failing some indication of admissible vocabulary, but still there is the hint of a procedure in the point about subvisible structure. If we allow our theory to include a relative term 'M' corresponding to the words 'alike in molecular structure' in some appropriate sense, then we can paraphrase 'x is soluble' and 'x is fragile' in rough outline thus:

$$(\exists y)(Mxy \text{ and } y \text{ dissolves}), \quad (\exists y)(Mxy \text{ and } y \text{ breaks})$$

with the verbs understood as tenseless. Correspondingly also perhaps, with change of 'M', for some other sets of disposition terms. Such paraphrases would be strictly for regimentation of theory, of course, not epistemological reduction.

Between subjunctive conditionals in a reasonably dispositional spirit and subjunctive conditionals at their wildest there is no boundary, but only a gradation of better and worse. There is such a gradation also among the etymologically explicit disposition terms. Which of these to accommodate in a canonical notation by systematic considerations of the above sort, which to admit separately as irreducible general terms, and which to ban—these are matters to decide with an eye to projects in hand and not once and for all.

The farther a disposition is from those that can confidently be pinned on molecular structure or something comparably firm, the more our talk of it tends to depend on a vague factor of *"caeteris paribus."* This factor was what was elusive likewise in indirect quotation; and it was what obstructed general analysis of the implicitly dispositional constructions represented by 'Tabby eats mice (§ 36). That the idioms involving it remain useful is due to those clues to the scope of *"caeteris paribus"* that are afforded by the context or other special circumstances of the particular utterance. This is why the paraphrasing of such idioms into a satisfactorily explicit canonical notation is often practicable occasion by occasion and altogether hopeless idiom by idiom.

From recent paragraphs it becomes evident not only that the subjunctive conditional has no place in an austere canonical notation for science, but also that the ban on it is less restrictive than would at first appear. We remain free to allow ourselves one by one any general terms we like, however subjunctive or dispositional their explanations. (Doubtless 'stimulus-synonymous' would be one.) What we exclude is the subjunctive conditional or the dispositional operator '-ble' as a freely applicable ingredient of canonical notation. Much of the general force even of these constructions is still available in other forms, moreover, thanks to the universally quantified indicative conditional and thanks also to such relative terms as 'M', which we remain free to adopt. For the rest, our renunciation seems only in keeping with the trend of science itself: the favoring of definite mechanisms, assumed or discovered, over unqualified causality.[2]

[2] A view of the residual subjunctive conditionals as unscientific language has been suggested also by Hampshire, who speaks of subjunctive conditionals that "are not intended to be replaceable by falsifiable general statements plus statements of initial conditions; when so used, they can be described as ex-

As for the indicative conditional, it presents no problem. In its unquantified form 'If p then q' it is perhaps best represented as suffering a truth-value gap (§ 37) whenever its antecedent is false. The gap is awkward for the same reason noted in connection with singular terms: it cannot be spotted by notational form. If in the spirit of good canonical notation we proceed to close it, what we come out with (like Philo of Megara and Frege before us) is simply the material conditional (§ 41), a truth function.[3]

Undue denunciation of the material conditional was provoked by Russell's word 'implication' (cf. § 41), but there would have been some protesting anyway. I should not want to rest the case for the material conditional on the claim that it differs none from the indicative conditional of ordinary usage except over the truth-value gap; for, here as at other points touching canonical notation, usage is not the issue. Let us not ask whether the material conditional constitutes a genuine semantical analysis, somehow, of the ordinary indicative conditional; let us merely notice that it, reinforced sometimes by universal quantification, proves on the whole to help us over humps of communication where we might otherwise have brought in an ordinary indicative conditional. In particular this is borne out wherever an indicative 'if-then' has found its way into the formulas of foregoing pages; it can satisfactorily be construed as the material conditional at each such point.

§ 47. A FRAMEWORK FOR THEORY

Our canonical notation in Chapter V continued to admit indicator words after tense and singular terms were eliminated. There was no limitation of its sentences to eternal ones. There is a certain premium on eternal sentences, though, and has been since writing began. Insofar as some utterances of a sentence can be true

pressing judgments, or interpretations of the facts, to distinguish them from their use in strictly scientific discourse." And see Russell, *Our Knowledge of the External World*, p. 220. On subjunctive conditionals and disposition terms see further Carnap, "Methodological character of theoretical concepts," pp. 62–69, and "Testability and meaning"; Goodman, *Fact, Fiction, and Forecast*; Pap, "Disposition concepts and extensional logic"; Reichenbach, §§ 60–63, and my review; and Sellars.

[3] See my *Elementary Logic*, § 7. But the claim applies to the indicative conditional only in its "semi-adjunctive" use, according to Reichenbach (pp. 389 f.), and not in what he calls its "connective" use.

and other utterances of it false, demands are placed on our knowledge of the circumstances of utterance; and such knowledge is scarcer for script than for speech.

Writing is essential to serious science, as rendering it cumulative; and the longer the preservation, the dimmer the circumstances of utterance. Furthermore, the spirit of theoretical science encourages fixity of truth values also apart from the demands of writing. What is true here-now tends the more to be true also there-then, the more it is of the sort that scientists aspire to discover. Though scientific data go back to observation sentences, which are true only utterance by utterance, the sentences of the theory that is projected from those data tend to be eternal.

A consequence of this tendency, and one which encourages it, is simplification of logical theory. Laws of logical inference refer to recurrences of sentences, on the assumption that a sentence true in one occurrence will be true in the next. Even inference of 'p' from 'p and q' (where 'p' and 'q' represent sentences) is a case in point. Any plan not predicated thus on fixity of truth values would be unrewardingly complex.

We do apply logic to sentences whose truth values vary with time and speaker. We leave temporal and pronominal references unfixed, and even the senses of ambiguous words, simply because the circumstances that would settle these matters on any particular occasion of utterance may be expected to settle them uniformly for the space of the argument. Occasionally this expectation fails and we have the *fallacy of equivocation*. Appliers of logical theory must keep alert to this hazard and, when it threatens, expand the offending sentences: not into eternal sentences, but just enough to mark any differences that would otherwise be brought out by vicissitudes of the argument.[1] The relation of eternal sentences to our logic is like that of silver dollars to our economy: mostly we do not see them, but we reckon in terms of them.

The primary distinction of eternal sentences is that they are the repository of truth itself, and so of all science. Insofar as a sentence can be said simply to be true, and not just true now or in this mouth, it is an eternal sentence. When our objective is an austere canonical form for the system of the world, we are not to rest with the renunciation of propositional attitudes and the subjunctive conditional; we

---

[1] Cf. my *Methods of Logic*, pp. xvi, 43.

must renounce also the indicator words and other sources of truth-value fluctuation.

'Because' and like idioms of causal type go the way of the sub-junctive conditional. With these and the propositional attitudes set aside, and modality and intensional abstraction dropped (§§ 41, 44), and quotation reduced to spelling (§ 30), and the indicative conditional canalized (§ 46), no evident reason remains for imbedding sentences within sentences otherwise than by truth functions and quantification. How powerful this combination is has been borne out by extensive logical regimentations of parts of science, especially mathematics, at the hands of Frege, Peano, and their successors.

Taking the canonical notation thus austerely, and holding also to the formal economies of Chapter V, we have just these basic con-structions: predication, universal quantification (cf. § 34), and the truth functions (reducible to one [2]). The ultimate components are the variables and general terms; and these combine in predication to form the atomic open sentences. What thus confronts us as a scheme for systems of the world is that structure so well understood by present-day logicians, the logic of quantification or calculus of predicates.

Not that the idioms thus renounced are supposed to be unneeded in the market place or in the laboratory. Not that indicator words and subjunctive conditionals are supposed to be unneeded in teaching the very terms—'soluble', 'Greenwich', 'A.D.', 'Polaris'—on which the canonical formulations may proceed. The doctrine is only that such a canonical idiom can be abstracted and then adhered to in the statement of one's scientific theory. The doctrine is that all traits of reality worthy of the name can be set down in an idiom of this austere form if in any idiom.

It is in spirit a philosophical doctrine of categories, except that it is peculiarly relative in its import. Of itself it sets no limits to the vocabulary of unanalyzed general terms admissible to science. But it sets limits to the ways of deriving complex predicates, com-plex conditions or open sentences, from those undictated components. It is a doctrine that limits what can be said of things to (a) such "prime traits" or general terms as may be expressly admitted sever-

[2] This is Sheffer's familiar reduction. See e.g. my *Mathematical Logic*, pp. 45 ff., or *Methods of Logic*, p. 11.

ally on merits beyond this doctrine's purely relativistic concerns, and (*b*) such "derivative traits" as can be formulated in those primary terms with help of predication, quantification, and truth functions alone. It delimits what counts as scientifically admissible construction, and declares that whatever is not thus constructible from given terms must either be conceded the status of one more irreducibly given term or eschewed. The doctrine is philosophical in its breadth, however continuous with science in its motivation.

Short of fixing the totality of admissible unanalyzed general terms, one might still consider distinguishing some absolute philosophical categories of such terms. Also, short of fixing the universe of admissible objects, or values of variables of quantification, one might consider distinguishing some categories in the way of basically diverse subuniverses: thus physical objects versus classes versus perhaps sundry other conspicuously distinct sorts of things. One might then go on to declare that terms in only certain of the categories of terms are significantly predicable of things in certain of the subuniverses. An example is the theory of types which Russell propounded as a means of coping with the antinomies of naïve set theory. Also apart from that technical context there has been a concern among philosophers to declare meaningless, rather than trivially false, such predications as 'This stone is thinking about Vienna' (Carnap) and 'Quadruplicity drinks procrastination' (Russell). Here we witness sometimes just a spontaneous revulsion against silly sentences and sometimes a remote project of cutting meaningful language down to something like empirical size. But since the philosophers who would build such categorial fences are not generally resolved to banish from language all falsehoods of mathematics and like absurdities, I fail to see much benefit in the partial exclusions that they do undertake; for the forms concerned would remain still quite under control if admitted rather, like self-contradictions, as false (and false by meaning, if one likes). Tolerance of the don't-cares (§ 38) is a major source of simplicity of theory; and in the present instance it counts double, sparing us as it does both the settling of categories and the respecting of them.

As for the technical motivation in set theory, alternative courses to Russell's are well known which depend on no language bans; indeed Russell's own substantive theory is easily so transcribed as to avoid that expedient.[3] All in all, I find an overwhelming case for a single unpartitioned universe of values of bound variables, and a simple grammar of predication which admits general terms all on an equal footing. Subsidiary distinctions can still be drawn as one pleases, both on methodological considerations and on considerations of natural kind; but we may think of them as distinctions special to the sciences and unreflected in the structure of our notation.

Still nothing has been said as to the make-up of the admissible vocabulary of unanalyzed general terms. But of this particular we may be sure: '$=$' will in effect be present, whether as an unanalyzed general term or in complex paraphrase, at least provided that the vocabulary of unanalyzed general terms is finite. For, write 'if Fx then Fy' and vice versa with each of the absolute general terms of the vocabulary in place of 'F'; also '(z)(if Fxz then Fyz)' and '(z) (if Fzx then Fzy)', and vice versa, with each of the dyadic relative terms in place of 'F'; and so on to '$(z)(w)$(if $Fxzw$ then $Fyzw$)' etc. The conjunction of all these formulas is coextensive with '$x = y$' if any formula constructible from the given vocabulary is; and otherwise we can without conflict adopt that conjunction as our version of identity.[4] In so doing we impose a certain identification of indiscernibles,[5] but only in a mild way.

Thus let us call two objects *absolutely* discernible (in a notation) if some open sentence with one free variable is fulfilled by only one of the two objects, and let us call them *relatively* discernible if some open sentence with two free variables is fulfilled by the two objects in only one order. What the described version of identity does is declare identical just those objects that are not relatively discernible. It does not declare identical all objects that are not absolutely discernible. For there can be objects x and y and a relative term (say 'F') such that Fxy and neither Fxx nor Fyy; and under these circumstances x and y need not be absolutely discernible, yet neither will they count as identical, since not (z)(if Fxz then Fyz).

The observation that identity thus implicitly accompanies any

---

[3] The outcome is not what Russell called typical ambiguity, but something like Zermelo's set theory. See my "Unification of universes."

[4] Cf. Hilbert and Bernays, pp. 381 f.

[5] See my *From a Logical Point of View*, pp. 70 ff., 107 ff., 117 ff., 123, for illustrative effects on the compositions of various universes of discourse.

finite vocabulary of general terms is a fitting scholium to §§ 12, 19, 20, 24, where I stressed the relevance of identity to the referential function of general terms. Also it gives a kind of justification of one's tendency to view '=', more than other general terms, as a "logical" constant.

Let us return now for a further word on our canonical grammar, which is down to predication, quantification, and truth functions. There is a technical reason for settling thus what constructions to allow even while leaving the fund of general terms open. For, various laws about logical transformations are proved by mathematical induction over sentence structure. That is, the laws are shown to hold for the simplest sentences and to hold also for sentences next more complex than sentences for which they hold, whereupon the conclusion is drawn that they hold for all. To argue thus we need to know the allowable constructions exhaustively, but only some few generally shared traits of the available simple sentences. When the constructions on sentences are limited to quantification and truth functions, one law that is easily proved by such induction is that of extensionality (§ 31).

Another reason for settling the constructions apart from the general terms is that the canonical forms are often wanted also in resolving confusions and programming deductive techniques where there is no thought of ultimate forms. Stopping short of the full course of rejections and reductions is no bar to applying the logic of quantification; we merely apply it as deep as the appropriate analysis happens to have penetrated. Surviving idioms of an extraneous sort—indicator words, intensional abstracts, or whatever—can remain buried in larger wholes which behave for the nonce as unanalyzed general terms.

But may we not still aspire to the discovery of some fundamental set of general terms on the basis of which all traits and states of everything could in principle be formulated? No; we can prove that openness is unavoidable, as long anyway as the sentences of a theory are included as objects in the universe of the theory. For, let S_1, S_2, ... be the sentences in the notation of a theory θ that have 'x' as sole free variable. Each of them is, for each object of the universe as value of 'x', true or false of that object; hence each of them, being also an object of the universe, is true or false of itself. We easily show that no general term definable in θ is true of exactly those of S_1, S_2, ... that are false of themselves. (For, if 'F' were such a term, then 'Fx' would be true of itself if and only if false of itself.[6]) Such a term can be added, irreducibly supplementing θ.

Yet it is possible in general to subject general terms to a striking formal condensation. If the assumed universe of objects includes at least a modest fund of classes—actually none of more than two members are required for the purpose—then it can be shown that any vocabulary (finite or infinite) of general terms (absolute or relative) is reducible by paraphrase to a single dyadic relative term.[7] Thus, at each stage in the supplementation of an open stock of general terms, we can encapsulate the whole stock in a single dyadic term. When new terms are added we can again do similarly; but the new single dyadic term will differ from the old in point of what pairs of objects it is true of.

Once we have said of a proposed theory that its constructions are to be predication, quantification, and the truth functions, we have settled just the logic of the theory. Questions then remain not only of its vocabulary of general terms, but also of its universe of discourse: the range of values of its variables of quantification. The very meaningfulness of quantification would seem to presuppose some notion as to what objects are to count as values of variables. Complete explicitness on this point is rendered unnecessary, however, by the fact that our quantifications usually depend for their truth upon only rather special denizens of a universe that admits of free variation in other respects. This is obvious for existential quantifications. That it is widely true also of universal quantifications becomes apparent when we reflect how commonly these take the form '$(x)($ if ... x ... then --- x ---$)$'; here only those special objects matter that fulfill the antecedent.

But if full explicitness on an aggregate universe of discourse for science is not required, still some broad normative and methodological considerations relating to the topic are in order. I shall devote the remaining chapter to them.

---

[6] This argument is in principle Cantor's. The form I have given it is reminiscent also of Grelling's paradox, and the use made of it is reminiscent of Tarski.

[7] See my "Reduction to a dyadic predicate," and references therein to Kalmár and Craig. The recent remark on identity, which depended on finitude of the number of general terms, is strengthened by this result.

CHAPTER SEVEN

Ontic Decision

§ 48. NOMINALISM AND REALISM[1]

One finds or can imagine disagreement on whether there are wombats, unicorns, angels, neutrinos, classes, points, miles, propositions. Philosophy and the special sciences afford infinite scope for disagreement on what there is. One such issue that has traditionally divided philosophers is whether there are abstract objects. *Nominalists* have held that there are not; *realists* (in a special sense of the word), or *Platonists* (as they have been called to avoid the troubles of 'realist'), have held that there are.

General definition of the term 'abstract', or 'universal', and its opposite 'concrete', or 'particular', need not detain us.[2] No matter if there are things whose status under the dichotomy remains enigmatic—"abstract particulars" such as the Equator and the North Pole, for instance; for no capital will be made of the dichotomy as such. It will suffice for now to cite classes, attributes, propositions, numbers, relations, and functions as typical abstract objects, and physical objects as concrete objects *par excellence,* and to consider the ontological issue as it touches such typical cases.

That more confidence should be felt in there being physical objects than in there being classes, attributes, and the like is not to

[1] A penultimate draft of much of Chapter VII was presented under the title "The Assuming of Objects" at the University of California, Berkeley, on May 13, 1959, as the Howison Lecture in Philosophy.

[2] Strawson's ingenious partial formulation of the distinction in "Particular and general," p. 257, presupposes a general notion of analyticity.

233

be wondered. For one thing, terms for physical objects belong to a more basic stage in our acquisition of language than abstract terms do. Concrete reference is felt as more secure than abstract reference because it is more deeply rooted in our formative past. For another thing, terms for intersubjectively observable physical things are at the focus of the most successful of unprepared communication, as between strangers in the marketplace. Surely such rapport tends to encourage confidence, however unconsciously, that one is making no mistake about his objects. Third, our terms for physical objects are commonly learned through fairly direct conditioning to stimulatory effects of the denoted objects. The empirical evidence for such physical objects, if not immediate, is at any rate less farfetched and so less suspect than that for objects whose terms are learned only in deep context. Note that whereas the first two causes for relative confidence in physical objects were causes only, this third one is a defensible reason.

Defensible but still contestable, on two counts: that it makes no case for physical objects of highly inferential sorts, and that it makes yet more of a case for sense data or sense qualities than for physical objects. Now the former of these two objections might be answered by appeal to continuity. If some physical objects are better attested than any abstract ones, then other and more conjectural physical objects are likewise more to be welcomed than abstract ones, because their acceptance along with those well-attested objects entails less loss of homogeneity, hence less loss of simplicity (*caeteris paribus*), than would acceptance of the abstract objects.

The other objection, insofar as it champions sense data in the sense of concrete sensory events (as against recurrent qualities), is an objection at most to physicalism and not to nominalism. But no matter; the likely rejoinder to the objection is independent of whether the subjective sensory objects envisaged are events or qualities. It is that no sufficient purpose is served by positing subjective sensory objects. This rejoinder would need sustaining on perhaps three counts, as follows, corresponding to three real or fancied purposes of positing such objects. (*a*) It would be argued that we cannot hope to make such objects suffice to the exclusion of physical objects. This point, urged in § 1, seems pretty widely acknowledged nowadays. (*b*) It would be argued (against Roderick Firth, for instance) that we do not need them in addition to physical objects, as means e.g. of reporting illusions and uncertainties. Thus one might claim that such purposes are adequately met by a propositional-attitude construction in which 'seems that' or the like is made to govern a subsidiary sentence about physical objects. One might claim that special objects of illusion are then no more called for than peculiar non-physical objects of quest or desire were called for in § 32. True, this argument is threatened by our high line on propositional attitudes in §§ 45 and 47; but perhaps appearance deserves no better, after all, than the *demimondain* status accorded to propositional attitudes generally. (c) It would be argued that we also do not need sensory objects to account for our knowledge or discourse of physical objects themselves. The claim here would be that the relevance of sensory stimulation to sentences about physical objects can as well (and better) be explored and explained in terms directly of the conditioning of such sentences or their parts to physical irritations of the subject's surfaces. Intervening neural activity goes on, but the claim is that nothing is clarified, nothing but excess baggage is added, by positing intermediary subjective objects of apprehension anterior to the physical objects overtly alleged in the spoken sentences themselves. The supposed function of sense-datum reports, in contributing a component of something like certainty to the formulations of empirical knowledge, may more realistically be assigned to observation sentences in the sense of § 10. These enjoy a privileged evidential position, in the directness of their correlation with non-verbal stimulation; yet they are not, typically, about sense data.

Points (a), (b), and (c) reflect my own general attitude. What perhaps basically distinguishes this from the attitude of sense-datum philosophers is that I favor treating cognition from within our own evolving theory of a cognized world, not fancying that firmer ground exists somehow outside all that. However, such cursory remarks as these on the philosophy of sense data can aspire at most to sort out issues and sketch a position; not to persuade.[3]

Let us now locate all this in its immediate context. What had been confronting us was the plea in behalf of sense data that if some physical objects are to be preferred to abstract ones on the score of comparative directness of association with sensory stimulation,

---

[3] For further representations against sense data, and bibliographical references, see Chisholm, *Perceiving*, pp. 117–125, 151–157, and Pasch, Ch. III. Further see § 54, below, and my note "On mental entities."

then sense data are to be preferred *a fortiori*. The answer proposed was predicated on utility for theory: that sense data neither suffice to the exclusion of physical objects nor are needed in addition. Now here we begin to witness the collision of two standards. Comparative directness of association with sensory stimulation was counted in favor of physical objects, but then we raised against the sense data themselves a second standard: utility for theory. Does one then have simply to weigh opposing considerations? No; on maturer reflection the picture changes. For let us recall the predicament in radical translation, which showed that a full knowledge of the stimulus meaning of an observation sentence is not sufficient for translating or even spotting a term. In our own language, by the same token, the stimulus meaning of an observation sentence in no way settles whether any part of the sentence should be distinguished as a term for sense data, or as a term for physical objects, or as a term at all. How directly the sentence and its words are associated with sensory stimulation, or how confidently the sentence may be affirmed on the strength of a given sensory stimulation, does not settle whether to posit objects of one sort or another for words of the sentence to denote in the capacity of terms.

We may be perceived to have posited the objects only when we have brought the contemplated terms into suitable interplay with the whole distinctively objectificatory apparatus of our language: articles and pronouns and the idioms of identity, plurality, and predication, or, in canonical notation, quantification. Even a superficially termlike occurrence is no proof of termhood, failing systematic interplay with the key idioms generally. Thus we habitually say 'for the sake of', with 'sake' seemingly in term position, and never thereby convict ourselves of positing any such objects as sakes, for we do not bring the rest of the apparatus to bear: we never use 'sake' as antecedent of 'it', nor do we predicate 'sake' of anything. 'Sake' figures in effect as an invariable fragment of a preposition 'for the sake of', or 'for 's sake'.

Let a word, therefore, have occurred as a fragment of ever so many empirically well-attested sentential wholes; even as a rather termlike fragment, by superficial appearances. Still, the question whether to treat it as a term is the question whether to give it general access to positions appropriate to general terms, or perhaps to singular terms, subject to the usual laws of such contexts. Whether to do so may reasonably be decided by considerations of systematic efficacy, utility for theory.

But if nominalism and realism are to be adjudicated on such grounds, nominalism's claims dwindle. The reason for admitting numbers as objects is precisely their efficacy in organizing and expediting the sciences. The reason for admitting classes is much the same. Examples have been noted (§ 43) of the access of power that comes with classes. A further example is Frege's celebrated definition of 'x is ancestor of y':

(z)(if all parents of members of z belong to z and $y \in z$ then $x \in z$).

Simplicity ensues, since we are spared separate, piecemeal provision for the things that classes provide. The efficacy of classes becomes yet more impressive when we find that they can be made to serve the purposes also of a great lot of further abstract objects of undeniable utility: relations, functions, numbers themselves (§§ 53–55).

We gain a perhaps more fundamental insight into the unifying force of the class concept when we observe how classes help us get by with quantifiers as the sole variable-binding operators. Thus think of '$\ldots z \ldots$' as some open sentence. *Concretion* [4] is the transformation that carries '$x \in \hat{z}(\ldots z \ldots)$' into '$\ldots x \ldots$'. Now let '$\Phi_x$' represent some variable-binding operator that builds sentences from sentences. If we suppose merely that 'Φ_x' is such that the substitutivity of concretion holds under it, we can drop 'Φ_x' in favor of a general term 'G'. For, take 'G' as true of just the classes y such that $\Phi_x(x \in y)$; then '$\Phi_x(\ldots x \ldots)$' can be rendered '$G\,\hat{x}(\ldots x \ldots)$'. Finally the operator of class abstraction in '$G\,\hat{x}(\ldots x \ldots)$' can be reduced to description, and description to quantifiers. (Cf. §§ 34, 38. But see also § 55.)

Closeness of association with stimulation has stood up poorly as an argument for giving physical objects preferential status. But something could still perhaps be salvaged from it. For, grant that the question whether to dignify given words as terms is a question whether to admit them freely to all term positions. Then instead of what was said earlier for physical objects, viz. that terms for them are fairly directly associated with sensory stimulation, perhaps we could say this: sentences fairly directly associated with sensory

---

[4] So called in my dissertation, Harvard, 1932, and in *A System of Logistic*.

stimulation exhibit terms for physical objects in all sorts of term positions, not just in rather special positions. It seems plausible that common terms for physical objects come out better by such a standard than abstract terms do.[5] But I shall not try to establish the point.

The case that emerged meanwhile for classes rested on systematic efficacy. Now it is certainly a case against nominalism's negative claims, but still it is no case against a preferential status for physical objects. In a contest for sheer systematic utility to science, the notion of physical object still leads the field.[6] On this score alone, therefore, one might still put a premium on explanations that appeal to physical objects and not to abstract ones, even if abstract objects be grudgingly admitted too for their efficacy elsewhere in the theory.

Nor let us scorn those two earlier causes for confidence in physical objects—the causes that were not recognized as reasons. One was that terms for such objects are so basic to our language; the other was that they are at the focus of such successful communication. To show why certain terms are felt as comfortable termini of explanation is not, after all, to render them otherwise.

§ 49. FALSE PREDILECTIONS. ONTIC COMMITMENT

We have considered the predilection for concrete objects and the case, despite such predilection, for admitting abstract objects. For symmetry let us now ponder the positive predilection for abstract objects; for it is not unknown.

An apparent reason for favoring physical objects was proximity to stimulation. This seemed all the more reason for favoring sensory objects of some sort, even sense qualities. Then, if attributes generally are held to be broadly analogous to sense qualities (as are the inferential particles of physics to common-sense bodies), the same appeal to continuity can be made in support of attributes as was made in support of the particles (§ 48). Here, I think, is one cause of the predilection that is sometimes manifested for attributes.

Not that I accept the line of reasoning. That argument for

[5] Cf. Alston, note 7.
[6] Cf. Strawson, *Individuals*, pp. 38–58.

sensory objects is offset, as urged in § 48, if we hold that such objects are neither adequate in lieu of physical objects nor helpful in addition to them.   Moreover, to project non-sensory attributes purely on the analogy of sense qualities, hence as recurrent characters somehow of a subjective show within the mind, betrays surely a cavalier attitude toward psychological processes and a lack of curiosity about the mechanisms of behavior.

Such is one likely cause of a predilection for attributes (apart from motives of systematic utility).   There is also a second.   Some of us are carried away by the object-directed pattern of our thinking, to the point of seeking the gist of every sentence in things it is about.   When a general term occurs predicatively alongside a name, the sentence thus formed will be seen by such a person as "about" not just the named object, but the named object and an attribute symbolized by the general term.[1]   He will feel therefore that any general term for physical objects, such as 'round' or 'dog', simultaneously symbolizes an attribute.   But then, he will reason, any argument for physical objects from the utility of such terms must, *ipso facto*, support attributes as well *and even better;* for the terms neatly symbolize one precise attribute apiece, while standing in no such pat correspondence to the indefinitely numerous physical objects that they purport to be true of.   (Much the same argument can be used also to support classes instead of attributes, since a general term can as well be said to symbolize its extension as its intension if we appropriately shade the sense of 'symbolize'.)

In this reasoning the mistake is not just the initial one of overdoing the object matter.   There is a subsequent fallacy in the idea that the utility of a word counts, of itself, in favor of all associated objects.   A word can prove useful in such positions as to favor the assumption of objects for it to be true of, without thereby favoring the assumption of objects related to it in other ways, e.g., as extension or intension.   Let us reflect on the mechanism.

Typical of the positions proper to general terms are the postarticular and the predicative.   The one position is contained in

---

[1] Thus for Locke general terms were names of general ideas (Bk. II, Ch. XI, paragraph 9).   Again Bergmann: "Who admits a single primitive predicate admits properties among the building stones of his world" ("Two types of linguistic philosophy," p. 430).   And see Baylis, where he argues in effect that to understand a general term is to grasp its meaning, and hence that there are such meanings, or attributes.   The fallacy of subtraction noted at the beginning of § 43, above, has doubtless encouraged the tendency to overdo 'about'.

singular terms; the other accompanies singular terms (which can be variables). These singular terms in turn are marked as singular terms by their occurrences as subjects of other predicatively occurring general terms, notably '=', and in variable-binding operators. And where do objects come in? The purported objects of whatever sort, concrete or abstract, are just what the singular terms in their several ways name, refer to, take as values.[2] They are what count as cases when, quantifying, we say that everything, or something, is thus and so. So when on grounds of systematic efficacy we decide to allow a word—'glint', say, to take a debatable case—full currency as general term, the effect is only that the glints, not glinthood or glintkind, are made to count as objects.

Actually, the effect is not even quite that much; for a general term in good standing can still, like 'unicorn', be true of nothing. But what typically happens is the following. Already while we debate whether our sentences may best be so analyzed and extended as to count 'glint' a full-fledged general term, we have before us certain incompletely analyzed but useful truths of theory or observation that contain the word; and then our taking 'glint' as a general term settles the analysis of these sentences in such a way that some of them come to affirm or imply '$(\exists x)(x$ is a glint)'.

So if 'round' and 'dog' have acquitted themselves to the glory of physical objects, they have done so as general terms true of physical objects and not as singular terms naming attributes or classes. The case for attributes or classes remains open as a separate question, however analogous. The general terms relevant to it are not 'round', 'dog', and the like, but 'trait', 'species', and the like; and the relevant singular terms are not such as 'Sputnik I' and 'Fido', but such as 'roundness', 'caninity', 'dogkind'.

The offenders who have called forth the past few pages are those who, through a confusion that I have just now tried to clear up, take it for granted that everyone in his use of general terms talks directly of attributes (or classes), *ipso facto* and willy nilly. The offenders are not those who make a considered argument for the existence of an attribute or class for every general term. Such an argument, coming under the head of what was tolerantly viewed in § 48, would be predicated on the systematic efficacy of admitting abstract general and perhaps abstract singular terms and using

[2] See § 40, note 1.

them in such a way as to bring attributes or classes into the universe of discourse as values, in effect, of the variables of quantification.   The merits of such a course are considered further in §§ 43 and 55.

The offenders may be depended upon to dismiss the distinction between concrete general terms like 'round' and abstract singular terms like 'roundness' as an insignificant quirk of grammar.   Now let me not seem to be making capital of any pedantic distinction in word forms.   This distinction is only a convenient and dispensable way of marking an underlying difference that can be uncovered anyway in a distinction of functions, as lately outlined.   But I venture to say that a failure to appreciate the underlying difference correlates nicely with the dismissal of the verbal distinction.

Along with the offenders last touched on there are others who, likewise making light of the distinction between abstract singular and concrete general terms, decide *against* abstract objects.   Apparently these thinkers have appreciated, for whatever reasons, that concrete general terms carry no commitment to attributes or classes, and then have concluded the same for the corresponding abstract singular terms, by dint of drawing no distinction.   This line of thought derives wishful vigor from a distaste for abstract objects coupled with a taste for their systematic efficacy.   The motivation has proved sufficient to induce remarkable extremes.   We find philosophers allowing themselves not only abstract terms but even pretty unmistakable quantifications over abstract objects ("There are concepts with which...," "...some of which propositions...," " ... there is something that he doubts or believes"), and still blandly disavowing, within the paragraph, any claim that there are such objects.[3]

Pressed, they may explain that abstract objects do not exist the way physical ones do.   The difference is not, they say, just a difference in two sorts of objects, one in space-time and one not, but a difference in two senses of 'there are'; so that, in the sense in which there are concrete objects, there are no abstract ones.   But then there remain two difficulties, a little one and a big one.   The little one is that the philosopher who would repudiate abstract objects seems to be left saying that there are such after all, in the sense of

[3] See Church, "Ontological commitment," for discussion of illustrative texts from Ayer and Ryle.

'there are' appropriate to them. The big one is that the distinction between there being one sense of 'there are' for concrete objects and another for abstract ones, and there being just one sense of 'there are' for both, makes no sense.[4]

Such philosophical double talk, which would repudiate an ontology while enjoying its benefits, thrives on vagaries of ordinary language. The trouble is that at best there is no simple correlation between the outward forms of ordinary affirmations and the existences implied. Thus, granted that the construction exemplified by 'Agnes has fleas' can very often be accorded the forthrightly existential sense intended by '$(\exists x)(Fx$ and $Gx)$', there remain abundant cases like 'Tabby eats mice' (§ 28) and 'Ernest hunts lions' (§ 32) that cannot. Reflective persons unswayed by wishful thinking can themselves now and again have cause to wonder what, if anything, they are talking about.

In our canonical notation of quantification, then, we find the restoration of law and order. Insofar as we adhere to this notation, the objects we are to be understood to admit are precisely the objects which we reckon to the universe of values over which the bound variables of quantification are to be considered to range. Such is simply the intended sense of the quantifiers '(x)' and '$(\exists x)$': 'every object x is such that', 'there is an object x such that'. The quantifiers are encapsulations of these specially selected, unequivocally referential idioms of ordinary language. To paraphrase a sentence into the canonical notation of quantification is, first and foremost, to make its ontic content explicit, quantification being a device for talking in general of objects.

The moot or controversial part of the question of the ontic import of a sentence may of course survive in a new guise, as the question how to paraphrase the sentence into canonical notation. But the change of guise conveniently shifts the burden of claims and disavowals. Futile caviling over ontic implications gives way to an invitation to reformulate one's point in canonical notation. We cannot paraphrase our opponent's sentences into canonical notation for him and convict him of the consequences, for there is no synonymy; rather we must ask him what canonical sentences he is pre-

---

[4] Cf. § 27. But the familiar vague notion that the assumption of abstract entities is somehow a purely formal expedient, as against the more factual character of the assumption of physical objects, may still not be wholly beyond making sense of; see Putnam, "Mathematics and the existence of abstract entities."

pared to offer, consonantly with his own inadequately expressed purposes. If he declines to play this game, the argument terminates. To decline to explain oneself in terms of quantification, or in terms of those special idioms of ordinary language by which quantification is directly explained, is simply to decline to disclose one's referential intent. We saw in our consideration of radical translation that an alien language may well fail to share, by any universal standard, the object-positing pattern of our own; and now our supposititious opponent is simply standing, however legalistically, on his alien rights. We remain free as always to project analytical hypotheses (§§ 15 f.) and translate his sentences into canonical notation as seems most reasonable; but he is no more bound by our conclusions than the native by the field linguist's.[5]

§ 50. ENTIA NON GRATA

The resort to canonical notation as an aid to clarifying ontic commitments is of limited polemical power, as just now explained. But it does help us who are agreeable to the canonical forms to judge what we care to consider there to be. We can face the question squarely as a question what to admit to the universe of values of our variables of quantification.

Economy is a consideration, but economy of theory and not just

[5] For more on quantification as avenue of ontic commitment see my *From a Logical Point of View*, Essays 1 and 6. On pp. 19 and 103 thereof it is stressed that I look to variables and quantification for evidence as to what a theory says that there is, not for evidence as to what there is; but the point can be missed, as by Henderson, pp. 279 f. — A more accountable misapprehension is that I am a nominalist. I must correct it; my best efforts to write clearly about reference, referential position, and ontic commitment will fail of communication to readers who, like Mates ("Synonymity," p. 213) and Braithwaite (review), endeavor in all good will to reconcile my words with a supposed nominalist doctrine. In all books and most papers I have appealed to classes and recognized them as abstract objects. I have indeed inveighed against making and imputing platonistic assumptions gratuitously, but equally against obscuring them. Where I have speculated on what can be got from a nominalistic basis, I have stressed the difficulties and limitations. True, my 1947 paper with Goodman opened on a nominalist declaration; readers cannot be blamed. For consistency with my general attitude early and late, that sentence needs demotion to the status of a mere statement of conditions for the construction in hand; cf. *From a Logical Point of View*, top of p. 174.

of objects. Also some objects may be preferable to others in the way suggested for physical objects late in § 48: representative sentences in which they are treated as objects may be relatively closely associated with sensory stimulation.

We have looked into the benefits of admitting physical objects and classes (§ 48), though there will be more to say of classes (§ 55). We considered also the claims and the difficulties of attributes and propositions (§§ 42 f.), and the weakness of the case for sense data (§§ 1, 48). At the extreme, finally, are the sakes and behalves. No one wants these, but the form of the argument for their exclusion is instructive. It is that 'sake' and 'behalf' have their uses only in the clichés 'for the sake of' and 'in behalf of' and their variants; hence these clichés can be left unanalyzed as simple prepositions. (From the point of view of canonical notation, prepositions in turn ordinarily get bundled off into relative terms; cf. § 22.)

Units of measure turn out somewhat like sakes and behalves. 'Mile', 'minute', 'degree Fahrenheit', and the like resemble 'sake' and 'behalf' in being *defective* nouns: they are normally used only in a limited selection of the usual term positions. Their defectiveness, though less extreme than that of 'sake' and 'behalf', is easily exposed in absurd interrogation. Are miles alike? If so, how can they count as many? And if they cannot, what of the two hundred between Boston and New York?

Questions about identity of attributes or of propositions are in their turn less absurd, on the face of them, than these about identity of miles. Still the lack of a standard of identity for attributes and propositions can be viewed similarly, as a case of defectiveness on the part of 'attribute' and 'proposition'. Philosophers undertook, however unsuccessfully, to supply this defect by devising a standard of identity, because they were persuaded of the advantages, in systematic utility or whatever, of taking 'attribute' and 'proposition' as full-fledged terms and so admitting attributes and propositions to the universe of discourse. This line is debatable on its specific merits, and we have debated it. The case of 'mile', 'degree Fahrenheit', and the like is clearer: no purpose is served by making units of measure accessible to variables of quantification. We can adequately accommodate these nouns as parts of relative terms 'length in miles', 'temperature in degrees Fahrenheit'.[1]

[1] So Carnap, *Physikalische Begriffsbildung.*

Just as the relative term 'author' is true of this and that man relative to this and that book, so 'length in miles' is to be understood as true of this and that number relative to this and that body or region. Thus instead of 'length of Manhattan = 11 miles' we would now say 'length-in-miles of Manhattan = 11' (form 'F of $b = a$') or '11 is length-in-miles-of Manhattan' (form 'Fab').

This leaves us recognizing numbers as objects. For the numeral '11' figures here as a singular term, on a par with 'Manhattan'. If we were to push forward to minimum canonical notation by eliminating singular terms as in Chapter V we would find our quantifiers calling for the number and the island unmistakably enough:

$$(\exists x)(\exists y)(x \text{ is-11 and } y \text{ is-Manhattan and } x \text{ is-length-in-miles-of } y).$$

And indeed we may expect numbers to be very much wanted, not only for this example, as values of our variables; they are nearly as useful as classes.

In *possible* concrete objects, unactualized possibles, we have another category of doubtful objects whose doubtfulness can be laid to defective nouns, with as good reason at least as in the case of attributes and propositions. For here again, and more glaringly than in the case of intensions, there is perplexity over identity; cf. § 8. Even when a position is specified, as in 'the possible new church on that corner', 'the possible hotel on that corner', the identity of position does not make the possible objects identical. Happily we can cut through all this, sometimes by retreating to universals as in § 8, and more usually by just absorbing the 'possible' of 'possible object' appropriately into the context and so not treating 'possible object' as a term. A sentence about possible churches can usually be paraphrased satisfactorily enough into a sentence that treats of churches and is governed, as a whole, by a modal operator of possibility. One may still ask what kind of modality is wanted, how to make sense of it, and how to cope with other problems that the modalities of one or another sort have been known to raise; but talk of possible objects would have been no better off with respect to such questions.

The notion of possible objects has been encouraged by two philosophical quandaries. One of them is raised by the verbs 'hunting', 'wanting', and the like, which cannot in general be looked upon as relating the agent to actual objects (cf. §§ 28, 32). Possible lions, possible unicorns, possible sloops suggest themselves as surrogate objects for such activities. But these matters can be handled more illuminatingly by paraphrase, as seen, into the idioms of propositional attitude. One is left with the problems of propositional attitude, but those, unlike the vagaries of unactualized possibles, are with us anyway.

The other quandary is raised by terms in want of objects: what are we talking about when we say there are no unicorns, or that there is no such thing as Pegasus? Partly this quandary comes of being carried away by the object-directed pattern of our thinking— if not to the extreme talked of in § 49, at least to the point of trying to see every sentence as "about" certain objects. Actually 'unicorn' and 'Pegasus' can be perfectly good terms, well understood in that their contexts are well enough linked to sensory stimulation or to intervening theory, without there being unicorns or Pegasus. Mainly it is on singular terms like 'Pegasus' that the quandary has centered rather than general ones like 'unicorn'; for it is there that under ordinary usage the truth-value gaps set in (§ 37), in a philosophically uncomfortable way. However, the canonical expedient of reparsing singular terms regularizes these matters and so ends, one may hope, any temptation to venture out on the morass of unactualized possibles.[2]

The notions of possible object and proposition are two that were encouraged by philosophical quandaries. A third is that of fact. The word 'fact' is commonplace enough, but where the philosophical motivation enters is in choosing to admit facts as objects rather than fob the word off with the lower-grade sort of treatment accorded 'sake' and 'mile'.

Part of what encouraged admission of propositions was a wish for eternal truth-value vehicles independent of particular languages (§ 40). Part of what encourages admission of facts is perhaps a wish to defer the question what makes a sentence or proposition true: those are true that state facts. Another force that has encouraged both acceptances is, again, the tendency to be carried away by object-directed thinking: a tendency, in this case, to liken sentences to names and then posit objects for them to name. It is perhaps where this force is the dominant one that we encounter readiness, as we occasionally do, to identify facts with propositions (viz., with some or all of the true ones).

[2] See Russell, "On denoting".

An additional connotation that often invests the word 'fact', both in philosophy and in lay usage, is that of unvarnished objectivity plus a certain accessibility to observation. In philosophical usage this connotation is sometimes adopted and widened in such wise that facts come to be posited corresponding to all the "synthetic" truths and withheld only from the "analytic" ones. So here that same analytic-synthetic dichotomy intrudes which we have found so dubious (§ 14); and it intrudes in a most implausibly absolute guise, independent apparently of all choice of language. The disarmingly commonplace ring of the word 'fact' comes even to lend the dichotomy a spurious air of intelligibility: the analytic sentences (or propositions) are the true ones that lack factual content.

There is a tendency—not among those who take facts as propositions—to think of facts as concrete. This is fostered by the commonplace ring of the word and the hint of bruteness, and is of a piece, for that matter, with the basic conception that it is facts that make sentences true. Yet what can they be, and be concrete? The sentences 'Fifth Avenue is six miles long' and 'Fifth Avenue is a hundred feet wide', if we suppose them true, presumably state different facts; yet the only concrete or at any rate physical object involved is Fifth Avenue. I resolved (§ 48) not to cavil over 'concrete', but I suspect that the sense of 'concrete' in which facts are concrete is not one that need endear them to us.

Facts, moreover, are in the same difficulty over a standard of identity as propositions were seen to be. And surely they cannot be seriously supposed to help us explain truth. Our two sentences last quoted are true because of Fifth Avenue, because it is a hundred feet wide and six miles long, because it was planned and made that way, and because of the way we use our words; only indirection results from positing facts, in the image of sentences, as intermediaries. Probably no such temptation would arise if the word were not already there performing an overlapping though unphilosophical function for ordinary discourse.

In ordinary usage 'fact' often occurs where we could without loss say 'true sentence' or (if it is our way) 'true proposition'. But its main utility seems to be rather as a reinforcement of the flimsy 'that' of propositional abstraction (§ 34). It is wanted there merely because of the idiomatic unnaturalness, in many substantival positions, of a pure 'that'-clause. (Yet it is limited in this syntactical service to 'that'-clauses that are taken to be true; for 'fact' persists in imputing truth.)   It has a further use still in abbreviated cross-reference: we often manage to avoid repeating a long previous affirmation by saying 'that fact'.   Now so far as these uses go there is no call to posit facts, certainly not over and above propositions, nor any difficulty in absorbing or paraphrasing away the word. Nor have the peculiarly philosophical appeals to fact impressed us.

§ 51.   LIMIT MYTHS

We were able to abjure sakes, measures, unactualized possibles, and facts without a pang, having satisfied ourselves that to admit them would serve no good purpose.   Examples are not far to seek, on the other hand, of supposed objects that are absurd or troublesome and yet such that their banishment from the domain of values of our variables threatens to impair our apparatus.   A classic example of such conflict and its resolution is afforded by the *infinitesimal*.

The notion of the infinitesimal emerged from the question how to deal with rates, e.g. instantaneous velocities.   What does it mean to say of a particle that at a momentary time t its velocity is ten feet a second?   Not precisely that during some actual period of s seconds (say a hundredth of a second), spanning t, the particle traverses the appropriate distance of $10s$ feet (a tenth of a foot); for the velocity may change during that and every poriod.   Newton and Leibnitz answered, in their differential calculus, by positing infinitesimals: quantities infinitely close to zero and yet, absurdly enough, distinct from one another.   A particle traveling ten feet a second at time t was said to traverse a certain infinitesimal distance d at time t, and a particle traveling twenty feet a second at time t was said to traverse a different infinitesimal distance $2d$ at time t, the elapsed time in both cases being zero.   Though the idea of infinitesimals was absurd, the differential calculus, in which infinitesimals were reckoned as values of the variables, gave true and valuable results.

The conflict was resolved by Weierstrass, who showed by his theory of limits how the sentences of the differential calculus could be systematically reconstrued so as to draw only on proper numbers as values of the variables, without impairing the utility of the calculus.   On his analysis, to say that the particle is traveling ten feet a second at t is to say that by narrowing the time span s around t you can get the distance as close to $10s$ as you like; i.e.,

(x)(if $x > 0$ then $(\exists s)$(distance in feet traversed during s seconds around t is between $10s - x$ and $10s + x$)).

A case with certain parallels to that of the infinitesimals is presented by the *ideal objects* that seem to be talked of in expositions of mechanics: mass points, frictionless surfaces, isolated systems. Just as infinitesimal numbers were contrary to arithmetic, so a point with mass, a surface without friction, or a system immune to outside forces would be contrary to physical theory. At the same time the elementary laws of mechanics are regularly formulated in terms of these ideal objects, as was once the differential calculus in terms of infinitesimals.

The appeal to ideal objects in mechanics occurs regularly through universal conditionals: thus (x)(if x is a mass point then ...). The non-existence of ideal objects consequently does not falsify mechanics; it leaves such sentences vacuously true for lack of counter-instances. Thus mechanics may seem better off with respect to ideal objects than the differential calculus had once been with respect to the infinitesimals. But the contrast is superficial. What should worry us about the ideal objects is the following. If by physical laws there are no such objects, and hence by physical laws all universal conditionals concerning them are trivially true, then how is it that some of these conditionals, rather than others, still evidently impart useful scientific theory?

This quandary over ideal objects, like that over infinitesimals, has its solution in the theory of limits. When one asserts that mass points behave thus and so, he can be understood as saying roughly this: that particles of given mass behave the more nearly thus and so the smaller their volumes. When one speaks of an isolated system of particles as behaving thus and so, he can be understood as saying that a system of particles behaves the more nearly thus and so the smaller the proportion of energy transferred from or to the outside world. This, broadly speaking, is how one's succinct talk of ideal objects would presumably be paraphrased when challenged.

The doctrine of ideal objects in physics is "symbolic," as this word is used by literary critics, psychoanalysts, and philosophers of religion. It is a deliberate myth, useful for the vividness, beauty, and substantial correctness with which it portrays certain aspects of nature even while, on a literal reading, it falsifies nature in other respects. It is useful also for the simplicity that it brings to certain computations. Now simplicity, in a theory that squares with observation sentences so far as its contacts with them go, is the best evidence of truth we can ask; no better can be claimed for the doctrines of molecules and electrons. What makes for the mythicalness of the doctrine of ideal objects, as against the literal truth (by today's lights) of the doctrines of molecules and electrons, is that the former works its simplifications in a limited domain of statements at the cost of more seriously complicating a more inclusive domain. When we paraphrase our talk of ideal objects in the Weierstrassian spirit as sketched above, we are merely switching from a theory that is conveniently simple in a short view and complex in a long view to a theory of opposite character. Since the latter, if either, is the one to count as true, the former gets the inferior rating of convenient myth, purely symbolic of that ulterior truth. Definition, meanwhile, or rule of paraphrase, enables us to enjoy the best of both worlds. (Cf. § 39.)

It is once more relevant to remind ourselves that paraphrase makes no synonymy claim. It only coordinates the uses one makes of diverse theories for diverse advantages. Hold, if you will, that the myth of ideal objects is merely convenient and not quite true, and that the paraphrase is what is true; or hold, if you will, that the myth of ideal objects is strictly true by virtue of having the paraphrase as its true meaning. Either of these philosophies is acceptable as long as both are recognized as loose formulations of one and the same situation; that they seem opposed is due to fancying, in 'true meaning', a more than impressionistic manner of speaking.

Much the same relationship that we have been observing between the doctrine of ideal objects and full-dress physical theory may be said also nowadays to obtain between Newtonian physics and relativity theory. Being simpler, Newton's laws are conveniently retained for use where the departures from strict truth thus entailed are slight enough not to obstruct one's purposes. Thus, in the same sense in which we called the doctrine of ideal objects a convenient myth, symbolic of truths other than its manifest content, we might equally call Newtonian physics a convenient myth, symbolic of that ulterior truth (by today's lights) which is relativity theory. The paraphrase of myth into literally accepted theory would proceed, here also, along Weierstrassian lines: each Newtonian sentence, to the effect that bodies behave thus and so, would be treated as saying that bodies behave the more nearly thus and so the smaller their relative velocities.

Such reflections partake of what churchmen call higher criticism. They are directed at reconciling some limitedly useful lesser theory with a more sweeping theory which on a literal-minded reading it contradicts: the infinitesimal calculus with the classical mathematics of number, the mechanics of ideal objects with general physics, and Newton's physics with Einstein's. But meanwhile let us keep in mind also that knowledge normally develops in a multiplicity of theories, each with its limited utility and each, unless it harbors more danger than utility, with its internal consistency.[1] These theories overlap very considerably, in their so-called logical laws and in much else, but that they add up to an integrated and consistent whole is only a worthy ideal and happily not a prerequisite of scientific progress. The continuing utility of the mechanics of ideal objects and of Newtonian mechanics is ample reason for treasuring and teaching these theories, whatever their conflicts with more august ones; and the same was true of the infinitesimal calculus before Weierstrass. This said, let the reconciliations proceed; each such step advances our understanding of the world.

§ 52. GEOMETRICAL OBJECTS

Traditionally geometry was the theory of relative position. For Poincaré and others influenced by the pluralism of non-Euclidean geometries, the geometries were a family rather of uninterpreted theory-forms, called geometries only because of structural resemblances to Euclid's original theory of position. The question of the nature of the objects of geometries in the latter sense need not detain us, secured as it is against an answer. But meanwhile geometry also in something like the traditional sense continues as a handmaiden, by whatever name, of natural science. Its objects would appear to be points, curves, surfaces, and solids, conceived as portions of a real space that bathes and permeates the physical world. They are objects which we are tempted to admit on a par with physical objects as values of our variables of quantification, as

[1] See Conant, pp. 98 ff.

when we say that Boston, Buffalo, and Detroit are cut by a great circle of the earth.

The objects of geometry can for some purposes be adequately explained away in the manner already contemplated for the ideal objects of mechanics; for we may think of points, curves, and geometrical surfaces as ideally small particles, ideally slender wires, and ideally thin sheets. This treatment conforms well enough to the pure universal statements of geometry—statements to the effect merely that any geometrical objects interrelated in such and such ways are interrelated in such and such further ways. But it ill fits the existential statements of geometry, which require there to be points, curves, surfaces, and solids everywhere.

May we then hold to the naïve view? Here we have a dualistic theory of spatiotemporal reality, whose two sorts of objects, physical and geometrical, interpenetrate without conflict. There is no conflict simply because the physical laws are not extended to the geometrical objects.

But if such a plan is tolerable here, why could we not equally in § 51 have admitted the ideal objects of mechanics in a single spatiotemporal universe along with the full-fledged physical objects, simply exempting them from some of the laws? Is it just that these two categories would be intuitively too much alike to make the separation of laws seem natural? No. There is a more substantial reason why mass points and the like, as objects supplementary to the full-fledged bodies, should be less welcome than geometrical objects. No sense has been made of their date and location. Evidently, to judge by what is said of them, mass points and such ideal objects are supposed to be in space-time of some sort, ours or another; but just where is each? And, if we waive location, there supervenes a perplexity of identity: when do mass points (or frictionless surfaces, etc.) count as one and when as two? Talk of ideal objects in mechanics, significantly enough, tends not to turn on such questions. There is in this circumstance strong reason to define the ideal objects away—say along the Weierstrassian lines of § 51—rather than to keep them and try to settle the perplexities of position or identity by multiplying artificialities. On the other hand geometrical objects raise no such evident problems of position or identity; they are positions outright.

But are we prepared to admit absolute positions, and therewith an absolute distinction between rest and motion? Is not motion relative rather, so that what would count from one point of view as an identical position twice over would count from another point of view as two distinct positions? No doubt. However, we can accommodate this relativistic scruple simply by adding a dimension and speaking of positions not in space but in space-time. Distinct point-instants are distinct absolutely, regardless of the relative movement of the point of view.

If motion is relative, then obviously the question whether a given spatiotemporal region (or aggregate of point-instants) is constant in shape through time, or whether its internal distances readjust through time, will depend on the relative movement of the point of view; and so will the question whether its shape at a time is spherical or elongated. But this is to say only that shape-at-a-time is relative to frames of reference; the geometrical objects whose shapes are concerned remain absolute aggregates of point-instants, however shaped and however specified.

Whether it was better to stay within the three spatial dimensions for our geometrical objects, or better to look beyond space into space-time for them, turned on whether it was wise to assume an absolute distinction between rest and motion. This question, in turn, is the question what theory will best systematize the data of physics. Thus we may fairly say that the question of the nature of the geometrical objects is, like the question of the nature of the elementary particles of physics, a question of physical theory. Granted, laboratory data only incline and do not constrain us in our geometrizing; but likewise they only incline and do not constrain us in our invention of a physical theory. Let fashion and terminology not mislead us into viewing geometry too differently from physics.

And the fact is that Einstein's physical theorizing included geometrical decisions also beyond the relativity of motion. Considerations of overall theoretical simplicity of physical theory induced him to settle for a non-Euclidean form of geometry, simpler though the Euclidean is when considered apart. Accepting then this four-dimensional non-Euclidean geometry along with relativity physics as the literal truth (by today's lights), we may view Euclidean geometry on a par with Newtonian physics (cf. § 51) as a convenient myth, simpler for some purposes but symbolic of that ulterior truth. The geometrical objects of Euclidean geometry then take on, relative to the "real" geometrical objects of the non-Euclidean "true" geometry of ideal objects, the status of manners of speaking, limit myths, explicable in principle by paraphrasing our sentences along Weierstrassian lines.

There remain also other geometries, other in various ways. There are the more abstract ones, culminating in topology, which treat of the geometrical objects in decreasingly specific detail. These geometries raise no further ontic problem, for their objects can be taken to be our same old geometrical objects; we can look upon these geometries as merely saying less about them.

And there remain geometries that are not just more abstract than, but actually contrary to, our "true" geometry of relativity physics. Shall we rate these as simply false? or seek ways of reconstruing their words that would make them true after all, whether of our same old geometrical objects or of something else? We need do none of this; an uninterpreted theory-form can be worthy of study for its structure without its talking about anything. When it is brought into connection with the quantifiers of a broader scientific context in such a way as to purport to talk unfeignedly of objects of some sort, then is time enough to wonder what the objects are.

Up to now I have defended geometrical objects not because I think it is best to admit them as part of the furniture of our universe, but only in order to exhibit relevant considerations. Meanwhile there remains, obviously, an objection to geometrical objects, on the score of economy of objects. Let us now consider how we may manage without them.

The only sentences we need try to paraphrase, for elimination of reference to geometrical objects, are those that cannot be facilely dismissed as gibberish of an uninterpreted calculus: those that contribute, rather, like sentences about the Equator or the one about Boston, Buffalo, and Detroit, to discourse about the real world outside geometry. Now sentences about the Equator can all probably be satisfactorily paraphrased into forms in which 'Equator' has the immediate context 'nearer the Equator than'; and these four words can be treated as a simple relative term or even defined away in terms of centrifugal force or mean solar elevation. The more serious cases are sentences which, like that about Boston, Buffalo, and Detroit, ostensibly call for a geometrical object as value of a variable of quantification.

But the reference to geometrical objects in such cases is an auxiliary merely to what we want to say about the movements and spatiotemporal relations of bodies; and we can hope to by-pass the geometrical objects by falling back on a relative term of distance (cf. § 50), or spatiotemporal interval, conceived as relating physical bodies and numbers. This course involves accepting numbers as objects along with bodies, but spares us assuming geometrical objects in addition. The elements are thus simplified. The practical convenience of geometrical objects can still be preserved by reinstating definitionally (cf. § 39) whatever idioms we analyze away.

The elimination can be systematized along the lines of analytical geometry. In its minimum essentials the idea is as follows, for our four-dimensional space-time. We pick five particle-events a, b, c, d, e, not quite at random. (The requirement is merely that they mark the vertices of a full-fledged four-dimensional "hypersolid," rather than all lying in a plane or a three-dimensional solid.) We can think of the five as given by proper names, or, what comes to the same (cf. § 37), by general terms true uniquely of each. Now every point (or point-instant) in space-time is uniquely determined once we specify its "distance" (or interval: the analogue of distance in four-dimensional space-time) from each of the five. The position of a body in space-time is therefore determined by the distance of its various extremes from each of the five reference particle-events. The attribution of (four-dimensional) shapes to bodies can be paraphrased as attribution of appropriate arithmetical conditions to the classes of ordered quintuples of numbers that fix the bodies' boundaries. Correspondingly for the attribution of collinearity or other geometrical relations.

We could take the further step, if we wish, of nominally restituting geometrical objects by *identifying* points (actually point-instants) with the appropriate ordered quintuples of numbers, and identifying the rest of the geometrical objects with the classes of their constituent points in that sense. Whether to speak of geometrical objects as by-passed or as reconstrued is a matter of indifference.

The five-point type of coordinate system thus simply described would be prohibitively awkward in practice. The least of its inelegances is that it ill exploits its numerical resources. For instance, distances from a and b that do not accord with the distance from a to b would never be wanted in the same quintuple of numbers. The compatible distances from the five points make up a quite special and not quickly recognizable class of quintuples. The more strictly Cartesian scheme, of fixing each point by its distance from each of various mutually perpendicular planes, is far superior: it gets by with quadruples of numbers instead of quintuples, it wastes no quadruples, and, above all, it correlates the important geometrical conditions with far simpler arithmetical conditions than our five-point method would do. Certainly one would want to set up a system of Cartesian coordinates. But its construction, given as starting point only a distance measure and selected reference particles, is a long story. The five-point method is a more readily describable one to the same theoretical effect, and suffices for conveying some concrete sense of what the elimination of geometrical objects means.

To the same end it may be worth while now to turn more specific still: to cut through the whole apparatus of systematic reference points and quadruples or quintuples of real numbers, and consider rather how some very definite geometrical remark about physical bodies, considered simply by itself, might be paraphrased into terms of distance without geometrical objects. Let us take the sentence to the effect that there is a line passing through the bodies A, B, and C, where B is the one in the middle.

A simple paraphrase that does not quite fill the bill is this: there are particles x, y, and z, respectively in A, B, and C, such that the distance from x to z is the sum of those from x to y and from y to z. The trouble with it is that it makes no allowance for gaps between the component particles (or particle-events) of a body. It does not allow for the possibility that every line through A, B, and C that hits particles of both A and C passes between particles of B, hitting none.

There is a way through this difficulty which may most readily be grasped in principle if we suppose that we are working in just two dimensions. So A, B, and C are now clusters of dots on a page; and we want to say in effect that there is a geometrical line through A, B, and C, without actually referring to any objects but the dots and their clusters, nor relating them otherwise than in point of distance. We suppose still that of these three clusters (if a line does cut through them) the middle one is B. What we want in effect to say, then, though within the allotted means, is that there are a dot x of A, a dot z of C, and dots y and y' of B (same or different), such that the geometrical line xz hits y or y' or passes between them. But xz hits y or y' or passes between them if and only if the area of the triangle xyz plus the area of the triangle $xy'z$ equals the area of the triangle xyy' plus the area of the triangle zyy'. But the area of a triangle is a known function f of the lengths of the sides. The following, then, is a formulation to our purpose, where 'dxy' means 'distance from x to y':

> There are a dot x of A, a dot z of C, and dots y and y' of B such that $f(dxy, dyz, dxz) + f(dxy', dy'z, dxz) = f(dxy, dyy', dxy') + f(dzy, dyy', dzy')$.

§ 53. THE ORDERED PAIR AS PHILOSOPHICAL PARADIGM

A pattern repeatedly illustrated in recent sections is that of the defective noun that proves undeserving of objects and is dismissed as an irreferential fragment of a few containing phrases. But sometimes a defective noun fares oppositely: its utility is found to turn on the admission of denoted objects as values of the variables of quantification. In such a case our job is to devise interpretations for it in the term positions where, in its defectiveness, it had not used to occur.

We shall find that a peculiarly clear-cut case of the latter sort is provided by the ordered pair, a device for treating objects two at a time as if we were treating objects of some sort one at a time. A typical use of the device is in assimilating relations to classes, by taking them as classes of ordered pairs.[1] The father relation becomes the class of just those ordered pairs which, like ⟨Abraham, Isaac⟩,[2] have a male and one of his offspring as their respective components.

Now just what is an ordered pair? See Peirce's answer:

> The Dyad is a mental Diagram consisting of two images of two objects, one existentially connected with one member of the pair, the other with the other; the one having attached to it, as representing it, a Symbol whose meaning is "First," and the other a Symbol whose meaning is "Second." [3]

---

[1] Relations as they concern us here are "relations-in-extension." They are to relations-in-intension (§ 43) as classes are to attributes. Anyone who persists in recognizing intensional objects can take relations-in-intension, analogously, as attributes of ordered pairs.

[2] The traditional notation '$x;y$' of Frege and Peano, for the ordered pair of x and y, is giving way nowadays to '⟨x, y⟩'.

[3] Peirce, vol. 2, paragraph 316.

We do better to face the fact that 'ordered pair' is (pending added conventions) a defective noun, not at home in all the questions and answers in which we are accustomed to imbed terms at their full-fledged best.

For illustrative purposes a special virtue of the notion of ordered pair is that mathematicians pretty deliberately introduced it, subject in effect to the single postulate:

(1) If $\langle x, y \rangle = \langle z, w \rangle$ then $x = z$ and $y = w$.

Pending added conventions, the expressions of the form '$\langle x, y \rangle$' are, like 'ordered pair' itself, defective nouns, their normal occurrences being limited to special sorts of context where (1) can be exploited.

Yet it is central to the purposes of the notion of ordered pair to admit ordered pairs as objects. If relations are to be assimilated to classes as classes of ordered pairs, ordered pairs must be available on a par with other objects as members of classes. The demands of further uses in mathematics of the notion of ordered pair are similar; in every case the very point of the ordered pair is its role of object— of a single object doing the work of two. A notion of ordered pair would fail of all purpose without ordered pairs as values of the variables of quantification.

The problem of suitably eking out the use of these defective nouns can be solved once for all by systematically fixing upon some suitable already-recognized object, for each x and y, with which to identify $\langle x, y \rangle$. The problem is a neat one, for we have in (1) a single explicit standard whereby to judge whether a version is suitable.

There are many solutions. The earliest, put forward by Wiener in 1914, ran (nearly enough) as follows: $\langle x, y \rangle$ is identified with the class $\{\{x\}, \{y, \Lambda\}\}$, whose members are just (a) the class $\{x\}$, whose sole member is x, and (b) the class $\{y, \Lambda\}$, whose sole members are y and the empty class.

This construction is paradigmatic of what we are most typically up to when in a philosophical spirit we offer an "analysis" or "explication" of some hitherto inadequately formulated "idea" or expression. We do not claim synonymy. We do not claim to make clear and explicit what the users of the unclear expression had unconsciously in mind all along. We do not expose hidden meanings, as the words 'analysis' and 'explication' would suggest; we supply lacks. We fix on the particular functions of the unclear expression that make it worth troubling about, and then devise a substitute, clear and couched in terms to our liking, that fills those functions. Beyond those conditions of partial agreement, dictated by our interests and purposes, any traits of the explicans come under the head of "don't-cares" (§ 38). Under this head we are free to allow the explicans all manner of novel connotations never associated with the explicandum. This point is strikingly illustrated by Wiener's $\{\{x\}, \{y, \Lambda\}\}$. Our example is atypical in just one respect: the demands of partial agreement are preternaturally succinct and explicit, in (1).

Philosophical analysis, explication, has not always been seen in this way.[4] Only the reading of a synonymy claim into analysis could engender the so-called paradox of analysis, which runs thus: how can a correct analysis be informative, since to understand it we must already know the meanings of its terms, and hence already know that the terms which it equates are synonymous?[5] The notion that analysis must consist somehow in the uncovering of hidden meanings underlies also the recent tendency of some of the Oxford philosophers to take as their business an examination of the subtle irregularities of ordinary language. And there is no mistaking the obliviousness of various writers to the point about the don't-cares. If nobody has objected to Wiener's definition as falsifying the ordinary notion of ordered pair, e.g. in that it makes x and y members of members of $\langle x, y \rangle$, the reason is perhaps that here the relevant considerations are so clearly on view; or perhaps only that 'ordered pair' is not ordinary language. Analogous objections to other and more classical philosophical analyses, at any rate, are not wanting. Russell's theory of descriptions has been called wrong because of what it does to the truth-value gaps.[6] Frege's definition of number has been called wrong because it says of numbers that they have classes as members, which was not so before. But I anticipate.

Before we turn to number, there is still a point about ordered pairs worth exploiting: that Wiener's version of ordered pairs is but one among many possible. A later and better known one is Kuratowski's, which identifies $\langle x, y \rangle$ rather with $\{\{x\}, \{x, y\}\}$. If one happens to be working in pure number theory, it can be desirable to construe ordered pairs of numbers in such a way rather as not to carry us outside the domain of natural numbers; and this again can be accom-

---

[4] By Carnap, yes; see *Meaning and Necessity*, pp. 7 f.

[5] On this issue see Carnap, *op. cit.*, pp. 63 f.; White, "On the Church-Frege solution"; and further references therein.

[6] Strawson, *Introduction to Logical Theory*, pp. 185 ff.

plished in an infinite variety of ways—e.g., by taking $\langle x, y \rangle$ as $2^x \cdot 3^y$, or as $3^x \cdot 2^y$, or as $x + (x + y)^2$. Each of these versions of the ordered pair conflicts with all the others, but each fulfills (1).

Which is right? All are; all fulfill (1), and conflict with one another only out among the don't-cares. Any air of paradox comes only of supposing that there is a unique right analysis—a mistake that is encouraged by the practice, otherwise convenient, of using the term 'ordered pair' for each version. On this and other points, the nature of explication as illustrated by the ordered pair may be made wholly evident by retelling the story of Wiener, Kuratowski, and the ordered pair in a modified terminology. In the beginning there was the notion of the ordered pair, defective and perplexing but serviceable. Then men found that whatever good had been accomplished by talking of an ordered pair $\langle x, y \rangle$ could be accomplished by talking instead of the class $\{\{x\}, \{y, \Lambda\}\}$—or, for that matter, of $\{\{x\}, \{x, y\}\}$.

A similar view can be taken of every case of explication: *explication is elimination.* We have, to begin with, an expression or form of expression that is somehow troublesome. It behaves partly like a term but not enough so, or it is vague in ways that bother us, or it puts kinks in a theory or encourages one or another confusion. But also it serves certain purposes that are not to be abandoned. Then we find a way of accomplishing those same purposes through other channels, using other and less troublesome forms of expression. The old perplexities are resolved.

According to an influential doctrine of Wittgenstein's, the task of philosophy is not to solve problems but to dissolve them by showing that there were really none there. This doctrine has its limitations, but it aptly fits explication. For when explication banishes a problem it does so by showing it to be in an important sense unreal; viz., in the sense of proceeding only from needless usages.[7]

The ordered pair has had illustrative value because of the crispness of requirement (1) and because of the multiplicity and the conspicuous artificiality of the explications. But what it illustrates as to the nature of explication applies very widely. In the case of the ordered pair the initial philosophical problem, summed up in the question 'What is an ordered pair?', is dissolved by showing how we can dispense with ordered pairs in any problematic sense in favor of certain clearer notions. In the case of singular descrip-

[7] See Alston, p. 16; Lazerowitz, pp. 21 f.

tions, the initial problems are the inconvenience of truth-value gaps and the paradoxes of talking of what does not exist; and Russell dissolves them by showing how we can dispense with singular descriptions, in any problematic sense, in favor of certain uses of identity and quantifiers. In the case of the indicative conditional, the initial problems are the inconvenience of truth-value gaps and the obscurity of truth conditions; and they are dissolved by making evident that we can in general dispense with the indicative conditional, in any problematic sense, in favor of a truth function. In the case of 'nothing', 'everything', and 'something', the initial problems (to dignify them) are those that come of handling these words too much like proper names; and they are dissolved by dispensing with the offending words in favor of quantification. In all these cases, problems have been dissolved in the important sense of being shown to be purely verbal, and purely verbal in the important sense of arising from usages that can be avoided in favor of ones that engender no such problems.

It is ironical that those philosophers most influenced by Wittgenstein are largely the ones who most deplore the explications just now enumerated. In steadfast laymanship they deplore them as departures from ordinary usage, failing to appreciate that it is precisely by showing how to circumvent the problematic parts of ordinary usage that we show the problems to be purely verbal.

Explication is elimination but not all elimination is explication. Showing how the useful purposes of some perplexing expression can be accomplished through new channels would seem to count as explication just in case the new channels parallel the old ones sufficiently for there to be a striking if partial parallelism of function between the old troublesome form of expression and some form of expression figuring in the new method. In this case we are likely to view the latter form of expression as an explicans of the old, and, if it is longer, even abbreviate it by the old word. If there was a question of objects, and the partial parallelism which we are now picturing obtains, the corresponding objects of the new scheme will tend to be looked upon as the old mysterious objects minus the mystery. Clearly this is merely a way of phrasing matters, and wrong only as it threatens the immunity of the don't-cares and suggests that one of two divergent explicantia must be wrong.

The contrast drawn at the beginning of this section, between the defective noun whose objects we dispense with and the defective noun whose defectiveness we are at pains to eke out so as to keep the objects, can then be put more simply: it is just a matter of whether the ostensible objects of the defective noun played roles that still want playing by some sort of object.

§ 54. NUMBERS, MIND, AND BODY

But for its greater antiquity and its concern with a more venerable notion, the philosophical question 'What is a number?' is on a par with the corresponding question about ordered pairs. Frege dealt with the one question, as Wiener did with the other, by showing how the work for which the objects in question might be wanted could be done by objects whose nature was presumed to be less in question. He identified—as one says—each natural number n with a certain class N of classes, as follows: 0 with $\{\Lambda\}$, and $n + 1$, for each n, with the class of all those classes which come to belong to N when deprived of a member. Thus, to put the matter circularly, each n is identified with the class of all n-member classes.[1]

After § 53, nothing needs be said in rebuttal of those critics, from Peano onward, who have rejected Frege's version because there are things about classes of classes that we have not been prone to say about numbers.[2] Nothing, indeed, is more logical than to say that if numbers and classes of classes have different properties then numbers are not classes of classes; but what is overlooked is the point of explication.

Von Neumann, playing Kuratowski to Frege's Wiener, offered a different identification: 0 with Λ, and $n + 1$, for each n, with the class of all the classes identified with $0, 1, \ldots, n$.

The condition upon all acceptable explications of number (that is, of the natural numbers $0, 1, 2, \ldots$) can be put almost as succinctly as (1) of § 53: any *progression*—i.e., any infinite series each of whose members has only finitely many precursors—will do nicely. Russell once held[3] that a further condition had to be met, to the

---

[1] Frege, *Grundlagen*, § 68. In detail the version I am using comes rather from Russell, *Principles*, Ch. XI.

[2] Peano's phrase: "... *car ces objets ont des propriétés différentes*" (*Formulaire*, p. 70).

[3] *Introduction to Mathematical Philosophy*, p. 10.

effect that there be a way of applying one's would-be numbers to the measurement of multiplicity: a way of saying that

(1) There are n objects x such that Fx.

This, however, was a mistake; any progression can be fitted to that further condition. For, (1) can be paraphrased as saying that the numbers less than n admit of correlation with the objects x such that Fx. This requires that our apparatus include enough of the elementary theory of relations for talk of correlation, or one-one relation; but it requires nothing special about numbers except that they form a progression.

Over and above the strict condition one might still argue for the intuitiveness of Frege's version, as follows. A natural number n serves primarily to measure multiplicity, and may hence be naturally viewed as an attribute of classes, viz., the attribute of having n members; or, if we favor classes over attributes, the class of the n-member classes. One might argue differently for the intuitiveness of von Neumann's version: a number is to count with. When we count the members of an n-member class we pair them with the first n numbers; and n itself is, for von Neumann, the class precisely of those first n numbers. (We have to count from 0 instead of 1 to make this come out right, but this is little to ask.)

Actually there has been no dispute that I know of over the relative intuitiveness of the two versions. One uses Frege's version or von Neumann's or yet another, such as Zermelo's, opportunistically to suit the job in hand, if the job is one that calls for providing a version of number at all. The situation is unlike matrimony. Frege's progression, von Neumann's, and Zermelo's are three progressions of classes, all present in our universe of values of variables (if we accept a usual theory of classes), and available for selective use as convenient. That all are adequate as explications of natural number means that natural numbers, in any distinctive sense, do not need to be reckoned into our universe in addition. Each of the three progressions or any other will do the work of natural numbers, and each happens to be geared also to further jobs to which the others are not.

It is thus borne in on us, as in the case of ordered pairs, that explication is elimination. The step is to be seen as depending, usually, on a compensatory revision of adjacent text. Thus consider again

Frege's explication of number, under which 'x has n members' can be paraphrased as '$x \,\epsilon\, n$'. If we picture his explication not as identifying each number n with a class of classes N but as avoiding reference to n by recourse to N, then what is afoot with 'has-...-members' is not an equating of it to 'ϵ', but a compensatory revision of it as 'ϵ'; a paraphrasing of 'has n members' not as '$\epsilon\, n$' but as '$\epsilon\, N$'. There are those whom an appreciation of the role of compensatory revision would have spared the error of objecting to Frege's version of number that 'has-...-members' does not mean 'ϵ', or parallel errors elsewhere in philosophy.

I hardly need add that I wholly approve of playing Frege's game straight, with 'n' for 'N' and '$x \,\epsilon\, n$' for 'x has n members', when one is not engaged in this particular project of clarification.

That explication is elimination, and hence conversely that elimination can often be allowed the gentler air of explication, is an observation about a philosophical activity that far transcends the philosophy of mathematics, even if the best examples are there. Before we drop the topic, we may do well to note the bearing of that observation on the philosophical issue over mind and body. Let me lead up to the matter with a defense of physicalism.

As illustrated by 'Ouch' (§ 2), any subjective talk of mental events proceeds necessarily in terms that are acquired and understood through their associations, direct or indirect, with the socially observable behavior of physical objects. If there is a case for mental events and mental states, it must be just that the positing of them, like the positing of molecules, has some indirect systematic efficacy in the development of theory. But if a certain organization of theory is achieved by thus positing distinctive mental states and events behind physical behavior, surely as much organization could be achieved by positing merely certain correlative physiological states and events instead. Nor need we spot special centers in the body for these seizures; physical states of the undivided organism will serve, whatever their finer physiology. Lack of a detailed physiological explanation of the states is scarcely an objection to acknowledging them as states of human bodies, when we reflect that those who posit the mental states and events have no details of appropriate mechanisms to offer nor, what with their mind-body problem, prospects of any. The bodily states exist anyway; why add the others? Thus introspection may be seen as a witnessing to one's own bodily condition, as in introspecting an acid stomach, even though the introspector be vague on the medical details. Granted, my words 'vague' and 'witnessing' here are mentalistic. But then my argument is directed to mentalists; physicalists do not need it.

This brief for physicalism adds little to foreshadowings in earlier pages, and nothing to what others have said.[4] But I assemble it here with an eye to the somewhat mitigating consideration afforded by our thoughts on explication and elimination. Is physicalism a repudiation of mental objects after all, or a theory of them? Does it repudiate the mental state of pain or anger in favor of its physical concomitant, or does it identify the mental state with a state of the physical organism (and so a state of the physical organism with the mental state)? The latter version sounds less drastic. Even ordinary language, in its least self-conscious attributions, falls neatly in with physicalism thus mildly conceived; one says 'Jones is in pain', 'Jones is angry', of quite the same object as 'Jones is tall'. What may primarily be said in characterization of physicalism thus mildly conceived is that it declares no unbridgeable differences in kind between the mental and the physical. Some may therefore find comfort in reflecting that the distinction between an eliminative and an explicative physicalism is unreal.[5]

For a further parallel consider the molecular theory. Does it repudiate our familiar solids and declare for swarms of molecules in their stead, or does it keep the solids and explain them as subvisibly swarming with molecules? Eddington took the former line in his opening paragraphs; common sense, with Miss Stebbing as spokeswoman, took the latter.[6] The option, again, is unreal. Nor is this surprising enough to be of much interest, except as a further analogical aid to appreciating the status of physicalism.

Not to discriminate between elimination and explication, there remains an important sense in which the physicalism contemplated above may be said to be less clearly *reductive* than Frege's version of number.[7] When Frege explains numbers as classes of classes, or

[4] See Carnap, *The Unity of Science;* Feigl, "The 'mental' and the 'physical' "; and, in Feigl, hundreds of further references. In particular see Feigl, pp. 417 f., for separation of physicalism from the intentionality issue of § 45.

[5] Perhaps this distinction is basically what is renounced in saying that "Philosophical behaviorism is not a metaphysical theory: it is the denial of a metaphysical theory. Consequently, it asserts nothing" (Ziff, p. 136).

[6] See Urmson.

[7] I am indebted to Davidson in the ensuing remarks, and to Feigl, p. 425.

eliminates them in favor of classes of classes, he paraphrases the standard contexts of numerical expressions into antecedently significant contexts of the corresponding expressions for classes; thus 'has-...-members' gives way to 'ϵ', and arithmetical operators such as '$+$' give way to appropriately definable class-theoretic operators. But when we explain mental states as bodily states, or eliminate them in favor of bodily states, in the easy fashion here envisaged, we do not paraphrase the standard contexts of the mental terms into independently explained contexts of physical terms. Thus the 'Jones is in' of 'Jones is in pain', the 'Jones is' of 'Jones is angry', remain unchanged, but merely come to be thought of as taking physicalistic rather than mentalistic complements. The radical reduction that would resolve the mental states into the independently recognized elements of physiological theory is a separate and far more ambitious program.

§ 55.   WHITHER CLASSES?

The infinitesimals and the ideal objects were supposed objects whose recognition was *prima facie* useful to theory and, at the same time, troublesome. (Cf. § 51.) Now classes are another example of the same, but they seem to resist similar treatment. Ways of serving the theoretical purposes of infinitesimals and ideal objects were found which did not call for these troublesome objects after all, and the objects were accordingly dropped. On the other hand no similar circumvention of classes suggests itself; one is impelled rather to the opposite course, that of keeping classes and coping with the trouble they make. Let us examine this matter.

Where classes offend is not just on the score, so doubtfully offensive, of their abstractness. Numbers likewise are abstract; but classes, if uncritically accepted, lead to absurdities. There are infinitely many such paradoxes of classes; the simplest is Russell's familiar one of the class $\hat{x}(x \notin x)$, which is a member of itself if it is not and is not if it is.

Yet the admission of classes as values of variables of quantification brings power that is not lightly to be surrendered. Examples of this access of power were noted in §§ 43 and 48, and have been added to since. Classes can do the work of ordered pairs and hence also of relations (§ 53), and they can do the work of natural numbers (§ 54). They can do the work of the richer sorts of numbers too—rational, real, complex; for these can be variously explicated on the basis of natural numbers by suitable constructions of classes and relations.

Numerical functions, in turn, can be explicated as certain relations of numbers. All in all the universe of classes leaves no further objects to be desired for the whole of classical mathematics.

The versatility of classes in thus serving the purposes of widely varied sorts of abstract objects is best seen in mathematics, but it spills over, as illustrated by relations. Again, consider a disease; it can be taken as the class of all the appropriately afflicted temporal segments of its victims. Correspondingly for anger and other states. Intensional objects aside, the abstract objects that it is useful to admit to the universe of discourse at all seem to be adequately explicable in terms of a universe comprising just physical objects and all classes of the objects in the universe (hence classes of physical objects, classes of such classes, etc.). At any rate I think of no persuasive exceptions.

Such is the power of the notion of class to unify our abstract ontology. To surrender this benefit and face the old abstract objects again in all their primeval disorder would be a wrench, worth making if it were all. But we must remember that the utility of classes is not limited to explication of the various other sorts of abstract objects. The power of the notion on other counts, glimpsed in §§ 43 and 48, keeps it in continuing demand in mathematics and elsewhere as a working notion in its own right: not only in the protean guises of number, function, state, and all else that it has served to explicate, but also straight. It confers a power that is not known to be available through less objectionable channels.

Let it not be supposed that attributes, despite the special difficulties enveloping them (cf. § 43), bear consideration as a means of dispensing with classes. For they are obviously involved also in paradoxes exactly parallel to those of classes. Two reasons for making little of this point are that attributes are badly off anyway, and that any remedy for the class paradoxes would presumably work for attributes too.

Thus it is that one resolves to keep classes and somehow excise the paradoxes. Now it is not to be wondered that a self-contradictory notion of class should have proved powerful. No holds are barred. It is too powerful for anyone's good, enabling one as it does to prove truths and falsehoods indiscriminately. The problem, then, is that of weakening it enough but not too much for future service.

Various ways are known. They have their several strengths and weaknesses, and none stands out clearly as the most satisfactory. All of them restrict, in some fashion, the universal applicability of the operator '$\hat{x}$' of class abstraction.[1] There ceases to be the old guarantee that for each open sentence there is a class whose members are just the values of the variable for which the sentence comes out true.[2] Whether classes continue to do all the services claimed for them, e.g. in foregoing pages and chapters, has then to be checked up with an eye to the specific restricted theory adopted. One argument that would call for qualifications is the one in § 48 which eliminated 'Φ_x'. On the whole, however, one manages to salvage most of the utility that the old class theory seemed (in happy ignorance of the paradoxes) to afford, apart from simplicity of governing principles. Naturalness, for whatever it is worth, is of course lost; a multitude of mutually alternative, mutually incompatible systems of class theory arises, each with only the most bleakly pragmatic claims to attention. Insofar as a leaning or tolerance toward classes may have turned on considerations of naturalness, nominalism scores.

Initial reason for favoring physical objects over abstract objects was urged at the end of § 48. Moved further by these latest reflections, one may wistfully survey the chances of getting by as a nominalist. One can afford to sacrifice some surely of the systematic benefits of abstract objects, as offset by a twofold gain: elimination of the less welcome objects, and elimination of a drastic dualism of categories.

In such a program the basic problem is how to say what one wants to say of physical objects without invoking abstract objects as auxiliaries. Thus, interested in whooping cranes and not at all in numbers, one still wants to say there are six whooping cranes. Here in fact there is no difficulty. The form 'There are n objects x such that Fx' can, for each specific n, be paraphrased with help of '=' and quantifiers (cf. § 24), and makes no demand upon numbers as values of variables of quantification. Again there is no difficulty in bringing in a time variable when we please, and even quantifying it; for times can be taken as physical objects, according to § 36.

[1] Note that the universally applicable '$\hat{x}$' of my *Mathematical Logic* has a different use: it collects "elements," not objects generally.

[2] Russell gets the same effect by a method that preserves, indeed, the letter if not the spirit of the old guarantee: he excises part of the domain of open sentences. See above, § 47.

'There are just as many husbands as wives' is where difficulties begin. '($\exists n$)(there are n husbands and there are n wives)' will not do, for it requires numbers as values of quantified variables. Neither will 'There is a correlation between husbands and wives', for it requires relations as values of variables. And problems like that of 'just as many' are raised again by 'more than', 'twice as many', and the like.

Another difficulty is that the nominalist deprives himself of Frege's technique of paraphrasing 'ancestor' in terms of 'parent' and quantification over classes (§ 48). He is still free to accept 'ancestor' and 'parent' each as a relative term, but he loses the theory that links them. Such a law as that ancestors of ancestors are ancestors he has to take as irreducible, rather than seeing it as implicit in Frege's paraphrase. The 'ancestor' example, moreover, is one among countless. For every open sentence in two variables another is wanted that stands to it as 'x is ancestor of y' stands to 'x is parent of y'. The connection is an important one to be able to exploit in general.

In the face of these difficulties the nominalist is not quite helpless. With some loss in naturalness, simplicity, and generality, he can devise alternative paraphrases of 'ancestor', 'just as many', etc. that quantify over physical objects instead of abstract ones.[3] But these are only samples of the difficulties that continue to beset him. He is going to have to accommodate his natural sciences unaided by mathematics; for mathematics, except for some trivial portions such as very elementary arithmetic, is irredeemably committed to quantification over abstract objects.[4]

If a thoroughgoing nominalist doctrine is too much to live up to, there are compromises. The logical paradoxes, which just now seemed to provide at least a last small push toward nominalism, would never have threatened if classes had been held to classes of concrete objects, classes of such, and so on, up to some fixed level and not beyond. This restriction would impair the explication of

[3] See Goodman and Quine.

[4] The nominalist program seems already and painlessly achieved if Whitehead and Russell's elimination of classes by a theory of incomplete symbols is thought to bear. But it does not; it only eliminates classes in favor of attributes. See my "Whitehead and the rise of modern logic." For more on the scope of nominalism see my *From a Logical Point of View*, Essay 6; Goodman, *Structure of Appearance*, Ch. II; Martin, *Truth and Denotation*, Ch. XIII; Stegmüller.

numbers as well as further work in mathematics, but it would be less austere than nominalism; and numbers, in particular, could be thrown in without explication if desired. Most such compromises, of course, are pointless as general philosophies because of the arbitrariness of their stopping places. One is led on to further indulgences as occasions arise.

Scope still remains for nominalism, however, and for various intermediate grades of abnegation of abstract objects, when with Conant we think of science not as one evolving world view but as a multiplicity of working theories. (See end of § 51.) The nominalist can realize his predilection in special branches, and point with pride to a theoretical improvement of those branches. In the same spirit even the mathematician, realist *ex officio,* is always glad to find that some particular mathematical results that had been thought to depend on functions or classes of numbers, for instance, can be proved anew without appealing to objects other than numbers. It is generally conducive to understanding to keep track of our presuppositions, in point of objects and otherwise, project by project; and to welcome ontological economy in connection with one project even if a more lavish ontology is needed for the next. But it is also important to have the less economical and more powerful mathematical theories well in hand as engines of discovery, for swift use in unforeseen places—even though in each such case we take pains afterward to find more economical ways of gaining the same result.

§ 56. SEMANTIC ASCENT

This chapter has been centrally occupied with the question what objects to recognize. Yet it has treated of words as much as its predecessors. Part of our concern here has been with the question what a theory's commitments to objects consist in (§ 49), and of course this second-order question is about words. But what is noteworthy is that we have talked more of words than of objects even when most concerned to decide what there really is: what objects to admit on our own account.

This would not have happened if and insofar as we had lingered over the question whether in particular there are wombats, or whether there are unicorns. Discourse about non-linguistic objects would have been an excellent medium in which to debate those issues. But when the debate shifts to whether there are points, miles, numbers, attributes, propositions, facts, or classes, it takes on an in some sense philosophical cast, and straightway we find ourselves talking of words almost to the exclusion of the non-linguistic objects under debate.

Carnap has long held that the questions of philosophy, when real at all, are questions of language; and the present observation would seem to illustrate his point. He holds that the philosophical questions of what there is are questions of how we may most conveniently fashion our "linguistic framework," and not, as in the case of the wombat or unicorn, questions about extralinguistic reality.[1] He holds that those philosophical questions are only apparently about sorts of objects, and are really pragmatic questions of language policy.

But why should this be true of the philosophical questions and not of theoretical questions generally? Such a distinction of status is of a piece with the notion of analyticity (§ 14), and as little to be trusted. After all, theoretical sentences in general are defensible only pragmatically; we can but assess the structural merits of the theory which embraces them along with sentences directly conditioned to multifarious stimulations. How then can Carnap draw a line across this theoretical part and hold that the sentences this side of the line enjoy non-verbal content or meaning in a way that those beyond the line do not? His own appeal to convenience of linguistic framework allows pragmatic connections across the line. What other sort of connection can be asked anywhere, short of direct conditioning to non-verbal stimulations?

Yet we do recognize a shift from talk of objects to talk of words as debate progresses from existence of wombats and unicorns to existence of points, miles, classes, and the rest. How can we account for this? Amply, I think, by proper account of a useful and much used manoeuvre which I shall call *semantic ascent*.

It is the shift from talk of miles to talk of 'mile'. It is what leads from the material (*inhaltlich*) mode into the formal mode, to invoke an old terminology of Carnap's. It is the shift from talking in certain terms to talking about them. It is precisely the shift that Carnap thinks of as divesting philosophical questions of a deceptive guise and setting them forth in their true colors. But this tenet of Carnap's is the part that I do not accept. Semantic ascent, as I

---

[1] Carnap, "Empiricism, semantics, and ontology."

speak of it, applies anywhere.[2] 'There are wombats in Tasmania' might be paraphrased as ''Wombat' is true of some creatures in Tasmania', if there were any point in it. But it does happen that semantic ascent is more useful in philosophical connections than in most, and I think I can explain why.

Consider what it would be like to debate over the existence of miles without ascending to talk of 'mile'. "Of course there are miles. Wherever you have 1760 yards you have a mile." "But there are no yards either. Only bodies of various lengths." "Are the earth and moon separated by bodies of various lengths?" The continuation is lost in a jumble of invective and question-begging. When on the other hand we ascend to 'mile' and ask which of its contexts are useful and for what purposes, we can get on; we are no longer caught in the toils of our opposed uses.

The strategy of semantic ascent is that it carries the discussion into a domain where both parties are better agreed on the objects (viz., words) and on the main terms concerning them. Words, or their inscriptions, unlike points, miles, classes, and the rest, are tangible objects of the size so popular in the marketplace, where men of unlike conceptual schemes communicate at their best. The strategy is one of ascending to a common part of two fundamentally disparate conceptual schemes, the better to discuss the disparate foundations. No wonder it helps in philosophy.

But it also figures in the natural sciences. Einstein's theory of relativity was accepted in consequence not just of reflections on time, light, headlong bodies, and the perturbations of Mercury, but of reflections also on the theory itself, as discourse, and its simplicity in comparison with alternative theories. Its departure from classical conceptions of absolute time and length is too radical to be efficiently debated at the level of object talk unaided by semantic ascent. The case was similar, if in lesser degrees, for the disruptions of traditional outlook occasioned by the doctrines of molecules and electrons. These particles come after wombats and unicorns, and before points and miles, in a significant gradation.

The device of semantic ascent has been used much and carefully in axiomatic studies in mathematics, for the avoidance, again, of

---

[2] In a word, I reject Carnap's doctrine of "quasi-syntactic" or "pseudo-object" sentences, but accept his distinction between the material and the formal mode. See his *Logical Syntax*, §§ 63–64. (It was indeed I, if I may reminisce, who in 1934 proposed 'material mode' to him as translation of his German.)

question-begging. In axiomatizing some already familiar theory, geometry say, one used to be in danger of imagining that he had deduced some familiar truth of the theory purely from his axioms when actually he had made inadvertent use of further geometrical knowledge. As a precaution against this danger, a device other than semantic ascent was at first resorted to: the device of disinterpretation. One feigned to understand only the logical vocabulary and not the distinctive terms of the axiom system concerned. This was an effective way of barring information extraneous to the axioms and thus limiting one's inferences to what the axioms logically implied. The device of disinterpretation had impressive side effects, some good, such as the rise of abstract algebra, and some bad, such as the notion that in pure mathematics "we never know what we are talking about, nor whether what we are saying is true." [3] At any rate, with Frege's achievement of a full formalization of logic, an alternative and more refined precaution against question-begging became available to axiomatic studies; and it is a case, precisely, of what I am calling semantic ascent. Given the deductive apparatus of logic in the form of specified operations on notational forms, the question whether a given formula follows logically from given axioms reduces to the question whether the specified operations on notational forms are capable of leading to that formula from the axioms. An affirmative answer to such a question can be established without disinterpretation, yet without fear of circularity, indeed without using the terms of the theory at all except to talk about them and the operations upon them.

We must also notice a further reason for semantic ascent in philosophy. This further reason holds also, and more strikingly, for logic; so let us look there first. Most truths of elementary logic contain extralogical terms; thus 'If all Greeks are men and all men are mortal . . .'. The main truths of physics, in contrast, contain terms of physics only. Thus whereas we can expound physics in its full generality without semantic ascent, we can expound logic in a general way only by talking of forms of sentences. The generality wanted in physics can be got by quantifying over non-linguistic objects, while the dimension of generality wanted for logic runs

[3] Russell, *Mysticism and Logic and Other Essays*, p. 75. The essay in question dates from 1901, and happily the aphorism expressed no enduring attitude on Russell's part. But the attitude expressed has been widespread.

crosswise to what can be got by such quantification. It is a difference in shape of field and not in content; the above syllogism about the Greeks need owe its truth no more peculiarly to language than other sentences do.

There are characteristic efforts in philosophy, those coping e.g. with perplexities of lion-hunting or believing (§§ 30–32), that resemble logic in their need of semantic ascent as a means of generalizing beyond examples.[4] Not that I would for a moment deny that when the perplexities about lion-hunting or believing and its analogues are cleared up they are cleared up by an improved structuring of discourse; but the same is true of an advance in physics. The same is true even though the latter restructuring be led up to (as often happens) within discourse of objects, and not by semantic ascent.

For it is not as though considerations of systematic efficacy, broadly pragmatic considerations, were operative only when we make a semantic ascent and talk of theory, and factual considerations of the behavior of objects in the world were operative only when we avoid semantic ascent and talk within the theory. Considerations of systematic efficacy are equally essential in both cases; it is just that in the one case we voice them and in the other we are tacitly guided by them. And considerations of the behavior of objects in the world, even behavior affecting our sensory surfaces by contact or radiation, are likewise essential in both cases.

There are two reasons why observation is felt to have no such bearing on logic and philosophy as it has on theoretical physics. One is traceable to misapprehensions about semantic ascent. The other is traceable to curriculum classifications. This latter factor tends likewise to make one feel that observation has no such bearing on mathematics as it has on theoretical physics. Theoretical assertions in physics, being terminologically physics, are generally conceded to owe a certain empirical content to the physical observations which, however indirectly, they help to systematize, whereas laws of so-called logic and mathematics, however useful in systematizing physical observations, are not considered to pick up any empirical substance thereby. A more reasonable attitude is that there are merely variations in degree of centrality to the theoretical

---

[4] Wittgenstein's characteristic style, in his later period, consisted in avoiding semantic ascent by sticking to the examples.

structure, and in degree of relevance to one or another set of observations.

In § 49 I spoke of dodges whereby philosophers have thought to enjoy the systematic benefits of abstract objects without suffering the objects. There is one more such dodge in what I have been inveighing against in these last pages: the suggestion that the acceptance of such objects is a linguistic convention distinct somehow from serious views about reality.

The question what there is is a shared concern of philosophy and most other non-fiction genres. The descriptive answer has been given only in part, but at some length. A representative assortment of land masses, seas, planets, and stars have been individually described in the geography and astronomy books, and an occasional biped or other middle-sized object in the biographies and art books. Description has been stepped up by mass production in zoology, botany, and mineralogy, where things are grouped by similarities and described collectively. Physics, by more ruthless abstraction from differences in detail, carries mass description farther still. And even pure mathematics belongs to the descriptive answer to the question what there is; for the things about which the question asks do not exclude the numbers, classes, functions, etc., if such there be, whereof pure mathematics treats.

What distinguishes between the ontological philosopher's concern and all this is only breadth of categories. Given physical objects in general, the natural scientist is the man to decide about wombats and unicorns. Given classes, or whatever other broad realm of objects the mathematician needs, it is for the mathematician to say whether in particular there are any even prime numbers or any cubic numbers that are sums of pairs of cubic numbers. On the other hand it is scrutiny of this uncritical acceptance of the realm of physical objects itself, or of classes, etc., that devolves upon ontology. Here is the task of making explicit what had been tacit, and precise what had been vague; of exposing and resolving paradoxes, smoothing kinks, lopping off vestigial growths, clearing ontological slums.

The philosopher's task differs from the others', then, in detail; but in no such drastic way as those suppose who imagine for the philosopher a vantage point outside the conceptual scheme that he takes in charge. There is no such cosmic exile. He cannot study and revise the fundamental conceptual scheme of science and common sense without having some conceptual scheme, whether the same or another no less in need of philosophical scrutiny, in which to work. He can scrutinize and improve the system from within, appealing to coherence and simplicity; but this is the theoretician's method generally. He has recourse to semantic ascent, but so has the scientist. And if the theoretical scientist in his remote way is bound to save the eventual connections with non-verbal stimulation, the philosopher in his remoter way is bound to save them too. True, no experiment may be expected to settle an ontological issue; but this is only because such issues are connected with surface irritations in such multifarious ways, through such a maze of intervening theory.

Bibliographical References

(Only those works are listed that are alluded to elsewhere in the book.)

Ajdukiewicz, Kazimierz. "Sprache und Sinn." *Erkenntnis* 4 (1934), pp. 100–138.

Aldrich, Virgil. "Mr. Quine on meaning, naming, and purporting to name." *Philosophical Studies* 6 (1955), pp. 17–26.

Alston, W. P. "Ontological commitment." *Philosophical Studies* 9 (1958), pp. 8–17.

Anrep, G. V. "The irradiation of conditioned reflexes." *Proceedings of the Royal Society of London* 94 (1923), pp. 404–426.

Apostel, L., W. Mays, A. Morf, and J. Piaget. *Les liaisons analytiques et synthétiques dans les comportements du sujet.* Paris: Presses Universitaires, 1957.

Ayer, A. J. *Language, Truth and Logic.* London: Gollancz, 1936, 1946.

Bar-Hillel, Yehoshua. "Bolzano's definition of analytic propositions." *Theoria* 16 (1950), pp. 91–117, and concurrently in *Methodos.*

Barcan, Ruth C. "A functional calculus of first order based on strict implication." *Journal of Symbolic Logic* 11 (1946), pp. 1–16.

—— "The identity of individuals in a strict functional calculus of second order." *Journal of Symbolic Logic* 12 (1947), pp. 12–15. (See *Journal of Symbolic Logic* 23, p. 342, for a correction of my review of this paper.)

Bass, M. J., and C. L. Hull. "The irradiation of a tactile conditioned reflex in man." *Journal of Comparative Psychology* 17 (1934), pp. 47–66.

Baylis, C. A. "Universals, communicable knowledge, and metaphysics." *Journal of Philosophy* 48 (1951), pp. 636–644.

Bedau, H. A. Review of Whorf. *Philosophy of Science* 24 (1957), pp. 289–293.

Bennett, Jonathan. "Analytic-synthetic." *Proceedings of the Aristotelian Society* 59 (1959), pp. 163–188.

Bergmann, Gustav. "Two types of linguistic philosophy." *Review of Metaphysics* 5 (1952), pp. 417–438.

—— "Intentionality." *Archivio di Filosofia* 1955, pp. 177–216.

Birkhoff, G. D. "Three public lectures on scientific subjects." *Rice Institute Pamphlet* 28 (1941), pp. 1–76.

Black, Max. *Critical Thinking.* New York: Prentice-Hall, 1952.

Bloomfield, Leonard. *Language.* New York: Holt, 1933.

Braithwaite, R. B. *Scientific Explanation*. Cambridge, England: University, 1953.

—— Review of Quine's *From a Logical Point of View*. *Cambridge Review* 75 (1954), pp. 417–418.

Brough, John. "Theories of general linguistics in the Sanskrit grammarians." *Transactions of the Philological Society* (Oxford) 1951, pp. 27–46.

—— "Some Indian theories of meaning." *Transactions of the Philological Society* (Oxford) 1953, pp. 161–176.

Brower, R. A. (ed.). *On Translation*. Cambridge, Mass.: Harvard, 1959.

Carnap, Rudolf. *Physikalische Begriffsbildung*. Karlsruhe, 1926.

—— *Der logische Aufbau der Welt*. Berlin, 1928.

—— "Ueberwindung der Metaphysik durch logische Analyse der Sprache." *Erkenntnis* 2 (1931), pp. 219–241.

—— *The Unity of Science*. London: Kegan Paul, 1934.

—— "Testability and meaning." *Philosophy of Science* 3 (1936), pp. 419–471; 4 (1937), pp. 1–40. Reprinted in Feigl and Brodbeck.

—— *The Logical Syntax of Language*. New York: Harcourt, Brace; and London: K. Paul, Trench, Trubner, 1937.

—— *Meaning and Necessity*, Chicago: University, 1947. 2d ed., with supplements, 1956.

—— "Empiricism, semantics, and ontology." *Revue Internationale de Philosophie* 11 (1950), pp. 208–228. Reprinted in Linsky, in P. P. Wiener, and in 2d ed. of Carnap's *Meaning and Necessity*.

—— "The methodological character of theoretical concepts." *Minnesota Studies in the Philosophy of Science* 1 (1956), pp. 38–76.

Cassirer, Ernst. *Language and Myth*. New York: Harper, 1946.

Chisholm, R. M. "Sentences about believing." *Proceedings of the Aristotelian Society* 56 (1956), pp. 125–148. Reprinted with revisions in *Minnesota Studies in the Philosophy of Science* 2 (1958), pp. 510–519.

—— *Perceiving: A Philosophical Study*. Ithaca: Cornell, 1957.

Chomsky, Noam. Review of Skinner's *Verbal Behavior*. *Language* 35 (1959), pp. 26–58.

Church, Alonzo. Review of Carnap's *Introduction to Semantics*. *Philosophical Review* 52 (1943), pp. 298–304.

—— Review of Quine's "Notes on existence and necessity." *Journal of Symbolic Logic* 8 (1943), pp. 45–47.

—— "On Carnap's analysis of statements of assertion and belief." *Analysis* 10 (1950), pp. 97–99.

—— "A formulation of the logic of sense and denotation." In Henle, Kallen, and Langer, pp. 3–24.

—— "Intensional isomorphism and identity of belief." *Philosophical Studies* 5 (1954), pp. 65–73.

—— "Ontological commitment." *Journal of Philosophy* 55 (1958), pp. 1008–1014.

—— Review of Quine's "On Frege's way out." *Journal of Symbolic Logic*, at press.

Conant, J. B. *Modern Science and Modern Man.* New York: Columbia University, 1952.

Duhem, Pierre. *La théorie physique: Son objet et sa structure.* Paris, 1906.

Eddington, A. S. *The Nature of the Physical World.* Cambridge, England, 1928.

Einstein, Albert. "Remarks on Bertrand Russell's theory of knowledge." In Schilpp, *The Philosophy of Bertrand Russell.*

Erdmann, K. O. *Die Bedeutung des Wortes.* Leipzig, 1900.

Evans-Pritchard, E. E. (ed.). *The Institutions of Primitive Society.* Oxford: Blackwell, 1954.

Feigl, Herbert. "The 'mental' and the 'physical'." *Minnesota Studies in the Philosophy of Science* 2 (1958), pp. 370–497.

—— and Wilfrid Sellars (eds.). *Readings in Philosophical Analysis.* New York: Appleton-Century-Crofts, 1949.

—— and May Brodbeck (eds.). *Readings in the Philosophy of Science.* New York: Appleton-Century-Crofts, 1953.

Firth, Raymond. *Elements of Social Organization.* London: Watts, 1951.

—— (ed.). *Man and Culture: An Evaluation of the Works of Malinowski.* London: Routledge and Kegan Paul, 1957.

Firth, Roderick. "Phenomenalism." American Philosophical Association suppl. vol., 1952 (*Science, Language, and Human Rights*), pp. 1–20.

Fitch, F. B. *Symbolic Logic.* New York: Ronald, 1952.

Flew, A. G. N. (ed.). *Logic and Language,* 1st series. Oxford: Blackwell, 1952.

Frank, Philipp. *Modern Science and its Philosophy.* Cambridge, Mass.: Harvard, 1950.

Frege, Gottlob. *Begriffsschrift.* Halle, 1879.

—— *Grundlagen der Arithmetik.* Breslau, 1884. Reprinted with English translation as *The Foundations of Arithmetic,* New York: Philosophical Library, and Oxford: Blackwell, 1950.

—— "Ueber Sinn und Bedeutung." *Zeitschrift für Philosophie und philosophische Kritik* 100 (1892), pp. 25–50. English translation ("On sense and reference") in Frege, *Philosophical Writings,* and also (as "On sense and nominatum") in Feigl and Sellars.

—— *Philosophical Writings.* (Peter Geach and Max Black, eds.) Oxford: Blackwell, 1952.

Geach, P. T. "Frege's *Grundlagen.*" *Philosophical Review* 60 (1951), pp. 535–544.

Gewirth, Alan. "The distinction between analytic and synthetic truths." *Journal of Philosophy* 50 (1953), pp. 397–426.

Goodman, Nelson. "On likeness of meaning." *Analysis* 10 (1949), pp. 1–7. Reprinted with revisions in Linsky.

—— *The Structure of Appearance.* Cambridge, Mass.: Harvard, 1951.

—— *Fact, Fiction, and Forecast.* Cambridge, Mass.: Harvard, 1955.

—— and W. V. Quine. "Steps toward a constructive nominalism." *Journal of Symbolic Logic* 12 (1947), pp. 105–122.

Grice, H. P., and P. F. Strawson. "In defense of a dogma." *Philosophical Review* 65 (1956), pp. 141–158.

Hampshire, Stuart. "Subjunctive conditionals." *Analysis* 9 (1948), pp. 9–14.

Heidegger, Martin. *Was ist Metaphysik?* Berlin, 1929.

Hempel, C. G. *Fundamentals of Concept Formation.* International Encyclopedia of Unified Science II, 7. Chicago: University, 1952.

—— "The theoretician's dilemma." *Minnesota Studies in the Philosophy of Science* 2 (1958), pp. 37–96.

Henderson, G. P. "Intensional entities and ontology." *Proceedings of the Aristotelian Society* 58 (1958), pp. 269–288.

Henle, Paul, H. M. Kallen, and S. K. Langer (eds.). *Structure, Method, and Meaning: Essays in Honor of H. M. Sheffer.* New York: Liberal Arts, 1951.

Hilbert, David, and Paul Bernays. *Grundlagen der Mathematik,* vol. 1. Berlin: Springer, 1934.

Hintikka, Jaakko. "Modality as referential multiplicity." *Eripainos Ajatus* 20 (1957), pp. 49–64.

Hochberg, Herbert. "The ontological operator." *Philosophy of Science* 23 (1956), pp. 250–259.

—— "On pegasizing." *Philosophy and Phenomenological Research* 17 (1957), pp. 551–554.

Hofstadter, Albert. "The myth of the whole: an examination of Quine's view of knowledge." *Journal of Philosophy* 51 (1954), pp. 397–417.

Hook, Sidney (ed.). *John Dewey: Philosopher of Science and Freedom.* New York: Dial, 1950.

—— (ed.). *American Philosophers at Work.* New York: Criterion, 1956.

Hovland, C. I. "The generalization of conditioned responses: I. The sensory generalization of conditioned responses with varying frequencies of tone." *Journal of General Psychology* 17 (1937), pp. 125–148.

Hume, David. *A Treatise of Human Nature.* 1739–1740. L. A. Selby-Bigge (ed.), Oxford, 1888.

Jakobson, Roman, and Morris Halle. *Fundamentals of Language.* The Hague: Mouton, 1956.

Jespersen, Otto. *Language: Its Nature, Development, and Origin.* New York, 1923.

—— *The Philosophy of Grammar.* New York, 1924.

Joos, M. A. *Acoustic Phonetics.* Baltimore: Linguistic Society, 1948.

Jourdain, P. E. B. *The Philosophy of Mr. B*rtr*nd R*ss*ll.* Chicago and London, 1918.

Kemeny, J. G. Review of Quine's "Two dogmas." *Journal of Symbolic Logic* 17 (1952), pp. 281–283.

—— "The use of simplicity in induction." *Philosophical Review* 62 (1953), pp. 391–408.

Korzybski, Alfred. *Science and Sanity.* Lancaster, Pa.: Science Press, 1933.

Krikorian, Y. H., and Abraham Edel (eds.). *Contemporary Philosophic Problems.* New York: Macmillan, 1959.

Kuratowski, Kazimierz. "Sur la notion de l'ordre dans la théorie des ensembles." *Fundamenta Mathematicae* 2 (1921), pp. 161–171.

Land, E. H. "Experiments in color vision." *Scientific American*, May 1959, pp. 84–99.

Langer, Suzanne K. *Philosophy in a New Key.* Cambridge, Mass.: Harvard, 1942.

Lazerowitz, Morris. *The Structure of Metaphysics.* London: Routledge and Kegan Paul, 1955.

Leach, E. R. "The epistemological background to Malinowski's empiricism." In Raymond Firth, *Man and Culture,* pp. 119–137.

Lee, Dorothy D. "Conceptual implications of an Indian language." *Philosophy of Science* 5 (1938), pp. 89–102.

Lee, O. H. (ed.). *Philosophical Essays for A. N. Whitehead.* New York: Longmans, 1936.

Lejewski, Czesław. "Logic and existence." *British Journal for the Philosophy of Science* 5 (1954), pp. 1–16.

Lenneberg, E. H., and J. M. Roberts. "The language of experience." *International Journal of American Linguistics,* suppl., 1956.

Leśniewski, Stanisław. "Ueber die Grundlagen der Ontologie." *Comptes rendus des séances de la Société des Sciences et des Lettres de Varsovie,* Classe III, 1930, pp. 111–132.

Lévy-Bruhl, Lucien. *Les Carnets.* Paris: Presses Universitaires, 1949.

Lewis, C. I. *A Survey of Symbolic Logic.* Berkeley, 1918.

—— "The modes of meaning." *Philosophy and Phenomenological Research* 4 (1944), pp. 236–249. Reprinted in Linsky.

—— and C. H. Langford. *Symbolic Logic.* New York: Century, 1932.

Lienhardt, Godfrey. "Modes of thought." In Evans-Pritchard, pp. 95–107.

Linsky, Leonard (ed.). *Semantics and the Philosophy of Language.* Urbana: University of Illinois, 1952.

Locke, John. *Essay concerning the Human Understanding.* 1690.

Malinowski, Bronisław. *Coral Gardens and Their Magic,* vol. 2. New York: American, 1935.

Mandelbrot, Benoît. "Structure formelle des textes et communication." *Word* 10 (1954), pp. 1–27; 11 (1955), p. 424.

Martin, R. M., "On 'analytic'." *Philosophical Studies* 3 (1952), pp. 42–47.

—— *Truth and Denotation.* Chicago: University, 1958.

Mates, Benson. "Synonymity." *University of California Publications in Philosophy* 25 (1950), pp. 201–226. Reprinted in Linsky.

—— "Analytic sentences." *Philosophical Review* 60 (1951), pp. 525–534.

Mill, John Stuart. *A System of Logic,* New York, 1867.

Mises, Richard von. *Positivism: A Study in Human Understanding.* Cambridge, Mass.: Harvard, 1951.

Naess, Arne. *Interpretation and Preciseness.* Oslo: Dybwad, 1953.

Neumann, J. von. "Zur Einführung der transfiniten Zahlen." *Acta Litterarum ac Scientiarum Regiae Universitatis Hungaricae Francisco-Josephinae,* sectio math., vol. 1 (1923), pp. 199–208.

Neurath, Otto. "Protokollsätze." *Erkenntnis* 3 (1932), pp. 204–214.

Osgood, C. E., and T. A. Sebeok (eds.). "Psycholinguistics." *International Journal of American Linguistics,* suppl., 1954.

Pap, Arthur. "Belief, synonymity, and analysis." *Philosophical Studies* 6 (1955), pp. 11–15.

—— "Belief and propositions." *Philosophy of Science* 24 (1957), pp. 123–136.

—— "Disposition concepts and extensional logic." *Minnesota Studies in the Philosophy of Science* 2 (1958), pp. 196–224.

—— *Semantics and Necessary Truth.* New Haven: Yale, 1958.

Pasch, Alan. *Experience and the Analytic.* Chicago: University, 1959.

Peano, Giuseppe. *Formulaire de mathématiques.* Paris, 1901.

—— *Opere scelte,* vol. 2. Rome: Cremonese, 1958.

Peirce, C. S. *Collected Papers,* vols. 2 and 5. Cambridge, Mass.: Harvard, 1932, 1934.

Perkins, Moreland, and Irving Singer. "Analyticity." *Journal of Philosophy* 48 (1951), pp. 485–497.

Pike, K. L. *Phonemics: A Technique for Reducing Languages to Writing.* Ann Arbor: University of Michigan, 1947.

Prior, A. N. *Time and Modality.* Oxford: Clarendon, 1957.

Putnam, Hilary. "Synonymity and the analysis of belief sentences." *Analysis* 14 (1954), pp. 114–122.

—— "Mathematics and the existence of abstract entities." *Philosophical Studies* 7 (1956), pp. 81–88.

—— "The analytic and the synthetic." *Minnesota Studies in the Philosophy of Science* 3, at press.

Quine, W. V. *A System of Logistic.* Cambridge, Mass.: Harvard, 1934.

—— "Truth by convention." In O. H. Lee, pp. 90–124. Reprinted in Feigl and Sellars.

—— *Mathematical Logic.* New York, 1940. Revised edition, Cambridge, Mass.: Harvard, 1951.

—— *Elementary Logic.* Boston: Ginn, 1941.

—— "Whitehead and the rise of modern logic." In Schilpp, *The Philosophy of Alfred North Whitehead,* pp. 125–163.

—— "Notes on existence and necessity." *Journal of Philosophy* 40 (1943), pp. 113–127. Reprinted in Linsky.

—— *O sentido da nova lógica.* São Paulo: Martins, 1944. Spanish edition, *El sentido de la nueva lógica,* Buenos Aires: Nueva Visión, 1958.

—— "The problem of interpreting modal logic." *Journal of Symbolic Logic* 12 (1947), pp. 43–48.

—— Review of Reichenbach. *Journal of Philosophy* 45 (1948), pp. 161–166.

—— *From a Logical Point of View.* Cambridge, Mass.: Harvard, 1953.

—— "On mental entities." *Proceedings of American Academy of Arts and Sciences* 80 (1953), pp. 198–203.

—— "Three grades of modal involvement." *Proceedings of XIth International Congress of Philosophy* (Brussels, 1953), vol. 14, pp. 65–81.

—— "Two dogmas of empiricism." See *From a Logical Point of View,* Essay 2.

—— "Carnap and logical truth." Mimeographed. Written early in 1954 at the request of P. A. Schilpp for a volume he had been planning. Published in Italian in *Rivista di filosofia* 48 (1957), pp. 3–29. Portions also published under the title "Logical truth" in Hook, *American Philosophers at Work*.

—— "Reduction to a dyadic predicate," *Journal of Symbolic Logic* 19 (1954), pp. 180–182.

—— "On Frege's way out." *Mind* 64 (1955), pp. 145–159.

—— "Unification of universes in set theory." *Journal of Symbolic Logic* 21 (1956), pp. 267–279.

—— "Speaking of objects." *Proceedings and Addresses of the American Philosophical Association* 31 (1958), pp. 5–22. Reprinted in Krikorian and Edel.

—— "Meaning and translation." In Brower, pp. 148–172.

—— *Methods of Logic.* Revised edition. New York: Holt, 1959.

Reichenbach, Hans. *Elements of Symbolic Logic.* New York: Macmillan, 1947.

Reid, J. R. "Analytic statements in semiosis." *Mind* 52 (1943), pp. 314–330.

Richards, I. A. *The Philosophy of Rhetoric.* London: Oxford, 1936.

Richman, R. J. "Neo-pragmatism." *Methodos* 8 (1956), pp. 35–45.

—— "Ambiguity and intuition." *Mind* 68 (1959), pp. 87–92.

Russell, Bertrand. *The Principles of Mathematics.* London, 1903.

—— "On denoting." *Mind* 14 (1905), pp. 479–493. Reprinted in Russell's *Logic and Knowledge,* and in Feigl and Sellars.

—— *The Problems of Philosophy.* New York, 1912.

—— *Our Knowledge of the External World.* London, 1914.

—— *Mysticism and Logic and Other Essays.* London, 1918. The essays date from 1901–1914.

—— *Introduction to Mathematical Philosophy.* New York and London, 1919.

—— *An Inquiry into Meaning and Truth.* New York: Norton, 1940.

—— "Mr. Strawson on referring." *Mind* 66 (1957), pp. 385–389.

—— *Logic and Knowledge.* London: Allen & Unwin, 1958.

Ryle, Gilbert. "Imaginary objects." Aristotelian Society suppl. vol. 12 (*Creativity, Politics, and the A Priori*), 1933, pp. 18–43.

—— *The Concept of Mind.* London: Hutchinson, 1949.

Rynin, David. "The dogma of logical pragmatism." *Mind* 65 (1956), pp 379–391.

Sapir, Edward. *Language.* New York, 1921.

Scheffler, Israel. "An inscriptional approach to indirect quotation." *Analysis* 14 (1954), pp. 83–90.

—— "On synonymy and indirect discourse." *Philosophy of Science* 22 (1955), pp. 39–44.

—— "Thoughts on teleology." *British Journal for the Philosophy of Science* 9 (1959), pp. 265–284.

Schilpp, P. A. (ed.). *The Philosophy of Alfred North Whitehead.* 1941. 2d ed., New York: Tudor, 1951.

—— (ed.). *The Philosophy of Bertrand Russell.* Evanston: Northwestern University, 1944.

Schönfinkel, Moses. "Ueber die Bausteine der mathematischen Logik." *Mathematische Annalen* 92 (1924), pp. 305–316.

Sellars, Wilfrid. "Counterfactuals, dispositions, and the causal modalities." *Minnesota Studies in the Philosophy of Science* 2 (1958), pp. 225–308.

Shannon, C. E., and Warren Weaver. *The Mathematical Theory of Communication.* Urbana: University of Illinois, 1949.

Skinner, B. F. *Science and Human Behavior.* New York: Macmillan, 1953.

—— *Verbal Behavior.* New York: Appleton-Century-Crofts, 1957.

Smith, John. "Tre tipi e due dogmi dell'empirismo." *Rivista di filosofia* 48 (1957), pp. 257–273.

Stanley, R. L. "A theory of subjunctive conditionals." *Philosophy and Phenomenological Research* 17 (1956), pp. 22–35.

Stebbing, L. Susan. *Philosophy and the Physicists.* London: Methuen, 1937.

Stegmüller, Wolfgang. "Das Universalien-problem einst und jetzt." *Archiv für Philosophie* 6 (1956?), pp. 192–225; 7 (1957?), pp. 45–81.

Strawson, P. F. *Introduction to Logical Theory.* London: Methuen, and New York: Wiley, 1952.

—— "Particular and general." *Proceedings of the Aristotelian Society* 54 (1954), pp. 233–260.

—— "A logician's landscape." *Philosophy* 30 (1955), pp. 229–237.

—— "Singular terms, ontology, and identity." *Mind* 65 (1956), pp. 433–454.

—— "Propositions, concepts, and logical truths." *Philosophical Quarterly* 7 (1957), pp. 15–25.

—— *Individuals.* London: Methuen, 1959.

Tarski, Alfred. *Logic, Semantics, Metamathematics.* Oxford: Clarendon, 1956.

Taylor, Richard. "Spatial and temporal analogies and the concept of identity." *Journal of Philosophy* 52 (1955), pp. 599–612.

Urmson, J. O. "Some questions concerning validity." *Revue Internationale de Philosophie* 7 (1953), pp. 217–229.

von Mises, see Mises.

von Neumann, see Neumann.

Waismann, Friedrich. "Verifiability." In Flew, pp. 117–144.

White, Morton. "On the Church-Frege solution of the paradox of analysis." *Philosophy and Phenomenological Research* 9 (1948), pp. 305–308.

—— "The analytic and the synthetic: An untenable dualism." In Hook, *John Dewey,* pp. 316–330.

—— *Toward Reunion in Philosophy.* Cambridge, Mass.: Harvard, 1956.

Whitehead, A. N. *Universal Algebra.* Cambridge, England, 1898.

—— and Bertrand Russell. *Principia Mathematica,* vol. 1. Cambridge, England, 1910. 2d ed., 1925.

Whorf, B. L. *Language, Thought, and Reality: Selected Writings of Benjamin Lee Whorf.* (J. B. Carroll, ed.) M.I.T.: Technology Press and New York: Wiley, 1956.

Wiener, Norbert. "Simplification of the logic of relations." *Proceedings of the Cambridge Philosophical Society* 17 (1912–1914), pp. 387–390.

Wiener, P. P. (ed.). *Philosophy of Science.* New York: Scribner's, 1953.

Williams, D. C. "The sea fight tomorrow." In Henle, Kallen, and Langer, pp. 282–306.

Wilson, N. L. "Substances without substrata." *Review of Metaphysics* 12 (1959), pp. 521–539.

Wittgenstein, Ludwig. *Tractatus Logico-Philosophicus.* New York and London, 1922.

—— *The Blue and Brown Books.* Oxford: Blackwell, 1958.

Woodger, J. H. *Biology and Language.* Cambridge, England: University, 1952.

Xenakis, Jason. "The logic of proper names." *Methodos* 7 (1955), pp. 13–24.

Ziff, Paul. "About behaviorism." *Analysis* 18 (1958), pp. 132–136.

Zipf, G. K. *The Psycho-Biology of Language.* Boston: Houghton Mifflin, 1935.

Index

About 239, 246

Abstract object 34, 52, 269; commitment to 119f, 123, 241ff; pro and con 122ff, 234, 237, 270

Abstraction: of classes 163ff, 209, 211f, 237. *See also* Intensional abstraction

Acquaintance 53n, 56, 178

Adjective 96f, 119; attributively used 103ff; predicatively used 96ff, 104; syncategorematic 103, 126, 132ff, 138, 175

Ajdukiewicz, Kazimierz 65n

Aldrich, Virgil 12n

Algebraic 112, 184f, 188f

Allen, J. H. 135

Alston, W. P. 238n, 260n

Alternation 57f, 134, 144

Ambiguity 81, 129–133, 183; of scope 138–141; of syntax 134–137. *See also* Vagueness

Analogy 9, 14ff, 19f

Analytic sentence 65ff, 182, 207, 220f, 247, 271; and modal 195f; stimulus-55, 65–69

Analytical hypotheses 68–71, 94; freedom of 72–76, 206, 221, 243; homophonic 59, 78, 203

Ancestor 237, 269

Anrep, G. V. 84n

Antinomy 229, 232n, 266ff

Apostel, Leo 67n

Application 106–110, 112

A priori 66

Aquinas, Thomas 116n

Aristotle 116n, 199

Article: definite, *see* Description; indefinite 96f, 118. *See also* Indefinite singular term

Assent 29f, 57, 62

Attribute 16f, 54, 118–123, 209ff, 233, 238ff; abstraction of 163ff, 169; identity of 209, 211, 244; versus class 123, 151, 166, 210, 257n, 267

Attributive position 103ff, 107, 112

Austerity 188, 210, 221, 225, 227

Ayer, A. J. 201n, 241n

Bar-Hillel, Yehoshua 65n

Barcan, Ruth C. 197f

Bass, M. J. 84n

Baylis, C. A. 239n

Bedau, H. A. 77n

Belief: -in 174; intensions as objects of 168f, 204; other objects for 211–216; transparent and opaque 145–150; with occasion sentences 217; with variables 166f, 214ff. *See also* Propositional attitude

Bennett, Jonathan 68n

THE M.I.T. PRESS PAPERBACK SERIES